Beethoven's Symphonies
and J. S. Dwight

JOHN S. DWIGHT (1813–1893)

BEETHOVEN'S SYMPHONIES AND J. S. DWIGHT

The Birth of American Music Criticism

ORA FRISHBERG SALOMAN

NORTHEASTERN UNIVERSITY PRESS • BOSTON

Music Advisor to Northeastern University Press
Gunther Schuller

Northeastern University Press
Copyright 1995 by Ora Frishberg Saloman

Library of Congress Cataloging-in-Publication Data

Saloman, Ora Frishberg, 1938–
Beethoven's symphonies and J. S. Dwight : the birth of American
music criticism / Ora Frishberg Saloman.
p. cm.
Includes bibliographical references.
ISBN 1–55553–216–0
1. Beethoven, Ludwig van, 1770–1827. Symphonies. 2. Beethoven,
Ludwig van, 1770–1827—Appreciation—United States. 3. Dwight, John
Sullivan, 1813–1893. 4. Musical criticism—United States.
I. Title.
ML410.B4S139 1995
784.2'184'092—dc20 94–34213
MN

Designed by Christine Leonard Raquepaw

Composed in Simoncini Garamond by Coghill Composition in Richmond, Virginia. Printed and bound by Thomson-Shore, Inc., in Dexter, Michigan. The paper is Glatfelter, an acid-free stock.

MANUFACTURED IN THE UNITED STATES OF AMERICA

99 98 97 96 95   5 4 3 2 1

To Ed

Contents

Acknowledgments

To the National Endowment for the Humanities, I express my thanks and gratitude for its generous award of a Fellowship for College Teachers and Independent Scholars enabling essential archival research. I am greatly obliged to Provost Lois Cronholm and Dean Norman Fainstein, School of Liberal Arts and Sciences, Baruch College of The City University of New York, for their valued support of this work with a publication subvention. Baruch College also provided a Fellowship Award and several grants of Released Time for which I am grateful.

For their courteous assistance, I acknowledge the staffs of many libraries: these include the Interlibrary Loan Service of the Baruch College Library; the Music Division and Special Collections of the New York Public Library for the Performing Arts at Lincoln Center and the Main Reading Room at 42nd Street; the Music Division, the Rare Book and Special Collections Division, and the Microform Reading Room of the Library of Congress, Washington D.C.; the Rare Book Room and the Music Department of the Boston Public Library; the Harvard Musical Association in Boston; the Houghton Library of Harvard University; the Massachusetts Historical Society; the Rare Book and Special Collections

Library of Columbia University; the Barnard College Library; and the New-York Historical Society.

All source materials from the Dwight Papers are quoted by courtesy of the Trustees of the Boston Public Library. Letters from the Autograph File and the Amy Lowell Autograph Collection of Houghton Library are quoted by permission of the Houghton Library, Harvard University. Archival documents from the Harvard Musical Association are published by permission of the Harvard Musical Association, Boston. A letter from the Bellows Papers is quoted by permission of the Massachusetts Historical Society.

Part of Chapter 6 originally appeared in the *Musical Quarterly;* my thanks to the journal, its editor at the time, Paul Wittke, and to Oxford University Press for permission to use the material in somewhat altered form.

I gratefully acknowledge the permission obtained from the Royal Musical Association to use material that originally appeared in the *Journal of the Royal Musical Association,* published by Oxford University Press. Parts of Chapters 2, 3, 8, and 9 are used in rather different form. For their thoughtful assistance, I am obliged to the editor of that journal, Mark Everist, to Ian Rumbold, and to the Secretary of the Royal Musical Association, Ewan West.

It is a pleasure to thank reference librarians who rendered particular assistance in the course of research, including Charles Sens of the Music Division of the Library of Congress, Natalie Palme of the Harvard Musical Association in Boston, and Giuseppe Bisaccia and Diane Ota of the Boston Public Library. I appreciate information provided by Kenneth Stuckey, Research Librarian of the Perkins School for the Blind in Watertown, Massachusetts.

I am especially indebted to Steven J. Ledbetter, Musicologist, Boston Symphony Orchestra, for his gracious encouragement to pursue this area of research and for his valued advice. My thanks as well to other scholars who expressed particular interest in the subject, responded helpfully to an inquiry, or engaged in stimulating discussion: these include John Graziano, Maria Rika Maniates, Christopher Hatch, Nicholas Temperley, Conrad L. Donakowski, William S. Newman, William Austin, Carol Berkin, Paul Charosh, Adrienne Fried Block, Pamela Fox, Jacklin Stopp, Ernestine Schlant, and Joel Myerson.

I owe many thanks to William Frohlich, director of Northeastern University Press, for his interest, consideration, and excellent handling of arrangements during the publication process.

For their unfailing moral support I shall always be indebted to my late father, Rabbi Naphtali Z. Frishberg, and to my mother, Lena Nidel Frishberg.

I express particular thanks and appreciation to my husband, Edward B. Saloman. I am immensely grateful for his highly supportive interest in all phases of the project, as well as for his invaluable assistance in resolving computer problems during preparation of the manuscript.

Introduction

American conceptions of symphonic structure and of Ludwig van Beethoven's symphonies in the 1840s were shaped significantly by the youthful John Sullivan Dwight (1813–1893) in the years before he gained his reputation as the editor of *Dwight's Journal of Music, A Paper of Art and Literature.*[1] As the first major American-born critic of music, Dwight founded that valuable journal in 1852, and it became the earliest long-lived music periodical in the United States. For twenty-nine years, until the *Journal* closed in 1881, Dwight vigorously championed the music of many European composers and the development of concert activity in America.

To support these goals, he wrote extended original essays on styles and composers and provided his own or other translations of German and French critical works. He published news of concerts and correspondence from abroad, as well as reprinting valuable material from English and Continental sources. Dwight pioneered in describing and reviewing numerous scholarly biographies, instruction manuals, and books on music. Subjects ranged from aesthetics, music criticism, and the psychology and sociology of music to acoustics and the state of education in music in conservatories and universities.

He also invited contributions to the *Journal* from other promiment writers on music. One of these was the respected American biographer of Beethoven, Alexander Wheelock Thayer,[2] who contributed about 325 articles, reviews, and letters from America and Europe. Dwight was the first to translate any part of Thayer's biography from the German back into English and to impress on his readers the significant scholarly achievement that it and similar European studies represented.[3]

Despite Dwight's stature in the cultural life of nineteenth-century America, however, very little is known about the formation of his approach to music criticism. By tracing his beginnings as a writer on Beethoven in the period following the composer's death in 1827, we can discover a dramatically new perspective on Dwight as critic. It offers a marked contrast to the existing literature, which is based almost exclusively on the readily accessible writings of Dwight's later years in the *Journal.*

This book identifies for the first time, and provides evidence of, specific European critical, biographical, musical, historiographical, literary, and historical foundations on which Dwight constructed his initial thought pertaining to Beethoven's symphonies. Four underlying and connected ideas shaped the research. First, Dwight's American reception of Beethoven's symphonies is comprehensible only from a perspective informed by his growing knowledge and transformation of related European intellectual traditions and critical approaches. A study of Dwight's musical learning connected to Beethoven provides a natural focus for that association.[4]

Second, he earned distinction by communicating to a literate but musically unsophisticated American public about the structure and importance of the symphony as a new kind of concert music.

Dwight chose Beethoven's symphonies as his prime modern exemplars of the genre before 1847.

Third, Dwight's search for, and development of, a higher criticism of music was unprecedented in the United States and was distinct from the journalistic chronicling of performances characteristic of the daily press. It evolved from his independent effort to understand music in its multiple facets as moral force, aesthetic art, and technical-scientific field. As a part of this process, he led in introducing a musical discourse and fostered the significant educative function of the music critic in American society.

Fourth, Dwight disseminated an idealistic vision of a universal Beethoven whose symphonic music he hoped would become emblematic of a new era marked by the amelioration of society. He also conceived of the symphony orchestra as a cooperative, rather than a competing, entity. This broad utopian view excluded the term "Romanticism," as Dwight will be shown to have used it, from any application to Beethoven's symphonies. However, he introduced to Americans a new Romantic outlook emphasizing the significance of symphonic music combined with constructive suggestions to guide readers in becoming informed listeners.

Dwight's texts are cultural documents. His interpretative comments, as well as references to books he read and other internal evidence, can be found in his manuscripts, unpublished letters, archival papers, and published articles and essays scattered in diverse, largely inaccessible periodicals or newspapers. Dwight's musical learning between 1835 and 1847 will be revealed to have been more extensive than has been known. As an examination of the European sources associated with American Beethoven criticism, this book opens an area that has not been treated previously in older twentieth-century assessments of the composer's impact on the Romantic imagination[5] or in more recent studies exploring the European criticism,[6] reception,[7] mystique,[8] or image[9] of Beethoven.

The earliest regular series of public orchestral performances of Beethoven's complete, rather than excerpted, symphonies in the United States occurred concurrently in New York and in Boston beginning in 1841.[10] These concerts coincided with a change in Dwight's career from Unitarian minister to a life in music as author, critic, and teacher. Among the small group of American-born writers in that era who attempted to create a listening public for Beethoven's music, only Dwight dared ultimately to forge a career in music.

He confronted formidable obstacles. In the 1820s and 1830s, American readers had learned of Beethoven's fame as a symphonic composer before they heard the music. Articles in the press and periodicals had reprinted or borrowed reports primarily from English publications that signaled the earlier popularity of his symphonies in London.[11] However, with few exceptions, these works presented complex challenges for performers, audiences, and writers in America before midcentury because of a relative absence of established musical and educational institutions, performance traditions, and a critical framework within which to locate symphonic and orchestral issues.

Dwight's musical curiosity and linguistic fluency equipped him to find and incorporate, but also to reject, varied European approaches to this new repertory. He developed a discourse attempting to extend beyond the level of superficial, or "acquaintance," knowledge to convey "discursive" knowledge as well.[12] In communicating with others for the common good, he hoped to instill in his compatriots a sense that music was a stimulating field of artistic and "scientific"significance rather than merely a pleasing diversion. Dwight's interest in European art music reflected his universal commitment to its concerns with moral and cultural idealism as part of what he conceived to be a shared heritage. Dwight also contributed in the nineteenth century to the general development of aesthetic perception and pleasure, considered, from a broad perspective, as an important phase in the history of civilization.[13]

It has been little recognized that when Dwight created his *Journal,* at the age of thirty-nine, he was then concluding the most optimistic and open-minded part of his career. Dwight's disappointment at the outbreak of the Mexican War in 1846 was compounded by a strong sense of loss on the closing in 1847 of Brook Farm, the experimental utopian community in West Roxbury, Massachusetts, which had been his home since 1841. In the early and mid-1840s, by contrast, he had flourished in musical as well as literary, educational, and reform activities. During those years of learning, Dwight had formulated his musical convictions as he heard many of Beethoven's large-scale works in orchestral performance, primarily in Boston. A review of the documents from the period before 1847 illuminates Dwight's pioneering role in articulating a musically progressive outlook atypical of that era in America.

PART ONE

———•———

*Approaches to
Beethoven's Symphonies,
1835–1842*

CHAPTER ONE

New Perspectives on
Dwight's Transcendentalism and
Posthumous Reputation

As one of the younger American Unitarian intellectual radicals of the 1830s, John S. Dwight was unusual in choosing a musical emphasis amid the range of religious, literary, social, and philosophical concerns that he and his colleagues utilized to express their discontent with perceived societal evils and orthodox theological dogma. American Transcendentalism of that decade, which took root in the religious heritage of liberal Unitarianism, opposed the Calvinist doctrine of sin with a central belief in the goodness, rather than the depravity, of human beings. It also reflected, and paralleled, diverse currents of philosophical, literary, and musical idealism.

Continuing religious controversies within Unitarianism had resulted in the formation of revolutionary positions by a first generation of Transcendentalist leaders, including not only Ralph Waldo Emerson but also George S. Ripley, the founder of Brook Farm. These and other "like-minded" thinkers, a number of whom were graduates of Harvard College and the Harvard Divinity School, sought the inspiration of an inner, personal God in human affairs. Their opposition to religious formalism and the rituals associated with organized religion ultimately led Emerson and Ripley to withdraw from the pulpit rather than serve the church as a conventional institution whose authority they had come to question. These struggles of conscience left a considerable impact on John S. Dwight, son of a Harvard-educated freethinker who had become a physician after studying for, then rejecting, the ministry.

The New England Transcendentalists participated in active discussions and created seven journals through which they expressed their widely disparate views. They accepted no binding affiliation, nor did they agree upon a single cause, except a belief in higher universal "Reason," or Soul, and a positive assertion of human worth based on an immanent connection with the divine. During the informal meetings of the group later called the Transcendental Club, which began in 1836, two perspectives emerged: Emerson championed the independence of the solitary individual, while Ripley defended the cooperative principle of individuals joining with each other to reform society. Among the participants in these exchanges, Amos Bronson Alcott, Margaret Fuller, and Henry David Thoreau affirmed Emerson's position; John Sullivan Dwight, among others, favored Ripley's vision of communal harmony.

Although Dwight admired Emerson's leadership, he thus looked to Ripley as his mentor. That distinction, often obscured in the pertinent musical scholarship, is basic to an understanding of Dwight's ethical conviction as it was expressed in the early and mid-1840s: all human beings were linked to each other in a common desire to achieve universal harmony as well as individual happiness. Dwight's belief in a shared destiny made an independent life of comparative solitude following Emerson's model inconceivable for him, and it provided the rationale for his cooperative vision in which all might contribute productively toward the fulfillment of human life. This high sense of common purpose invigorated his dedication to the aims of Brook Farm and motivated his particular conception of the orchestra's role in musical life. As well, it contributed to his active associations with diverse groups throughout his career.

The Transcendentalist fervor also included a strong cultural component. Here again Ripley, rather than Emerson, became Dwight's guide. Ripley was less heavily reliant than Emerson on American and English intellectual traditions; it was Ripley who founded the pathbreaking series of translations of recent Continental philosophical and literary works, *Specimens of Foreign Standard Literature,* to which Dwight and Fuller each contributed a volume.

As chief opponent of the conservative position defended by Andrews Norton, Ripley had led the liberal struggle against Unitarianism by articulating a radical refutation of its rationalist basis as posited in John Locke's material philosophy. According to Locke, human knowledge was acquired primarily through the senses rather than by direct intuition engaging the higher mental faculties. Ripley and other Transcendentalists, including Dwight, emphasized instead the human capacity to strive beyond the "Understanding" of the perceived physical world toward knowledge of higher truth and beauty through the realm of pure ideas, or "Reason," which transcended the experience of the senses. Ripley recognized a Kantian perspective as the foundation on which German idealist thinkers, in particular, had subsequently drawn.

It was Ripley's conviction that Transcendentalism was "the first major cultural rebellion in national history."[1] He, Dwight, and Fuller were in the vanguard of those seeking to lessen the impact of American conservative dependence on English models by providing access to Continental literature in translation. However, they shared the widespread Transcendentalist esteem for the works of the British writers Thomas Carlyle and Samuel Taylor Coleridge. Ripley and Dwight admired Carlyle's interpretative commentaries on German literature for English-speaking readers and his strong denunciation of the excesses of English materialism.

Ripley and Dwight established a lifelong friendship. The former delivered the sermon at Dwight's ordination in Northampton, Massachusetts, in May of 1840 on the same weekend during which Ripley decided finally to quit the ministry. The two remained in close contact during the period leading to Ripley's founding of Brook Farm and then long after its closing. In the mid-1840s, Ripley and Dwight agreed about the essential compatibility of individual development and communal activity, just as they shared a fundamental belief that all people were part of a single connected humanity. Ripley pursued his philosophical, political, and social reform interests vigorously; during that time, Dwight intensified his musical and literary studies but also assisted Ripley in advancing a program of social change. These ideas form the essential background of Dwight's early writings on Beethoven.

The youthful Dwight's key role in introducing the symphonic genre to the American public has not been examined in contemporary scholarship. This is so in part because his texts remain scattered but also because Dwight's later musical and social conservatism tended to obscure the pioneering nature of his initial Beethoven criticism. A brief survey of the major literature pertaining to him in the century since his death may explain how and why an image of the older Dwight has prevailed.

One of the most formidable shapers of Dwight's posthumous reputation was William Foster Apthorp, a contributor to *Dwight's Journal of Music* in its later years, who became music critic of the *Boston Evening Transcript.* He wrote the obituary of Dwight that first appeared there in 1893 before being reprinted in a volume of Apthorp's essays.[2] Thirty-five years Dwight's junior, Apthorp had benefited from a formal course of study in music at Harvard College. It had not existed there in Dwight's youth, despite his advocacy of its legitimacy in the undergraduate curriculum. As a critic and professor of music, Apthorp wrote about works by established as well as recent composers (then including Hector Berlioz, Robert Franz, and Richard Wagner).

Proudly advocating European "new music," he focused on Dwight's later and contrasting conservative preferences. Apthorp portrayed the critic he came to know as possessing a psychic animosity to the modern spirit and nervous energy that Apthorp believed characteristic of music by Berlioz and Wagner. He acknowledged that his older colleague had a "fair ear" and an "astonishingly accurate grasp of musical terminology." Dwight's musical perceptions were of the finest, and he had manifested an "inveterate instinct for culture," together with aesthetic sensibility. From Apthorp's perspective as a younger member of the musical establishment at the close of the nineteenth century, however, it was no longer pertinent to recall Dwight's progressive championship of Beethoven's music a half-century earlier, when Americans had regarded it as new, modern, and complex.

In his anecdotal appreciation of the older critic's direct views and literary facility, Apthorp contributed to the portrait presented by George Willis Cooke in the first standard biography of Dwight.[3] Appearing in 1898, it included warm reminiscences by students and friends, dating mostly from the 1870s or later, together with autobiographical incidents culled from Dwight's correspondence. Containing little specific documentation and no scholarly apparatus, it was a genteel tribute that briefly accounted for Dwight's early period through the blurred remembrances of later years.

Cooke's biography became the basis of diverse assessments of Dwight, ranging from those in an account of Brook Farm by Lindsay Swift,[4] to a brief entry by Eleanor Robinette Dobson in the *Dictionary of American Biography,*[5] to a significant critical article by Edward Waters. Although Waters's "John Sullivan Dwight" originally appeared in 1935, it acquired continuing influence by being republished as the introductory essay to the modern reprint edition of *Dwight's Journal of Music* issued in 1968.[6]

Apthorp's and Cooke's accounts of Dwight's enjoyment of fine food, wine, and convivial gatherings in privileged surroundings contributed to an impression of the critic in the later nineteenth century as a prominent member of the conservative Boston establishment. The descriptions were markedly at odds with his philosophical, financial, and social circumstances in the mid-1840s. Scholarship devoted to the social history of Boston reinforced and compounded that image of the elderly Dwight by reprinting his handwritten diagram showing the seating at one of the Parker House dinners held by the Saturday Club. Beginning in the 1870s, Dwight was active in this private group composed of illustrious writers, judges, senators, and doctors.[7]

Clarity in musical issues was further undermined by the appearance of an article shortly before the mid–twentieth century; it lauded Dwight's application of a connected poetic-musical lyrical approach, a homogeneous "Dicht-Tonkunst," to poetic translations and literary reviews. Its author underestimated Dwight's fundamentally musical outlook, exaggerated his influence in disseminating German literary Romanticism in America, and erred in concluding that the "poetic qualities of the German Romantic composers were the standard" by which Dwight had judged "all music."[8]

Two consequential studies appeared in the 1950s, one of which was the modern biography of Dwight by Walter L. Fertig.[9] His point of view became singularly influential through citations in later works, as well as Fertig's concise entry on the critic in *The New Grove Dictionary of American Music* issued in 1986.[10] As a scholar in the field of English, with an emphasis on American Studies, Fertig surveyed the literary, political, and artistic components of Dwight's large output more systematically than had Cooke. Although he mentioned briefly several musical works, a study of the sources associated with Dwight's musical thought avowedly was not part of his thesis.[11] Nevertheless, like Cooke, Fertig located Dwight primarily in the literary sphere as an amateur of music. According to Fertig, Dwight's limited musical education and abilities had resulted in music criticism that was "amateurish" if judged by modern standards. Unlike Cooke, Fertig sought to connect more closely the strands of Dwight's career with his Transcendentalist views, and he stressed Dwight's varied moods to achieve a more nuanced delineation of the critic's personality.

The other publication marking the midcentury decade was an article by Irving Lowens including a checklist of Transcendentalist writings on music between 1835 and 1850.[12] Lowens judged Dwight to have possessed the "keenest critical intelligence on the entire American scene." Asserting that "the Transcendental pope of music" was still in the "apprentice stage of his career" before 1850, he acknowledged nonetheless that it was then that Dwight worked out his ideas on the nature of music. Lowens built directly on Fertig's recent work to reinforce a prevailing but inappropriate notion: Dwight's criticism in later decades, which followed a long period of apprenticeship, was more significant in its culminating maturity and unquestioned authority. However, Lowens noted Dwight's early musical prescience and, through the checklist, gave bibliographical recognition to writings awaiting detailed examination.

In the decades since 1960, diverse articles and doctoral dissertations assessed Dwight's work as it appeared primarily in his *Journal* during the second half of the nineteenth century. These included Dwight's role in the American reception of Wagner's instrumental music from early works[13] and his participation in controversies concerning incipient American musical nationalism.[14] There were also studies of Dwight's Transcendentalist thought connected to contemporaneous authors from the perspectives of American Studies[15] and American literature[16] or as part of the intellectual background of Charles Ives's aesthetic theories.[17] *Dwight's Journal of Music* was the subject of systematic examination.[18] One author considered Dwight's writings, primarily from the *Journal,* in a general history of the reception of Beethoven's music in the United States before 1865.[19] The publication in 1986 of Irving Sablosky's compilation *What They Heard* enabled the general public to sample Dwight's views from the second half of the nineteenth century by assuring ready access to extracts from the *Journal*'s pages.[20]

Amid this considerable activity there were few signs that the early writings had been recovered for separate attention. Sterling F. Delano studied the various departments of the Associationist journal, *The Harbinger, Devoted to Social and Political Progress,* with one chapter devoted to Dwight's music criticism between 1845 and 1849.[21] My preliminary article in 1990 surveyed Dwight's early views on Beethoven's symphonies in comparison with diverse approaches by other Boston writers, including Margaret Fuller, Christopher Cranch, and William Wetmore Story.[22] Two of my subsequent articles, in 1992 and 1994, presented aspects of my recent research connecting European musical and literary sources to Dwight's criticism of Beethoven's Fifth and Ninth Symphonies, respectively.[23]

In 1992, Michael Broyles published an important study describing the musical and social origins of a distinction between elitism and populism in early-nineteenth-century Boston, with emphasis on developments in the 1820s and the 1830s.[24] Delineating a three-stage process, Broyles proposes that early-nineteenth-century Presbyterian-Congregational hymnodic reformers increased the devotional style of church music to enhance its religious and moral character. In the next phase, members of the predominantly Unitarian upper class brought about changes that shifted attention, particularly through the Boston Academy of Music, from sacred vocal music to secular instrumental music. Finally a few writers, including John S. Dwight, transformed the early Puritan emphasis on edification. They transferred the goals of the hymnodic reformers from sacred to secular realms in combination with aspects of New England Transcendentalism and European Romanticism.

According to Broyles, the application of religious rhetoric to abstract instrumental music by Dwight, among others, had the effect of imbuing it with a moral dignity leading to greater acceptance for its ethical values during the establishment of an American tradition of high culture. Broyles emphasizes that aspect in his treatment of Dwight, in whom he discerned elitist tendencies in the late 1830s and early 1840s. However, Broyles makes his judgments on the basis of only a few selected documents written by Dwight in those decades.

The full range of Dwight's writings about symphonic music before 1847 must be examined in order to evaluate his complex views. I will show that they include universal ideals combined with pragmatic educative aims. These encouraged many to join in collective cultural access as listeners by drawing on their intuitive capacities, interests in learning, or inclinations toward cultural experience. In those years, Dwight held a predominantly reformist vision. It included the idea that art music could exert a positive force toward a better future attainable by all working together instead of dividing according to social class.

In addition, although it is possible to locate religious rhetoric in particular essays before 1847, it is vital to recognize that between 1842 and the latter part of 1846, Dwight's radical disillusion with public forms of prayer and preaching was at its height. It was during that epoch of rebellion against religious formalism that he first wrote about Beethoven's symphonies.

Until 1844 (and by consensus), formal religious meetings or worship were prohibited at Brook Farm. Even then however, as efforts were being made to "spiritualize" social planning, no chapel existed on the premises; thoughts of building one were ultimately thwarted.[25] It was not until January of 1847 that Dwight joined with William H. Channing and others to form a Religious Union of Associationists, after which he participated in a liberal service consisting of readings and music. In the years before 1847, however—particularly between 1843 and 1846, when Dwight initially heard the orchestral performances of Beethoven's symphonies—religious rhetoric was superseded by his flexible consideration of musical, biographical, and critical issues.

Dwight's approach to Beethoven may be interpreted as an effort to reconcile, for the first time in the history of American criticism of abstract instrumental concert music, two apparently opposite perspectives. He affirmed the lofty ethical character of Beethoven's symphonies, but he also attempted to describe their musical and aesthetic qualities. Dwight's interest in their moral virtues may have been in part a reaction to utilitarian pressures in an expanding industrial society. It was also a recognition that those positive qualities enhanced the status of symphonic music in an environment in which secular instrumental music had been regarded as amusement rather than art.

At the same time, however, by locating Beethoven's symphonies beyond the material world in a realm of the ideal, Dwight encouraged American recognition of their musical significance as artistically shaped expressions of the highest inner human aspirations. The intellectual process through which he began to perceive their aesthetic and structural qualities will be the focus of this book.

CHAPTER TWO

———————►-◉-◄———————

Friedrich Schiller, Thomas Carlyle, and Dwight's Humanistic Conception of Beethoven's Music, 1835–1839

One of the most stimulating intellectual forces shaping Dwight's approach to Beethoven came from the ideals expressed in the poetry and aesthetic theories of Johann Christoph Friedrich Schiller (1759–1805). Between 1835 and 1839, Dwight's interest in particular works by Schiller led to a fresh perspective that informed his conception of Beethoven as a musical leader for the American critic's own epoch.

Dwight had been actively interested in instrumental music and in poetry well before 1835. While in his final year at the Boston Latin School in 1828, he had visited Harvard College on Exhibition Day to "catch a glimpse beforehand of the promised land." The experience had been memorable. In University Hall, he had witnessed an informal musical group with which he was to have an important future association, the Pierian Sodality. He recollected that occasion at which he, for the first time, "heard and *saw*, up there in the side (north) gallery, the little group of Pierians, with their ribbons and their medals, and their shining instruments, among them that protruding, long, and lengthening monster, the trombone":

Had any strains of band or orchestra ever sounded quite so
sweet to the expectant Freshman's ears as those? And was not
he, too, captivated and converted to the gospel of the college
flute, as the transcendent and most eloquent of instruments?
Nevertheless within a year or two he chose the reedy clarinet,
wherewith to lead a little preparatory club,—the purgatory which
half-fledged musicians of his own ilk had to pass through before
they could be candidates for the Pierian paradise. This was
called the Arionic Society, [sic] and if its utmost skill was discord, the struggle of its members for promotion into the higher
order was persistent.[1]

The manuscript "Records of the Arionic Sodality" state that the
group had been formed in 1813, the year of Dwight's birth, and
that he was inducted into it as a player of the "clarionett" on
September 17, 1829.[2] The minutes describe the election of officers
at that meeting: "J. S. Dwight was elected President," with respon-
sibilities to include collaboration in revising the old code of laws.
But the new president, then a college sophomore, intended his
first priority to be an improvement in music making. The following
unusually detailed entry conveys the flavor of his earnest efforts
with the ten-member group:

Sept. 30th [1829]

Tuesday. Met at no. 32 Hollis at 7 o'clock. Br. Dwight led the
band, and the music was pronounced, by competent judges, to
have been unusually good. The Society will now, we hope regain,
or surpass, its former standing. After playing till 8 o'clock, the
pres^t gave out the following tunes, to be played at next meeting.
Look out upon the stars (no. 3), Yellow haired Laddie (6), Boston Cadets March (No. 5), Buonaparte's quick step (No. 4).
The Society then adjourned, till the next Tuesday. Voted—that
the members copy the tunes into their books, under penalty of
a fine.

J. W. Gorham, Sec.[3]

That Dwight had sufficient musical proficiency to lead this preparatory group with enthusiasm and a measure of discipline, and that he flourished in situations combining music with good fellowship, can be deduced from the entries. He is listed as a member in 1829–30 and in 1830–31.

Dwight's progress as a clarinetist enabled him to gain admission to the Pierian Sodality as a college senior. This group, formed in 1808 as a student society for "mutual improvement in instrumental music," had passed through several stages. Dwight later referred to the 1830s and early 1840s as its "middle period," occupied primarily with "fluting, serenading, [and] exhibition-playing." When Dwight was a member in 1831–32, it comprised several each of first, second, and third flutes, a clarinet, two French horns, a cello, and "part of the time a nondescript bass horn." It was an extracurricular activity. There were then no formal courses in music offered within the official curriculum of the college.

University students who wished to play an instrument often chose the flute; during the early 1830s, there is little evidence of interest in strings or music for stringed instruments. A former Pierian recalled in a later nineteenth-century account that the violin had been held "in small repute" among gentlemen—(probably because of its early-nineteenth-century association with dancing)— and that he had been obliged to put aside his own when he arrived at Harvard College in favor of the more popular woodwind instrument. Its silver trills could be heard emanating "from every side of the quadrangle" at the close of morning study hours.

Samuel Jennison is a witness to another of Dwight's important musical activities during that period. Jennison's retrospective memoir of 1875 signals deference to his highly prominent contemporary: "A single piano, at which a graduate, a devoted amateur, rooming in Massachusetts, studied Beethoven's Sonatas, then just beginning to become known, seems now, with its superior character and capabilities, fitly to symbolize the advanced position already occupied by the critic who has ever since held the most influential musical pen in this community." A marginal note in Dwight's hand identifies the pianist and the date: "J. S. D. of 1832."[4] This evidence suggests that Dwight, having received early piano instruction from his father, had acquired sufficient keyboard skill by 1832, the year of his graduation from Harvard College, to study Beethoven's sonatas. They were then very little known in America, and it was a mark of the nineteen-year-old's advanced musical taste that he practiced these complex works with diligence and particular interest.

In his undergraduate years, Dwight had enthusiastically studied languages. He had also received recognition as poet for the Hasty Pudding Club, of which he was a member, and was class poet at his graduation.[5] During the spring and summer of 1832, Dwight obtained letters of recommendation from the president of Harvard University, Josiah Quincy, and from faculty members Cornelius C. Felton, instructor in Greek, and Charles Follen, professor of German language and literature. They attested to his excellent character, high rank among the students in his class, and notable attainments in the classics and in German. These qualified him "amply for the business of instruction, in which he proposes to engage after taking his degree."[6]

Following his graduation, Dwight avowed no career interest in medicine, law, or the ministry. He was gaining proficiency in literature, languages, and music. Although Dwight's accomplishments as a student of German would soon prove to be valued assets in acquiring musical knowledge, he did not then find a suitable teaching position. When he entered the Harvard Divinity School, therefore, he was not fully committed to the ministry as a profession. It is not surprising that he interrupted his course of study to become a tutor in Pennsylvania.

Dwight was not an avid correspondent; there are few extant letters from him but many more addressed to him concerning his thoughts in these years. While away from Massachusetts, Dwight received from a friend and former classmate, Samuel Osgood, a reply to a letter of his. To the question of how they might bring out their best powers to lead useful lives, Osgood asserted, "We are both of us given to speculation."

Suggesting that one of the best means of "ridding ourselves of mystical Expressions" was to read plays, in whose natural language the portrayal of strong emotions could be a vivid model, Osgood's main recommendation for their future happiness was to "learn to be free under restraint." The phrase appears twice in a letter alluding to fundamental mutual problems: they tended to resist conforming to the pressures and values of the surrounding society. Osgood reasoned that everything exacts its toll, even the most joyous things, but asked, "[M]ay not our hearts beat freely under the labors and restraints of artificial society?"[7]

Letters to Dwight from another good friend at the Divinity School, Charles Timothy Brooks, described acquaintances and activities of mutual interest, perhaps intended as gentle persuasion while Dwight pondered his situation. Christopher Cranch's flute continued to arouse them pleasantly each Saturday, Dr. Follen's German lectures remained notable, the religious and social ferment between orthodox and liberal theological views was exciting.[8] He also reported a debate held "on the use and value of Church Music—and on Sunday Mr. Ware gave a grand sermon in eulogy of ch. music."[9] Dwight returned to Harvard in August 1834.

It was during this period of graduate study that Dwight translated the revised version of Friedrich Schiller's ode "An die Freude." As "Hymn to Joy," it was published in *The New-England Magazine* of May 1835 without accompanying prose commentary and signed only with the initial "D." below the poem.[10] That

Dwight selected this poem for his first publication marks its high personal and professional significance to him. It also adumbrates his later decision to gather it and other admired poems by Schiller and by Goethe into a book of translations with interpretative notes.

After graduating from the Divinity School in 1836, Dwight entered upon a highly fruitful period that belied a friend's concern regarding his "nonconformity to circumstances." His steady achievement answered any concern whether his character might be "dreamy, irresolute, and impractical—with a consciousness all the while of a lofty destiny of usefulness in the world."[11] In 1837 and 1838, he purposefully gathered and drafted materials for the projected volume of Schiller's and Goethe's poems of which he was primary translator and editor. He also served various pulpits, including one at East Lexington, although he lacked a permanent ministerial position. In addition, he strengthened his organizational leadership in the Pierian Sodality and articulated his views on music.

Dwight acquired an excellent literary reputation on the appearance of his translation, with notes, entitled *Select Minor Poems, Translated from the German of Goethe and Schiller.*[12] It was published in 1839 as the third volume of Ripley's *Specimens of Foreign Standard Literature.* Dwight's decisive handling of the project and the clarity of his objectives emerge from one of several letters exchanged with colleagues who contributed translations to complete the substantial work. In his autograph letter of March 10, 1837, to James Freeman Clarke, editor of *The Western Messenger,* Dwight describes his intention to organize the lyrics of Goethe and Schiller to exhibit "as much as possible of their spirit" and in some measure to mark "the different *phases* thro' wh. their minds passed." He specified his method of translation, an organic rather than a literal one, as the preservation of the author's idea in "the *form* as well as the spirit, for in Lyric poetry the *form* is part of the *Substance*." His aim was to retain to the greatest possible extent the rhythm as well as the "fervor and grace of expression" of the original.[13]

Among the few poems from Schiller's early period that Dwight chose to translate for inclusion in the work were his preferred "An die Freude" and "Die Künstler" ("The Artists"). Both relate to each other and to Dwight's humanistic response to Beethoven, for they evoke fundamental images and concepts that he subsequently utilized in his essays about the composer's music. Dwight's commentary interprets both poems as expressions of Schiller's optimistic faith in the brotherhood of all human beings.

Dwight saw in "An die Freude" an image of a reunion of humanity, a holy jubilee celebrating a world free of sin that reflected Elysium or the Eternal Spirit. People could strive to meet on the holiest human ground possible, that "of the essential oneness of all souls," to be achieved through the identification of the interests and aims of all people.[14] The poem conveyed the possibility of a binding universal force to be attained through joy and fraternal sympathy. Its far-reaching ideal appealed to Dwight, who claimed that Schiller's fiery earlier poems glowed with "the same noble fervor, the same earnest philanthropy, world-embracing, as in the song 'To Joy,' which always characterized the poet and the man."[15]

Dwight's connection of Schiller's poetic vision of a united and ennobled humanity with Beethoven's expression of it through music is apparent in his discussion of a boundless yearning as the foundation of human existence. This yearning is experienced through a longing to "embrace the whole," which found its natural language in music. Dwight considered it interesting that Beethoven, whom he called "the most spiritual of composers," had turned to Schiller's ode as an expression of these human universal sentiments after reveling in the more abstract instrumental freedom of "pure harmony." He then cited a lengthy passage about Beethoven's Ninth Symphony in support of that direct link. (The passage's source will be identified and discussed in Chapter 3.)

Schiller's "Die Künstler" echoed the universality resounding in "An die Freude" and encompassed the earnest conviction that the highest unity could be achieved by beauty as an illuminating path to knowledge. It was a paean to the uniquely human province of art, which could lead toward the Elysium of reason and moral virtue. By learning art's laws, humanity would be ennobled and made free. Into the hands of artists the Godhead, as Creator of the Universe, had bestowed the possibility of bringing dignity to humanity; the soul's culture had both aesthetic and moral imperatives in its journey toward enlightenment and unity. "Die Künstler," which manifested the influence of Schiller's study of Kant, was "a noble Hymn to the spirit of all Art" whose conception and "fervent aspiration" deeply impressed Dwight.[16]

In Schiller's career "Die Künstler," in particular, had anticipated the message developed in his treatise of 1795, *Briefe über die aesthetische Erziehung des Menschen* (*On the Aesthetic Education of Man, in a Series of Letters*), which posited the indispensable role of aesthetic culture in the moral education of the complete human being in modern society. Mankind could be brought through cultivation toward the ideal of a higher harmony on individual and societal levels. As M. H. Abrams has explained, Schiller's series of letters on aesthetic education proposed that people strive toward an infinite artistic aim beyond human capacity rather than try to achieve a limited, accessible goal. This was one of the chief works of the era to stress the exalting possibilities of the life journey, rather than its aim, and it became a major source for the notion of elevating the boundless over the bounded in later Romantic writings.[17]

Dwight's formal study of German literature as an undergraduate and his extended reading of Schiller and Goethe in the course of preparing his book are likely to have assured his familiarity with Schiller's aesthetic treatise in the original German. Dwight's notes to Schiller's poetry provide evidence that he knew a key extract from a translation of the work on aesthetic education. He found it through the mediating impact of Thomas Carlyle. After consulting that author's chief American correspondent, Emerson, Dwight sought and received Carlyle's permission to dedicate the poetry volume to him "as a slight token of admiration and gratitude." In their different ways, Carlyle and Dwight shared a desire to disseminate knowledge of Schiller's writings and his artistic ideals among English-speaking readers.

Dwight cited favorably Carlyle's *Life of Friedrich Schiller,* which included commentary and translated sections of his works. In stressing the elevation of Schiller's idea of the poet's (artist's) life and calling, Dwight extracted from Carlyle's biography the following translated passage from *On the Aesthetic Education of Man.* I suggest that it formed a prominent aspect of Dwight's mental outlook as he handled materials about Beethoven's biography and works:

> But how is the Artist to guard himself from the corruptions of his time, which on every side assail him? By despising its decisions. Let him look upwards to his dignity and his mission, not downwards to his happiness and his wants. Free alike from the vain activity that longs to impress its traces on the fleeting instant, and from the discontented spirit of enthusiasm that measures by the scale of perfection the meagre product of reality, let him leave to *common sense,* which is here at home, the province of the actual; while *he* strives from the union of the possible with the necessary to bring out the ideal. This let him imprint and express in fiction and truth, imprint it in the sport of his imagination and the earnest of his actions, imprint it in all sensible and spiritual forms, and cast it silently into everlasting Time.—*Ueber die Aesthetische Erziehung des Menschen.*[18]

It was the artist's leadership in the process of striving beyond the bounds of time and the defined sphere of the actual that Dwight would first evoke in an essay appearing in 1843, fashioning it into his chief image in discussing Beethoven's Symphony no. 5 in C Minor, op. 67. Before 1847, Dwight had studied Beethoven's piano sonatas. He had also become acquainted with a few pieces of early chamber music, songs (including *Adelaïde,* op. 46), the oratorio *Christus am Oelberge,* op. 85, and the opera *Fidelio,* op. 72, as he came to know many of the symphonies. These works convinced Dwight that Beethoven was the musical artist of his century whose striving toward Elysium could restore the bonds of human fellowship torn by increasing individual alienation, competitive societal pressures, and the outbreak of war. In the two poems and the aesthetic treatise, Schiller had exalted fraternal, cooperative ties between people. He had then formulated a theory of art as a humanizing agent in civilization, a kind of "aesthetic utopianism,"[19] whose educative power could lead to a higher moral state. The impact of Schiller's views on Dwight's criticism of Beethoven's symphonies and on his perception of a link between aesthetic education and social progress was particularly strong between 1835 and 1846.

Carlyle lauded Schiller's principles as having been derived from the spiritual "inmost nature of man" rather than from material concerns. In Schiller's *On the Aesthetic Education of Man* (termed *Aesthetic Culture* by Carlyle), the British writer singled out its representation of sublime human feelings as stages in a progression toward the highest human grandeur. Carlyle exhorted the reader to overcome his earthly individual isolation and "war with Fate" by answering Schiller's call to rise toward that "height of internal activity and peace, and *be,* what he has fondly named himself, the god of this lower world." Retaining that goal would reward the exertions necessary to understand Schiller's ideas.

Carlyle's presentation, with its stress on Schiller's ethical content and search for moral verities, reinforced Dwight's similar convictions regarding the necessity to transcend worldly concerns through aesthetic education. In their early years, both Carlyle and Dwight idealized the high artistic and spiritual purpose of creative expression. The young American critic drew from Carlyle's account a passage from a translated letter by Schiller expressing his hope that art would reconcile both the creation of form and the free "play of inspiration" at a higher level.[20] This helped Dwight to recognize Schiller's struggle between two opposite mental processes, "the reflective and the spontaneous creative tendency." Although Dwight was then describing the challenge posed by these conflicting tendencies in translating Schiller's "Die Künstler," he returned strikingly to this thought when subsequently explaining the necessary coalescence of both to the higher criticism of art that he sought to shape.

Dwight also found Carlyle's discussion of the sympathetic relations between Goethe and Schiller to be valuable. For the sake of readers acquainted with English literature, Dwight included from that discussion a lengthy excerpt contrasting their differences by analogy to an imagined interview between Shakespeare and Milton.[21] In this instance, as elsewhere in Carlyle's biography, Schiller emerged as earnest, intense, impetuous, and aspiring, in contrast to the calm, natural, and "all-comprehending spirit" of Goethe. Dwight would come to associate with Beethoven personal qualities resembling those that he, as well as Carlyle, had most admired in Schiller.

Dwight benefited significantly from his study of Schiller's works and Carlyle's biography of the poet in still another way. Dwight sought to transmit to others in his country the earnest aims underlying the creation of art music as well as literature and the other arts. He found in Schiller's poetry and treatise, as in Carlyle's commentary, a way of conveying that high purpose. The German poet had emphasized the noble aim of literature; it did not exist to gratify selfishness, idleness, or mere spectacle. Schiller's fervor and the language with which Carlyle communicated Schiller's serious approach to his calling were to be echoed by Dwight in his response to music, and especially to Beethoven's works. Carlyle's explanation was notable:

> As Schiller viewed it, genuine literature includes the essence of philosophy, religion, art, whatever speaks to the immortal part of man. The daughter, she is likewise the nurse of all that is spiritual and exalted in our character.[22]

Schiller had shown from his perspective that literature's great boon was its capacity to lead humanity toward moral truth, that inward "truth of moral feeling," as Carlyle put it, by which human life was ennobled and inspired. This intense conviction may have inspired Dwight's plea that musical compositions also be regarded, studied, and promoted as literature, understood in this broad sense primarily as creative imaginative expression addressing the spiritual in humanity.

This interpretation provides an understanding of the full significance of Dwight's concept of music as literature, which was the basis of proposals intended initially to advance the cause of music, particularly as a field of learning at Harvard University. Handel and Beethoven should be honored just as much as Homer and Shakespeare, according to an 1837 report of the Pierian Sodality.[23] Dwight wrote it during the same year in which he was preparing his commentary on Schiller's poems for his volume of translations.

Ultimately, Dwight admired the works of Schiller and Goethe for their inherent qualities and because they could "inspire worthier aims and methods of culture" than prevailed at the time, according to his observation. He appears to have been drawn to Schiller's quest on another level as well. Dwight's preface to his volume of poetry translations includes the following striking passage that explains his particular admiration for Schiller's goals:

> From Schiller he [the student] learns lofty aspirations, and from Goethe how to realize them. The one speaks to him amid the hackneyed forms of life of a better ideal world, and warns him, inspires him, to trust all inward intimations of the True, the Beautiful, the Perfect, however contradicted by the Actual. The other shows him the riper practical wisdom, which makes much of the moment, and turns life into poetry.[24]

Dwight transferred this vital imagery regarding Schiller to his idealized conceptualization of Beethoven as musical leader.

Dwight attributed to Schiller and Goethe, through their literature and the strong ties of friendly association built between them, the beginning of a living movement addressing the authentic needs of humanity irrespective of class or nationality. Their works, especially the poetry, were significant to him in that period precisely because they spoke to the "*common* interests of all"; they told "how life, and thought, and poetry, and beauty, are the inheritance of Man, and not of any class, or age, or nation."[25] To Dwight, universality was an essential characteristic of enduring art that he sought and prized, particularly in the symphonic music of Beethoven.

Other artistic traits Dwight valued were organic unity and identification with the ideals of liberty. These, too, he praised in Schiller's *Wilhelm Tell* as he reviewed a translation by his friend Charles T. Brooks in 1839.[26] As before, Dwight underscored Schiller's capacity to create a "living work of Art" containing a complete vision, one culminating in freedom for a virtuous hero as it does for a nation within a framework of moral law.

Dwight's call to his readers can be interpreted broadly as a personal challenge: "From the poems and the lives of Goethe and Schiller, many a young mind has caught the watchword of self-culture; let him speed it onwards."[27] In this period, Dwight actively pursued his own musical learning and literary activity, joined to a desire to communicate with a larger public. How he found a direct connection between Schiller's aims and Beethoven's symphonic music is the subject of Chapter 3.

CHAPTER THREE

———————◆•○•◀———————

Dwight's Discovery
of German Music Criticism
in A. B. Marx's "Beethoven,"
1837–1838

While engaged in an effort to promulgate art music as an essential and humanizing factor in the lives of all people, Dwight discovered an essay that directly linked Schiller's ideals to the music of Beethoven. It also provided a model of German higher music criticism. A single reference in Dwight's *Select Minor Poems* provides only the title, *Universal-Lexicon der Tonkunst;* this led, however, to my identification of the author of a lengthy passage quoted in Dwight's notes to Schiller's "An die Freude."[1] He is Adolf Bernhard Marx (1795–1866), a contributor to the *Universal-Lexicon* who was then a professor and director at the Friedrich Wilhelm University of Berlin as well as former editor of the *Berliner allegemeine musikalische Zeitung.*[2]

The presence of the quotation in Dwight's volume of poetry translations confirms his knowledge of its original source during the time he prepared the manuscript in 1837 or 1838. He extracted and translated it from Marx's essay on Beethoven, which appeared in 1835 in the first volume of the *Encyclopädie der gesammten musikalischen Wissenschaften, oder Universal-Lexicon der Tonkunst (Encyclopedia of Complete Musical Knowledge, or Universal Lexicon of Music).*[3] Edited by Gustav Schilling, the six-volume work contains entries of varying length and prose style arranged alphabetically; it includes substantial essays on composers and genres by leading German theorists, aestheticians, critics, and professors of music. Dwight's access to it brought him into direct contact with a significant new resource for musical learning.

Interpreting the essence of Schiller's ode to be a "boundless yearning to embrace the whole" and linking it to music, Dwight found an affirmation of universality in the fact that Beethoven had utilized part of that very poem as the finale of a symphony with chorus. Its chronological position as the last of the nine symphonies seemed to him, on the basis of Marx's testimony, to represent a culmination of the composer's creativity. Although there is no evidence to suggest Dwight's acquaintance with the Symphony no. 9 in D Minor, op. 125, in any version as early as 1837, his interest in every facet of the composer's life and art led him to include a lengthy passage linking Beethoven to Schiller's ode.

Discovery of Marx's essay was significant to Dwight as a "glimpse into the deepest philosophy of the arts." It reinforced his conviction that both Beethoven and Schiller, as creative artists utilizing different means, had sought to communicate a longing for a better world through a work symbolizing the union of mankind. The original passage by Marx contains a reference, omitted by Dwight, to Beethoven's Choral Fantasy for Piano and Orchestra, op. 80.[4] Dwight's compressed translation reads as follows:

> As in outward life his had been a fruitless longing for the peaceful joys of the family circle, so in his art he returns with all the yearnings of memory and love to men; there grows in him a longing for *human* music, for song, and it leads him to the climax of his creative power. The ninth symphony, with chorus, is written. Here, in the widest reach of his art, he embraces all the results of his life. With giant force he summons around him the giant forces of the fullest and most active orchestra; they must,

they are obliged to play around him;—and their deep, murmuring tempest, and their light, frolic dances, waft his longing onward, till it dissolves into tenderest regret, into melancholy, sweet renunciation. But all this can satisfy no longer. The harmonies drop away; and the instruments themselves (in the style of recitative) pass into the manner of the human voice. Yet again do all those forms float dream-like over us, when human voices take up the recitative, and lead it into Schiller's song 'To Joy'—a union-song of all mankind. Nothing can be more moving, nothing lets us look so deeply into his breast, as when first the Basses, then the [other] singers, join so simply, so like a people's chorus, in the words 'Joy, thou brightest, heaven-lit spark,' and surrender themselves to the soft love and longing, which seeks but *men, only men!* requires only communion with men, and knows and will know nothing higher.*

*Universal-Lexicon der Tonkunst.[5]

Marx's original passage, and Dwight's selection of it, evince a characteristic belief in the interpenetration of life and art through an application of features from Schiller's poem to the biography and music of Beethoven.[6] According to this view, the essence of a "Bundeslied aller Menschen" ("union-song of all mankind") was its striving to achieve "die Gemeinschaft mit Menschen," communion with human beings, through universal artistic expression. Years before he joined a utopian community or heard the symphonies performed as complete orchestral works, Dwight cherished the ideal that Beethoven's music, like Schiller's poetry and aesthetics, could instill bonds between groups of people.

Dwight's knowledge of Marx's essay suggests its importance as one source of the American's other ideas concerning Beethoven's career and music. The essay mixed Marx's theories, knowledge of the compositions, and admiration for the composer. Marx perpetuated the notion, current during Beethoven's life, that the early works had drawn on traditions formulated by Haydn and Mozart before Beethoven forged his bold individual style. However, Marx was writing in the mid-1830s, almost a decade after Beethoven's death, from a perspective shaped by dynamic ideas of historical evolution: the German critic's Beethoven was not only a culminator and an innovator but a composer who traversed stylistic changes climaxing in the music of his later years.

Marx ardently championed those controversial works, which were deemed incomprehensible by writers attributing their complexity to Beethoven's altered perceptions resulting from his hearing loss. As a major composition of Beethoven's final period, the Ninth Symphony was exceptional in receiving a public orchestral performance in the United States before the 1850s. Its American première in 1846, to be discussed in Chapter 9, was a celebrated event attended and described by Dwight.

Marx's essay is permeated by key words delineating a spiritual framework for an approach to Beethoven's art. Those concepts that engendered Dwight's sympathetic response associated "Sehnsucht" ("longing") and "Geist" ("soul," "spirit") with Beethoven's music in its expression of "tiefwurzelnde Empfindung" ("deep-rooted feeling") conveyed "im Innern" ("in an inner sense"). Musical traits that appear to have been particularly suggestive to Dwight were Marx's emphasis on the importance of a work's, or movement's, initial melodic material, "Thema" ("theme"), and that material's elaboration through a unity of design pursued "in höchster Freiheit zu höchster Einheit" ("in highest freedom to the highest unity").

Crucial to Marx's thesis was his view of Beethoven as an instrumental composer for whom the piano was central. Unlike its less prominent role in the careers of Haydn or Mozart, this instrument had been the vehicle of his most characteristic utterances (together with the string quartets). Marx described Beethoven's ideal of keyboard sound, based on the full-spaced chords and orchestral approach to color, as richer, more powerful, more sonorous, and wider-ranging than that of his predecessors. In Dwight's subsequent statements about pianists, he echoed Marx's contention that, after Beethoven, there had been no additions of important expressive devices despite recent changes extending techniques of virtuoso brilliance. It was Beethoven who had developed the importance of the inner melodic lines, enriched the harmonies, and utilized the full disposition of the keyboard. Marx contended that the piano sonatas were a complete repository of Beethoven's techniques and his preferred medium of personal expression throughout his life.[7]

Similar formal and expressive tendencies, together with an unprecedented elaboration of thematic and motivic material, could be discovered in the symphonies, which displayed an entirely individual and grandly effective style. Marx emphasized that Beethoven had submerged himself in their abundant orchestral colors to create bold structures achieving varied textures in unified designs. Contrasting the textures of Johann Sebastian Bach and Beethoven, Marx explained that Bach had achieved polyphony through counterpoint, whereas harmony had been the foundation from which Beethoven's lines had acquired richness and freedom of movement.[8] The German critic's general approach was to have important ramifications for Dwight's 1846 outline of eras in the history of music.

Marx argued that just as Beethoven had responded with full sympathy to the inner voices of his instrumental world, he had been impeded by the nature of the human voice and speech when confronting the challenges of vocal composition. Although he praised particular works with voice, including the final movement of the Ninth Symphony, Marx asserted that Beethoven had sometimes allowed the orchestra to overwhelm solo voices or chorus.

The commentary by Marx appears to have been the earliest

writing on Beethoven in which Dwight encountered the technique of interpreting abstract instrumental music according to subtle or explicit programmatic elements. Such descriptions had begun to appear in quantity in about 1780.[9] They were connected, to a considerable degree, with the desire to explicate the "meaning" of instrumental music as it assumed increasing compositional significance and status in European concert life. In this essay, Marx introduced three concepts that associated particular works by Beethoven with a representational approach or a narrative element: "Seelenzuständen," or states of the soul; "Seelenbilder," or soul-images; and "Ideenreihe," a series of ideas.

With the first concept, Marx claimed that Beethoven had placed in certain instrumental works deeply rooted sentiments that sprang from states of the soul recognizable as their inner content. He chose as his example the Piano Sonata no. 26 in E-flat, op. 81a ("Les Adieux"), in which Beethoven had suggested an extramusical reference in the subtitle; Marx extended this reference to the specific situation of feelings represented by a loving couple on parting and reuniting. Marx also advanced a view of the Symphony no. 5 in C Minor, op. 67, as a triumphant victory attained after grievous struggles, but he quickly acknowledged that this work exalted high emotions in a way unachievable by words.

The second concept, "Seelenbilder," could involve more definite references, but Marx echoed Beethoven's specific caution when he described the Symphony no. 6 in F, op. 68 ("Pastoral"), as an example of a work whose soul-images arose not from the material reproduction of external conditions but from their reflection as the highest realization in an inner sense.[10]

The third concept, "Ideenreihe," held the greatest potential for explicit imagery applied to abstract, or nonprogrammatic, music. This potential could be realized through a series of ideas associated not merely with the Symphony no. 3 in E-flat, op. 55 ("Sinfonia eroica"), but also with the Symphony no. 7 in A, op. 92, the Piano Sonata no. 23 in F Minor, op. 57, and the last big sonatas. Marx explained that the series of ideas might be generated by an external idea, a generalized perception of human nature, or an autobiographical element. He also avowed that the works of composers like Haydn contained mere intimations of these associations, whereas Beethoven's instrumental music mightily awakened them.

I shall clarify in later chapters that Dwight's writings reveal an independent and consistently maintained antipathy to the direct association of specific extrinsic situations with Beethoven's instrumental music. He repeatedly attempted to clarify for his readers the distinctive nature of instrumental music that could not be represented by one plot, or "story." Although he acknowledged the presence in it of generalized expressive character or mood, he did not incorporate into his critical lexicon Marx's three representational concepts.

In other respects, however, the German writer's essay was significant in stimulating Dwight's early thinking. Marx's musical aesthetics, formulated earlier than his theoretical discussion of so-called sonata form, centered on the spiritual ennobling of the listener through art music, especially Beethoven's works. That thesis reinforced Dwight's fundamental convictions.

Scott Burnham has proposed that Marx was "the first to develop a critical approach to music based on a faith in the unerring coherence and spiritual elevation of Beethoven's masterworks, a faith we share today."[11] In his valuable study, Burnham interprets Marx's early articles written between 1824 and 1830 as editor in chief of the *Berliner allgemeine musikalische Zeitung.* His essay on Beethoven, published in 1835 in Gustav Schilling's *Universal-Lexicon,* touches on a few of those initial views. It also retains the central thought found in Marx's earlier material: the listener should approach an understanding of Beethoven's music on the basis of a spiritual communion with it. Dwight's intuitive tendencies accorded fully with Marx's enunciated vision. John S. Dwight was the first American writer on music to fashion a critical discourse that included, as an important element, a profound recognition of the inner essence of Beethoven's works. He remained a staunch advocate of this position for well over half a century.

Important distinctions must be noted, nevertheless. Unlike Marx, who was musically sophisticated and cognizant of a wide range of music as well as concert traditions, Dwight became acquainted only gradually with various genres of the repertory. Moreover, they approached subjective criticism from opposite perspectives: Marx upheld its autonomy despite his environment's traditional belief in the superiority of scientific, or technical, understanding,[12] whereas Dwight regarded subjective criticism as a valuable educative tool that might encourage prospective listeners in his society to become interested in comprehending stylistic features.

Dwight confronted the challenge of his American readers' lack of technical musical experience by addressing the role of music in general education. The impact of Schiller's aesthetic aims, and of Marx's ideas as applied to Beethoven's music, enabled Dwight to approach the topic with added insight and firm commitment. In May 1838, as his volume of poetry translations neared completion, the American critic contributed to a new and short-lived music journal, the *Boston Musical Gazette: A Semi-Monthly Journal Devoted to the Science of Music*. The front page carried his article "Music, as a Branch of Popular Education,"[13] in which he proposed a new conceptual approach to the problem.

Sustaining the cause of music as an indispensable branch of education and an "incalculable good," Dwight saluted organized efforts to teach the rudiments of music through common-school instruction and the Boston Academy of Music (without naming their perspicacious leader, Lowell Mason). Dwight emphasized his own interest in widening the focus to create an educated demand for music in the broad public by asking, "Why may not Music become a popular influence among us?" He elaborated on music as "the least exclusive" of all the arts, a view he had first expressed in "On Music," an unpublished manuscript essay, part of which had appeared in *The American Monthly Magazine* of November 1836.[14]

Dwight's advocacy of wide musical culture has been little acknowledged. Contemporary readers familiar with his writings of later decades may find surprising his statement in the *Boston Musical Gazette* that a "true idea of music forbids the thought that it is anything exclusive. Without looking at fact or experiment, I can readily believe in the capacity of all mankind for music, so long as I can believe that music supplies a genuine want of the soul."[15] Underlying that credo was Dwight's Transcendentalist faith in individual will and the positive view that, having a capacity to acquire knowledge through intuition, all people were spiritually equal. He added the necessity of developing a latent human capacity for thought that included the arts: it deserved to be "brought out, i.e. literally, *educated*" so that all people could have the opportunity to become acquainted with music.

This recognition of the fundamental importance of education linked to the soul's culture represented Dwight's actual conviction about the educability of a broad populace in a democracy beyond the institutional boundaries of public school or university. Reconsidering two positions advanced in 1837 in his *Report Made At a Meeting of the Honorary and Immediate Members of the Pierian Sodality,*[16] he adopted a wider framework. As a background for his new ideas, Dwight delineated the necessity for young people to be able to learn about Handel, Mozart, and Beethoven as well as

Socrates, Shakespeare, and Newton. In this instance, his pantheon implied a parallel ordering of figures to be honored by society: Beethoven's original discoveries in music were equal to Newton's in science. The American critic also expanded his earlier concept of music as a written literature of the world, in the imaginative Schillerian sense, to include a "pure Literature of the affections" made accessible to all.

Therefore, Dwight proposed educating "the public ear" in order to nurture innate musical talent in the young, open minds to the great masterworks, and stimulate demand for the composition or performance of music. Dwight reasoned that if the natural wants of the soul were broadly understood to include music, then early nurturing initially to its "mechanical" aspects (scales, intervals, rhythms) and then to its spirit would assure the eventual creation of a national music. It is striking that Dwight insisted on the priority of fundamental technical knowledge as a basis for higher mental cognition of music. Questioning whether a taste for art music could become universal, he asserted that sensitivity to it might become as common as that to poetry or fine writing. However, it is important to note his desire to include it as part of everyone's early experience without exclusion. He then arrived at his central thesis:

> The wider a mere power of discriminating sounds or what is
> called a "musical ear," is diffused, the higher will be the style
> and the standard of music in a community. Let the million be
> musical at all, and the one genius there is among them will be
> doubly strong and creative. The summit of the pyramid will rise
> in proportion to the width of its base.[17]

Dwight supported a wide base of community involvement in music as a means of establishing a healthy musical culture. Broad aesthetic cultivation, in the framework of Schiller's ideas, and an opportunity for the young to acquire a sound technical education in music were essential components of Dwight's recommendations. Calling for public musical education and concerts that could increase general knowledge of music as a literature while providing inspiring models, Dwight sought to foster a situation in which all would have access to art music, many might find it aesthetically satisfying, and a few could achieve the full flowering of their special compositional gifts. In that way, musical learning could provide the benefits of education for the entire community while also stimulating individual creativity.

CHAPTER FOUR

Dwight and William Gardiner, English Beethoven Enthusiast, 1835–1838

In Dwight's musically formative years, his approach to Beethoven's instrumental music was clarified by his knowledge of two books annotated or written by William Gardiner (1770–1853), an English writer on music and an amateur violist. Credited with having introduced Beethoven's music to England after procuring the Trio in E-flat, op. 3, in Bonn and performing it in Leicester in 1794,[1] this contemporary of Beethoven (a hosiery manufacturer by profession) had a varied impact on Dwight's early musical experiences. Although the two men never met, their mutual admiration for Beethoven's music strongly marked their activities. There is evidence that Dwight became acquainted with Gardiner's views in 1835.

The vital and stimulating character of English concert life in the early nineteenth century assured that "probably nowhere in the world outside of Vienna were as many works of Beethoven heard as in London."[2] In marked contrast to the United States, all of Beethoven's symphonies had been performed orchestrally in London during the first quarter of the nineteenth century.

During that period, Gardiner's name became known in America through his hymn-tune books and as a source for one of Lowell

Mason's celebrated compilations, *The Boston Handel and Haydn Society Collection of Church Music.*[3] Gardiner's earlier work of 1812, *Sacred Melodies, from Haydn, Mozart and Beethoven, Adapted to the best English Poets, and Appropriated to the use of the British Church,*[4] had enabled Americans to become acquainted with sacred vocal adaptations of melodies drawn from a largely instrumental repertory by composers, including the three associated with Vienna, then referred to as the "German school."

The varied objectives of Gardiner and Mason reflected the different musical situations in each country. Gardiner believed that he was improving English psalm singing by joining poetic texts to parts of predominantly slow movements of symphonies, chamber music, and sonatas. These originally instrumental melodies by Haydn, Mozart, Beethoven, and others represented the "new science" at that time. Mason adapted material from a wider group of English and Continental melodies for which he supplied three- and four-part harmony in an effort to reform the psalms and hymns used in American churches.

Gardiner addressed issues that were important to his compatriots in the early part of the century, one being varying practices between parish churches and large cathedrals. Another issue involved stylistic distinctions, strongly perceived in England, between the "ancient" music of composers like Corelli and Handel and the "modern" music of Haydn, Mozart, and Beethoven.

In his preface of 1822, however, Mason emphasized that in America the differing styles of many composers were not yet widely known. Therefore, Mason freely selected excerpts from both "ancient and modern authors" in a desire to add interest to psalmody and improve its practice in schools, societies, congregations, and family devotion.[5] Despite significant distortions of rhythm and character, melodies associated with Beethoven's name had thereby become known to many Americans in the 1820s and

1830s partly through the vocal collections by Gardiner and Mason, among others.

John Sullivan Dwight was sympathetic to Mason's reform ideas in the 1830s, despite the men's different backgrounds and aims. Mason, twenty-one years older than Dwight, was a prominent choir director in an orthodox Congregational church, a professor at the Boston Academy of Music, and a leader in the campaign to introduce the study of music into the public school curriculum.[6] As noted earlier, in 1835 Dwight was a graduate student and liberal Unitarian with strong interests in music, foreign languages, and literature. In his manuscript essay "On Music," Dwight praised two works published in 1834 that he considered to be "among the first fruits of a happy reformation" by the Boston Academy of Music to raise musical standards: the "Second Annual Report of the Boston Academy of Music" and "Manual of the Boston Academy of Music, for instruction in the elements of Vocal Music, on the system of Pestalozzi," by Lowell Mason. Despite his avowed support, however, Dwight's focus was on instrumental rather than vocal music.

His guiding principle was that music was important as a natural "language of feeling" just as words were a language of thought. Feelings, being infinite, could be represented best through flexible tones rather than by unyielding words limited to referential ideas. A harmonious binding connection to the universe, which Dwight would soon link to Beethoven's Ninth Symphony (through Schiller and Marx) and then to other Beethoven symphonies in the 1840s, became essential to his general commitment to music in the mid-1830s:

> We have said that the feelings are in their nature infinite—in them rests our faith in immortality. It would be to confine and do them violence, to connect them with mere words which are

but the *limited* forms of visible and palpable ideas. Love, striving to amalgamate with all—devotion, reaching forward to eternity—all that mysterious part of our nature, which binds us to one another, to the beauty of the world, to God and to an hereafter,—require[s] a different language from that common sense or intellect, which looks coldly upon the outward world, only to dissect it, and which occasions separations, instead of harmony, in human hearts.[7]

As the "least exclusive" among the arts, music was significant for its capacity to unite individuals and nations in common sympathies. Dwight was convinced that a blending of the ideal and the practical could achieve the highest state of society. When that goal was endangered by the selfish claims generated by "politicians or money-makers," music could help to restore societal balance by "familiarizing men with the beautiful and the infinite."[8] That, rather than an improvement in the singing of psalms, became Dwight's primary concern.

His preference for instrumental music led him to search for ways of describing a "language of feeling," whose characteristics appeared difficult to communicate effectively through written discourse. Dwight believed that he had found in Gardiner's writings a guide to a critical literature in English treating instrumental issues.

I have identified Gardiner as the author of an anonymous passage cited by Dwight in "On Music." He drew that quotation from the older writer's annotations to biographies of Haydn and Mozart. They had been translated and heavily based on varied sources by Stendhal (Marie-Henri Beyle). Readers learned of Gardiner's contributions to the work from its title page, announcing "Notes by the Author of *The Sacred Melodies.*"[9]

Dwight's incorporation of an extensive unidentified quotation, in manuscript and in the published excerpt, suggests its significance to him as a model of writing about a passage of instrumental music. His choice, Gardiner's description of a section from Haydn's oratorio *The Creation,* enabled American readers familiar with that work to consider instrumental activity not only in association with a text but as an appropriate subject of critical discourse. Dwight argued that Haydn's music did not exemplify the common music of the church but that it was an apt combination of expression and musical description capable of leading to a devotional influence.

To illustrate the higher power of music to express vast conceptions, Dwight noted briefly that Haydn's famous instrumental introduction, associated with the idea of chaos, displayed "occasional discords, struggling with and at last absorbed in the harmony—(fit image of the triumph of virtue)."[10] He then presented the more detailed, anonymous discussion of the same section:

> It commences with all the known instruments, displayed in twenty-three distinct parts. After these are amalgamated in one tremendous note, a slight motion is made perceptible in the lower parts of the band, to represent the rude masses of nature in a state of Chaos. Amidst this turbid modulation, the Basson [*sic*] is the first that makes an effort to rise, and extricate itself from the cumbrous mass. The sort of motion with which it ascends, communicates a like disposition to the surrounding materials, but which is stifled by the falling of the double basses, and the *Contrafagotto.*
>
> In this mingled confusion, the Clarionett struggles with more success, and the ethereal Flutes escape into air. A disposition verging to order is seen and felt, and every resolution would intimate shape, and adjustment, but not a concord ensues! After the volcanic eruptions of the Clarini and Tromboni, some arrangement is promised; a precipitation follows of the discordant sounds, and leaves a misty effect, which happily expresses the *"Spirit of God moving upon the face of the waters."* At the fiat: *"Let there be Light,"* the instruments are unmuted, and the audience is lost in the refulgence of the harmony.

Gardiner's descriptive prose associates an idea, based on the accompanying text, with particular woodwind and brass activity, melodic motion, changes of dynamics, timbral differentiation, and general reference to effects of consonance and dissonance. These features were suggestive to Dwight, but he recognized that others might find that quotation "extravagant." He stressed then, as he would throughout his career, that it "requires cultivation, to appreciate the higher productions of any art." Dwight's position was consistent: he maintained that music was the most accessible of arts, but additional preparation and study could increase its comprehension.

On the basis of the documentary citation, Dwight knew Gardiner's notes to Stendhal's *Life of Haydn* in 1835. What might he have learned from them about Beethoven's music? In contrast to Stendhal's heavily anecdotal text, Gardiner's annotations were more instructive regarding musical substance. Stendhal staunchly upheld the excellence of Italian melody and the vocal music of an older generation of composers, including Pergolesi, Leo, Durante, and Alessandro Scarlatti. Gardiner disagreed with Stendhal's perspective by pitting against it German (i.e., Viennese) strength, harmonic innovation, and instrumental sensitivity. According to Gardiner, these virtues were shared by what he called the "modern school" of Haydn, Mozart, and Beethoven.

To Stendhal's view that changing musical fashions declined into mediocrity, Gardiner countered with the opposite premise based on artistic "progress" that assured Beethoven's place in a compositional pantheon. Haydn's innovations as the "true inventor of the symphony" and in string quartets had been extended by Beethoven. The latter had also created, however, a different style, one associated with new harmonies and an increased use of dissonance.

> Nor can we imagine the art is on the decline, while so great a
> genius as Beethoven lives. This author, though less perfect in
> other respects than Haydn, exceeds him in power of imagina-
> tion; and, from recent specimens of his unbounded fancy, it is
> to be expected that he will extend the art in a way never contem-
> plated even by Haydn or Mozart.[11]

Recalling that Gardiner's original judgments date from 1811 and
1817, they exemplify a kind of criticism written during Beethoven's earlier career in which Haydn's music received praise for a
unity of design unmatched by the younger composer (whose claims
on the imagination, however, remained extraordinary).

In Beethoven's work Gardiner sensed a wholly new tone:

> Turn, for example, to his symphony in C major, the first note of
> which strikes the auditor by the new way in which its harmony is
> compounded. It begins with a discord, which imparts a bewail-
> ing, and dark effect to the wind instruments, and which rouses
> the imagination, and leaves the ear unguarded, for sudden and
> striking impressions.

Gardiner considered these symphonies, unlike Haydn's, to be "ro-
mances of the wildest invention, exhibiting a supernatural agency,
which powerfully affects the feelings and imagination."[12] According to this view, Beethoven's music seized the emotions of the
auditor and created an extraordinary impact through its unusual
harmonies, striking dissonances, and new instrumental effects.

Gardiner's conception of a "supernatural agency" operative in
Beethoven's symphonies, contrasted to the natural, human, and
comprehensible features of Haydn's works, was very close to that
proposed by E. T. A. Hoffmann, German author and music critic.
His famous characterizations of Haydn, Mozart, and Beethoven
had been widely disseminated in a Romantic manifesto first published in the Leipzig *Allgemeine musikalische Zeitung* of July 4 and

11, 1810; it was reprinted in a revised version in 1813 and published in book form in 1814.[13] Although the German critic's name does not appear directly in Dwight's early symphonic reviews, Hoffmann's influential criticism was the contemporary foundation for the differing commentaries on Beethoven written by Marx, Gardiner, [Karl] August Kahlert, and Gottfried Wilhelm Fink, among others. I shall further consider the connections between Hoffmann's and Dwight's ideas, which can be determined most precisely through Fink as one of several intermediaries, in Chapter 6.

Gardiner emphasized Beethoven's new instrumental techniques in chamber music as well as in symphonies. Beethoven had increased the importance of the cello part in string quartets and created independent yet connected interchange among the parts. His method superseded the "agreeable conversation" of a Haydn quartet, to which Stendhal's text alluded, to include "more mind" at a different level, reminding Gardiner of a "moral discourse."[14]

Gardiner also lauded the new era that had opened with the transition from harpsichord to pianoforte music: "It is the only instrument that will represent the effects of a full orchestra, and since its mechanism has been improved, Beethoven has displayed its powers in a way not contemplated even by Haydn himself."[15] Gardiner concluded additionally that in sacred music Beethoven was "pre-eminently great." The English writer's acquaintance with musical repertory not yet known in the United States and his assessment of Beethoven's position in the history of music provided a firm basis for the view that he was both a culminating composer and one whose "genius seems to anticipate a future age."[16]

In spite of Dwight's concurrence from his own perspective regarding the significance of Beethoven's achievement, he maintained an independent aesthetic stance that caused him to differ sharply with Gardiner in other respects. Stendhal's volume stimulated Dwight and other Bostonians to consider aesthetic issues raised by instrumental music. These included the extent to which the art of music was imitative. In his text, Stendhal had disparaged music as the least definite of the arts, asserting that the effect of symphonies could be increased if they were played in a theater while painted scenes, ostensibly analogous to the passages, were exhibited onstage. That author had also described two kinds of imitation of nature, the physical and the sentimental. Jean-Jacques Rousseau had previously differentiated between them, explaining that the second type retraced not the objects but "the feelings which they inspire."[17]

On this vital issue of music as imitation, Gardiner did not take the opportunity in his notes to contradict Stendhal. Gardiner's apparent assent was to be confirmed in his later book, *The Music of Nature*. In this area, Dwight strongly disagreed with Gardiner, according to his review-essay of 1838. That Dwight read Gardiner's *Music of Nature*[18] on its appearance in a Boston reprint edition during the preparation of *Select Minor Poems* is clear from a passing reference to it in his commentary on a poem by Friedrich Schiller.[19] His critique of Gardiner's book appeared in September 1838 in *The Christian Examiner and General Review*.[20] There he was listed, amid prominent ministers and Harvard professors, as a principal contributor. The article was immediately reprinted in full in two issues of the *Boston Musical Gazette*.[21] Dwight's review-essay, therefore, reached readers from academic, religious, and musical circles.

Gardiner had proposed that music was an imitation of physical nature in the animated world. The book moved from early chapters on topics such as "Noise and Sound" to material about vocal performers, human cries, and the song of birds. It presented informal, anecdotal characterizations of specific orchestral instruments before introducing comments on composition. Gardiner freely interpolated brief musical passages by different composers into his prose. These included quotations from Beethoven's instrumental works, which he occasionally supplied with text. He also cited his own previous arrangements in the *Sacred Melodies*.

Along with Gardiner's advocacy of Beethoven's bold style, then, the book contained naïve notions placed, according to Dwight, within a superficial medley of facts based on a fundamentally flawed premise. For example, Gardiner associated the staccato subject of the Scherzo in Beethoven's Third Symphony with the cackling of hens and quoted its opening three bars, in treble clef only, in that context.[22]

Gardiner's experience as a violist and his sensitivity to string techniques enabled him to comment about Beethoven's compositional control in achieving particular dynamic shadings and note articulations by precise markings instructing the performers. However, when he reiterated material from his earlier notes to Stendhal's *Life of Haydn* about Beethoven's innovations in quartets and symphonies, he emphasized their depiction of "some of the grandest effects of the natural world." Gardiner did not acknowledge the inherent contradiction that, having supplied texts for excerpts from Beethoven's instrumental music, he yet counted them as the "first specimens of instrumental music breathing a sentiment more powerful than words."[23]

Dwight did not consider *The Music of Nature* an answer to his avowed search for a "higher criticism of music." Vigorously refuting Gardiner's central thesis, he began by asserting the purpose of music in a way based on earlier statements from "On Music" and from his Divinity School graduation thesis, "On the Proper Character of Poetry and Music for Public Worship," published in *The Christian Examiner and General Review* in November 1836. In these, he had emphasized that music, whether instrumental or associated with a poetic text, was a natural language of feeling belonging to a higher realm shared by reason, imagination, and beauty.[24] Dwight disagreed with those who, like Gardiner, insisted on its faithful representation of things and lauded instead music's capacity for artistic idealization.

Adding new ideas in his review-essay of 1838, Dwight expressed the hope that a genuine philosophy of music could be built one day that would combine spontaneous and reflective tendencies capable of addressing the essential nature of music and its relation to the soul's culture. That fusion was rare, and Dwight surmised that it would await a future age in which purely instrumental music would receive belated recognition.[25] In 1838, Dwight affirmed a central tenet: music was unique for its capacity to combine the direct expression of natural sentiments with artistically shaped aspects of the beautiful. Both these elements could draw people together by merging their private interests in a universally shared sentiment.[26]

From Dwight's perspective, Beethoven had carried the recent instrumental art "up into the infinite, bounding all human conception since his own." The American critic was convinced that a true philosophy of music could be located only in the sphere of instrumental music, which was "music proper," with the orchestra as "its highest external development." On this credo Dwight would, within a few years, build his conception of the symphonic Beethoven. In 1838, however, he asserted that instrumental music was more flexible than song. He based this view particularly on his increasing knowledge of keyboard sonatas by Beethoven and Haydn, which expressed "all the deepest undefined yearnings of the soul" regardless of time or circumstances. Lacking access then to Beethoven's late string quartets, Dwight accepted Gardiner's positive judgment of them as anticipating feelings of "a future age."

In essence, Dwight supported Gardiner's championing of Beethoven's instrumental stature but refused to accept his fundamental aesthetic position regarding music as an imitative art. The younger man challenged Gardiner's view firmly, stating that even in instances in which music engaged in partial description it "never copies nature literally; if it does it fails. It uses the privilege of art to idealize whatever it represents."

Despite these substantial reservations about the book's main argument, Dwight hailed *The Music of Nature* as a symbol of the existence of a literature of music in the English language and of the possibility that musical sounds could be concretely discussed. In these respects, an important era had opened—it was "almost the first specimen we have had of anything like the *literature of music*." Wanting to find ways of writing about music to general audiences, Dwight perceived in Gardiner's work "an approach at least, not wholly unsuccessful, to a power of translating music into words." He proclaimed it an important contribution: "Here then is quite a discovery; music may be described."[27]

Dwight admired Gardiner's treatment of specific instrumental passages and his earlier acquaintance with a range of Beethoven's music as instrumentalist and auditor. Gardiner had shown that discrete features of composition could be recalled in prose distinctly enough to sustain critical comparison between passages. Dwight heralded this aspect of Gardiner's achievement: "In this way it is opening the door to a new branch of literature, *musical criticism*, a thing alike needed for the cause of pure taste, and for the vindication to music of her true place among the sister spirits of the Beautiful, of her equal share in human culture."

In this area, Dwight wanted to share with his readers the English author's "power of description." He chose two citations about instrumental activity, one concerned with Niccolò Paganini's violinistic virtuosity and the other with an evocative passage from a sinfonia in Haydn's *Creation*. In the latter instance, Dwight noticed Gardiner's characterization of instrumental participation in the same oratorio that he had selected three years earlier. Part of Gardiner's passage follows:

> In the commencement of this piece, our attention is attracted by a soft streaming note from the violins, which is scarcely discernible till the rays of sound which issue from the second violin diverge into the chord of the second; to which is gradually imparted a greater fulness of color, as the viols [sic] and violoncellos steal in with expanding harmony.[28]

This narrative may have suggested to Dwight a particular way of projecting, through descriptive prose, an association with a musical passage of unfolding instrumental color, combined with gradually intensifying dynamics and harmony, that could help listeners to remember it more clearly after hearing it. He would apply that highlighting of specific instrumental activity to his treatment of Beethoven's symphonies in the 1840s.

In his essay of 1838, Dwight disclosed another important reason for his interest in Gardiner's writings. Expressing regret that *The Music of Nature* had not contained all of Gardiner's notes to Stendhal's *Life of Haydn,* he urged that the earlier volume be reprinted. It had interested Dwight as "one of the very few works in English which treat at all worthily of the aesthetics of music." The qualification, "in English," indicates his knowledge of a literature concerned with musical aesthetics in a language other than English. By then, he knew, and had quoted from, Marx's essay on Beethoven from Schilling's *Universal-Lexicon.* That is the interpretative framework behind Dwight's assertion that "except among the Germans, little philosophy or higher criticism can be expected."[29]

Through Gardiner's writings, Dwight became aware of new instrumental repertory, controversial issues in musical aesthetics, and ways of shaping musical description. He also glimpsed opposing sides of a musical controversy between "ancients" and "moderns" in England and on the Continent. Although it was remote from his immediate musical experience, he recognized in it Gardiner's enthusiastic support of Beethoven as the chief among "modern" German instrumental composers.

CHAPTER FIVE

A German Musician and Editor in Boston:
H. Theodor Hach as Guide, 1839–1842

The arrival in Boston of H. Theodor Hach sometime during 1837 introduced directly into Dwight's life a person who possessed knowledge of European, especially German, musical traditions and whose particular interests in instrumental music and in Beethoven coincided with his own inclinations. Hach's way of encouraging musical learning beyond academic circles in the United States was through the dissemination of valuable information in a significant, if short-lived, music journal for which he was editor and critic.

Hach's founding in 1839, initially with T. B. Hayward, of *The Musical Magazine; or Repository of Musical Science, Literature, and Intelligence*,[1] initiated a forum for the circulation in America of recent musical ideas from the Continent and England. Sustained (with difficulty) for three years, it offered a diversity of views as well as publication opportunities to Dwight at a decisive period in his career. Dwight's writings from 1839 to 1842 can be placed in the framework of his interactions with Hach to establish the men's mutual regard, as well as Hach's role as a vital intermediary of Euopean Beethoven sources. I shall consider Hach's essay on two of Beethoven's symphonies and his pertinent activity as a professional cellist in Chapters 6 and 7, respectively.

Hach may have been encouraged to come to Boston by Lowell Mason, who became friendly with him during Mason's trip to Germany in 1837.[2] Hach had connections to Lübeck and to Hamburg, where he met Mason and assisted him with travel arrangements and translation; Mason did not speak German, but Hach was fluent in English. As a teacher of music, cellist, and writer, Hach possessed abilities that could contribute importantly to musical education, concert life, and music criticism in America. Mason had taught music from 1832 to 1836 at the Perkins Institution and Massachusetts Asylum for the Blind in Watertown.[3] During his years in Boston, Hach succeeded Mason there and held the position of principal teacher of music and general assistant. I have ascertained his professional connection to that institution on the basis of a heading in a letter in his hand reading "Institution for the Blind" and confirmed his position according to the *Fourteenth Annual Report of The Trustees of the Perkins Institution and Massachusetts Asylum For the Blind, to the Corporation.*[4]

During the year in which Hach was organizing his new periodical, Dwight was receiving praise for his recently published volume of poetry translations with notes. Among the congratulatory communications was one from Thomas Carlyle. Beyond taking pleasure in Dwight's dedication of the book to him and lauding the younger man's ability and skill ("I have heard from no English writer whatsoever as much truth as you write in these Notes about Goethe"), his response to a letter from Dwight indicates that the American had alluded to his serious financial situation, which offered no immediate prospect of a settled position. Carlyle advised Dwight not to be unduly depressed by poverty, since it is "no bad companion for a young man." He urged him, instead: "Heed not poverty. Speak to your fellow men what things you have made out by the grace of God."[5]

Between 1839 and 1842, Dwight maintained a continuing connection with Hach during a turbulent period in which he served congregations on a temporary basis, was ordained as pastor of the Second Congregational Church in Northampton, Massachusetts, for a year from 1840 to 1841, and ultimately rejected the ministry as a career to begin residence at Brook Farm in November 1841. The formation of many of Dwight's musical convictions coincided with aspects of European musical thought that became known to American readers through translated or reprinted excerpts appearing in *The Musical Magazine,* of which Hach became sole editor in 1840.

Situated as one of the earliest authoritative periodicals of its kind in America between the experimental Boston *Euterpeiad* of 1820–22 and *Dwight's Journal of Music* beginning in 1852, this magazine was unusual then for its inclusion of foreign extracts along with the essays supplied largely by the indefatigable Hach. It provided information in the areas of elementary theory, the pedagogy and performance practice of instrumental and vocal art music, the history of music, musical biography, and music criticism, supplemented by fiction, poetry, and newsworthy items.[6] In the last year of its existence, Hach stated that his goals for the periodical had been to increase America's understanding of art music by influencing "the mind and soul of man and of artist" by providing musical knowledge such as "our scant music literature does not furnish" and to raise a standard of musical taste through "true but encouraging criticism."[7]

Lacking Hach's professional background in music, Dwight welcomed his support on behalf of shared objectives. The earliest link of record between them can be traced to Hach's brief mention in 1839 of the Boston edition of Stendhal's *Life of Haydn,* with

Gardiner's notes. He quoted an unidentified writer's earlier encouragement that it be reprinted for its treatment of the aesthetics of music.[8] As I have pointed out, it was Dwight who had thus referred to it in an essay of 1838 for *The Christian Examiner*.

Dwight contributed three articles during this period to the Transcendentalist periodical, *The Dial*; all of them were channeled to its first editor, Margaret Fuller, through the managing editor, George Ripley. Two were revised sermons, while only one dealt with musical issues.[9] "The Religion of Beauty" linked Dwight's aesthetic vision to a high moral ideal as a beneficent shield against narrow utilitarianism;[10] "Ideals of Every-Day Life" extolled moral perfection as the consistent key to meaningful human striving.[11] His critical article of 1840, "The Concerts of the Past Winter" (first of a series of annual concert-review essays continued by John F. Tuckerman and Margaret Fuller), won praise from the demanding Ripley: "Your article on 'Concerts' is an atoning offering for the many sins of the 'Dial.' "[12]

Dwight and Hach seized on similar issues for comment. In two instances, Dwight elaborated on concerns that he had broached in 1838 in disagreeing with Stendhal. They were then raised by Hach in 1839 when he dissented from the French writer on the object of music and on the function of imitative passages in Haydn's *Creation*. Hach asserted that music was the highest of the arts, extending beyond gratification of the senses to reach the heart and intellect. He disagreed with Gardiner about his "favorite theory" and criticized Haydn's imitation of physical nature in his oratorio as insufficiently ideal.[13] Dwight reiterated the essence of both statements in his article for *The Dial*.

Encouraged by the greater interest shown that season in "genuine classic music," he restated his central belief that music represented the aspiration of the heart to the Infinite. Dwight was optimistic that as taste grew a preference for instrumental "music *pure"* would also increase. Indicating acquaintance with a version of Beethoven's Sixth Symphony, he praised its feeling of nature to the detriment of Haydn's *Creation*. Dwight rejoiced in the prominence of orchestral material in Haydn's work but, like Hach, misunderstood what he perceived to be its particularity of detail:

> Art [. . .] should breathe the pervading spirit of Nature, as a whole, and not copy too carefully the things that are in it. Whoever has studied the Pastoral Symphony, or the Pastoral Sonata of Beethoven, will feel the difference between music which flows from an inward feeling of nature, from a common consciousness (as it were) with nature, and the music which only copies, from without, her single features. These pieces bring all summer sensations over you, but they do not let you identify a note or a passage as standing for a stream, or a bird.[14]

Hach and Dwight, therefore, opposed the positions of Stendhal and Gardiner regarding the musical imitation of physical nature. In addition, Dwight's views markedly contrasted to a pictorial conception of Beethoven's music proposed by one of Dwight's friends, John F. Tuckerman. Tuckerman's review-essay of François-Joseph Fétis's entry on Beethoven for the *Biographie Universelle des Musiciens* appeared in July 1840 in *The Boston Quarterly Review* during the same month as Dwight's article on concerts in *The Dial*.[15]

Unlike Dwight, Tuckerman asserted that human passions as well as scenes of nature had explicit prototypes in sound. He transferred his general notion of music as a "picture of ideas" to Beethoven's works, which Tuckerman admired especially for their capacity to present to listeners "a true picture of his life." Tuckerman's praise of the powers of Beethoven as "pictorial, descriptive, imitative to the highest degree," combined with his avowal of a close connection between extrinsic literary references and instrumental music, constituted a sharply contrasting stance to that of Dwight concerning Beethoven's instrumental music.

Dwight's article on concerts for *The Dial* is also notable for its praise of what he would henceforth refer to as "the new school of Piano Forte playing" for its idiomatic keyboard qualities, originality, and novel technical features.[16] Compositions by Sigismund Thalberg, Theodor Döhler, Chopin, Adolf Henselt, and Liszt could be enjoyed "for what they are, without complaining that they are not something else." He expressed satisfaction in hearing them interpreted by the visiting European virtuosi Frederick Racke-mann [Rakemann] and Leopold Kossowski. However, as early as 1840, he tempered that enthusiasm with the admission that he would have been "much more pleased" to hear sonatas by Beethoven or other "true classic" works written only for musical reasons and the communication of inspired artistic feeling rather than for instrumental display. Dwight did not alter these mixed reactions about virtuosi when, in 1845, he considered the positive and negative aspects of their contributions. In 1846, as I shall indicate, he would reassert the importance of "the new school of Piano Forte playing" in an outline of stages in the history of music.

Like Hach, Dwight strongly encouraged increased orchestral performances. Addressing members of a large group gathered to pay tribute to the leader of the Boston Handel and Haydn Society's orchestra, Dwight urged them to practice together throughout the year in order to become an ensemble worthy of performing the major works of Haydn and Mozart. If that occurred, "orchestra and audience would improve together, and we might even hope to hear one day the '*Sinfonia Eroica*,' and the '*Pastorale*' of Beethoven."[17] Impeding steady progress, he thought, were a lack of frequent public performances of classic music and the absence of a constant audience, but Dwight believed that an initial nucleus of two or three hundred enthusiasts could lead to the building of a large and appreciative public. That was his hope and his goal.

The essay also clarifies Dwight's high esteem for Hach. Describing Joseph Knight's vocal recital, Dwight voiced dismay that Knight had not sung Beethoven's and Matthison's "Adelaïde" in the original German, instead of in Charles Horn's English bowdlerization called "Rosalie." Dwight's sensitivity in this matter can be attributed initially to the resulting linguistic and textual deformity rather than to a purist's desire for authenticity, but he also objected emphatically to the changed subject resulting in a different work. Always attuned to instrumental aspects, Dwight maintained that the performance of the second part of the piece had produced the effect of slighting "those magnificent chords of the accompaniment, which is as wonderful as the part for the voice." He then recommended that readers consult Hach's description of that event, since his informed commentary about "Adelaïde" had preceded Dwight's remarks:

> But for a just criticism of this and of the whole concert we would refer to the excellent "Musical Magazine" of Mr. Hach,—a work which we are glad to notice in passing; for, next to good music itself, good musical criticism should be hailed as among the encouraging signs.[18]

Dwight's admiration for Hach extended beyond his editorial and critical capabilities to his professional musicianship. The American critic recommended ways to increase the audience for art music, one of which was to introduce public instrumental concerts on the model of the Classic Concerts organized by Ignaz Moscheles in England. Dwight's proposal concerned repertory written primarily for chamber music ensembles, with the occasional addition of symphonies. The programs were to be repeated often enough to attain familiarity among a nucleus of several hundred subscribers, who would broaden into a large audience.

Again, Dwight's aim was to restrict the repertory through repetition, not to limit the size or nature of the eventual audience. On the contrary, he regretted that the audience in America for this type of music was then small, but he expressed the hope that repeated access and patient education, together with the availability of cheap tickets, would eventually draw a wider public to it. I shall point out in Chapter 7 that Dwight and Hach disagreed about the size of an audience appropriate for chamber music. In introducing his idea for a series in 1840, four years before the Harvard Musical Association sponsored a regular series of public chamber music concerts (with Hach as cellist), Dwight deemed the participation of Hach and other German-born musicians then resident in Boston essential to its success:

> Let a few of our most accomplished and refined musicians institute a series of cheap instrumental concerts. . . . The two or three hundred, who are scattered about and really long to hear and make acquaintance with Beethoven and Haydn, could easily be brought together by such an attraction, and would form a nucleus to whatever audience might be collected, and would give a tone to the whole, and secure attention. Why will not our friends, Messrs. Schmidt, Hach, Isenbech, &c. undertake this? It might be but a labor of love at the outset; but it would create in time the taste which would patronize it and reward it.[19]

Hach, in turn, again evinced his pleasure in Dwight's work when he reprinted, without attribution, three key sentences from the American writer's essay on concerts. They described Handel's *Messiah* as exemplifying musical unity and Haydn's *Creation* as illustrating musical variety.[20] Subsequently, Hach also extracted three pages from the same article by Dwight for republication in the next issue of *The Musical Magazine.* In this case Hach prefaced the comparison, still unattributed, by recommending it as "so true and beautiful."[21]

Hach began his third year as editor of *The Musical Magazine* with the news that henceforth articles would be contributed occasionally by prominent members of the community, including "Rev. J. T. [*sic*] Dwight, and other eminent literary amateurs of music."[22] In January 1841, with Dwight then in Northampton, Hach perceived him as a minister and noted literary critic whose strong musical interests and convictions had enabled him to write persuasively about the subject. Neither one could have foreseen Dwight's imminent departure from the pulpit later that year to undertake a career in music. Hach's announcement suggests that he had already requested, and received, an article from Dwight. The sole editor of *The Musical Magazine* welcomed assistance in appropriately filling its pages.

Shortly thereafter, a substantial extract appeared from Dwight's report of 1837 to the Pierian Sodality. While endorsing its views, which had been directed particularly to the Harvard University community, Hach stressed his individual position: music, as an art, could be perfected through the leadership of "educated men," although he acknowledged that successful efforts had been made to bring music "to the people."[23]

Dwight's tenure as pastor in Northampton, meanwhile, was drawing quietly to a close. The ordination had taken place on May 20, 1840, with George Ripley delivering a sermon that encouraged neither rules nor dogma but rather the establishment of spiritual experience through a personal relation with God. He had urged his younger friend to be a guide and public teacher in the search for truth.[24] Reverend William Ellery Channing had delivered a cautionary charge: knowing of the younger man's delight in "poetry and the fine arts," he exhorted him to discover truth for himself by helping others "to *see*," and to remember that "the divinest art is that, which studies and creates the beauty, not of outward form, but of immortal virtue."[25] Despite the good wishes of these and other prominent supporters, Dwight's contract was not renewed after his first year.

During his absence from Boston (which included a stay of several months in Northampton beyond the expiration of his contract), the Boston Academy of Music had inaugurated its orchestral series featuring Beethoven's symphonies. Dwight had heard about one of these concerts from Sophia Ripley, with whom he shared a warm friendship based, in part, on their interests in music and literature:

> If it were not so long passed, I would tell you of the last concert of the academy & their exquisite performance of one of the most magnificent & touching of Beethoven's Symphonies. Boston never has seen an eveg [*sic*] like that in her young annals— "Only think," said Charles Putnam, "the man who would enjoy this more than all the rest of us put together is a hundred miles off!"[26]

This and other correspondence provides evidence that by spring and early summer Dwight was seriously considering the option of joining the Ripleys in their new venture at Brook Farm, about which Sophia Ripley wrote positively and in detail.

Shortly thereafter, Dwight accepted an invitation extended to him "at the eleventh hour" to present the annual address before the Harvard Musical Association at its Commencement Day gathering.[27] Dwight's biographer, Walter L. Fertig, has asserted that the Harvard address assumed a "note of tragedy": after all, Dwight had left the pastorate and was preparing to join Brook Farm, unlike members of his audience who may have been "reservedly tolerant" or "openly disrespectful" of Ripley's experiment.[28] One might adopt a less drastic perspective and see the

address as a poignant autobiographical document marking its author's passage from one phase of his life to another. In November,
he would go to Brook Farm, where he would be free of external
pressures to sustain a livelihood in the church. He would also enjoy
a greater chance to study, teach, play, and write about music in a
pleasant environment. Disappointment and uncertainty mixed
with a new sense of opportunity as he reasserted his musical convictions.

Hach published Dwight's Harvard address in *The Musical Magazine* on August 28 (three days after the lecture to the Harvard
Musical Association on August 25, 1841), with attribution, and
without added comment by the editor, as the lead article on the
front page.[29] Unlike his position in the past, Dwight was no longer
constrained by ties to the Divinity School or formal connection to
the church. He could, and did, assert a modified approach.

In stating that all original music that ministered to the "wants
of the soul" could be considered holy, Dwight was asking the
members of his audience to be less influenced by the function
attached to music and thus to be more openly receptive to it.
Music transcended specific purposes, whether liturgical (sacred)
or recreational (secular). He thought music should be recognized
more broadly as an art, a language, and a prophecy. In principle, if
music could be approached without primary reference to its limit-
ing function, it would win greater public acceptance for its dual
capacity "to hallow pleasure and to naturalize religion."[30]

Works composed as spiritual revelations by an "artist-creator,"
rather than by a "mechanical" composer, might then attain the
highest consideration. Inevitably, therefore, he praised Beethoven's instrumental music for its aspiration beyond the linguistic
realm and cited his instrumental adagios, which could be viewed
as secular music or as the essence of prayer—"not formal prayer,
I grant, but earnest deep unspeakable aspiration." This issue was

important to Dwight personally and professionally: acknowledging that he had never felt "at home in this world of the finite and the artificial," the critic avowed his discovery in Beethoven's harmony of "another and an unseen world which only the heart knoweth, and which the pure in heart shall enter, though they are not of the successful ones after the world's way."

At this point of transition, Dwight renewed his commitment to enduring art music, and especially to Beethoven's instrumental music, for its capacity to instill a powerful consciousness of "new worlds within us; [these works] bring out the glow and grandeur of the world around us; they open a new communication between our hearts and nature, and assert the present Deity, without name, without creed."

He was suggesting his preference for music whose intimation of a higher existence could enable human beings to share in a "final reconciliation of the sacred and secular in all things." When Dwight asked members of the Harvard Musical Association to promote a taste in the larger community for Beethoven, Haydn, and Mozart, he was championing, from his perspective, musical experiences that afforded individuals the freedom to grow intellectually while also finding bulwarks against the artificiality and strife of the finite world.

As contributor to, and reader of, Hach's *Musical Magazine,* Dwight was in contact with stimulating musical issues even during his isolation in Northampton. Hach advocated increased presentations of large-scale instrumental music, an improvement in string playing, knowledge of music acquired through concert performances and historical essays, and the promotion of higher standards of taste. He urged the Boston Academy of Music to "get up an orchestra of its own."[31] When it expanded its operations into the instrumental field, he congratulated the Academy and offered suggestions; some of these were not always feasible to implement, such as the addition of time to regular weekly rehearsals. However, he praised a development that offered "classical instrumental concerts; classical in the choice of the music, and classical, as far as can be, in its performance; thus furnishing models for improving musical taste." Such concerts could increase what Hach regarded as a "pure taste" for music in its "highest forms (the Symphony, the Overture.)"[32]

As cellist, Hach played solos and chamber music as well as participating in orchestral concerts during his years in Boston. From at least 1840, four years before the Harvard Musical Association's chamber music series, there is evidence of his participation in independent chamber music performances on concert programs of a diverse nature. He appeared with other distinguished professional instrumentalists, including Henry Schmidt, professor of violin and leader of the Academy's orchestra (with whom Hach encouraged local amateurs to study), and Frederick Rackemann [Rakemann], one of the finest German pianists then touring in America. On one occasion, these three performed an early trio by Beethoven that was, according to Hach, "very favorably received, and this fresh, spirited, and yet so melodious composition, deserves to be a favorite."[33]

The editor's performances lent authority to his comments about the important role of musicians in communicating compositional intentions. He stressed the power of instrumental music to aspire beyond the perceived world of the Understanding to reach man's "higher part, his living soul" when composers gave expression to distinct character and form.[34] By regarding mechanical execution as subservient to thoughtful musicianship, the performer could connect the actual markings of the notated score to that spiritual aspect. This idealistic approach would enable the performer to convey a composition's meaning by fully entering into its spirit. Dwight echoed this conviction repeatedly in his criticism.

As long ago as 1927, Otto Kinkeldey noted Hach's particular activity in circulating and interpreting discussion of Beethoven and his music. Hach's "helpful criticisms and suggestions, his musicianly comments and analyses of the works performed are worthy of treatment by themselves."[35] The relative inaccessibility of Hach's journal in its entirety accounts, in part, for the subsequent neglect of his contributions to the reception of Beethoven's music in the United States.

As editor, translator, or writer, Hach provided Dwight and other readers of *The Musical Magazine* with access to a variety of commentary about Beethoven. He published an early direct glimpse of Beethoven's expressed dedication to his art in a translated excerpt from the Heiligenstadt Testament of 1802, known to English-speaking readers as the Will.[36] He included lengthy extracts from, or comments based on, the *Biographische Notizen über Ludwig van Beethoven* of 1838 by Franz Wegeler and Ferdinand Ries stressing Beethoven's independent nature, pianistic excellence, and increasing deafness.[37] Hach also carried Bettina Brentano von Arnim's characterization of the "spiritual" Beethoven, with his reported expression of closeness to God through his art.[38]

Additionally, Hach made available a translation of Fétis's complete essay on Beethoven originally published in his *Biographie Universelle des Musiciens*.[39] Although it appeared a few months after John F. Tuckerman's essay describing Fétis's work in *The Boston Quarterly Review,* the translation enabled Americans to read Fétis's essay directly in its entirety and thereby to connect information about Beethoven's artistic career to descriptions of his unfamiliar instrumental compositions.

Hach deemed interesting Margaret Fuller's biographical essay in *The Dial,* "Lives of the Great Composers, Haydn, Mozart, Handel, Bach, Beethoven," and reprinted large extracts from it.[40] Through his editorial selection, Hach reinforced Fuller's emphasis on the affirming power of music and its sustaining capacity in the lives of the five composers. He chose sections from her material on Beethoven (which had been based on a variety of Beethoven sources in addition to Anton Felix Schindler's *Biographie von Ludwig van Beethoven*) that stressed the composer's independence, private misfortunes, and necessity to "travel inward" to intense artistic concentration.

In determining his editorial choices, Hach emphasized the musical tradition, including particularly Haydn, on which Beethoven had built, as well as his originality. He also tried to separate fact from myth, asserting his desire to learn about the composers "as men" rather than revering them "as demi-gods."[41] In discussing Ignaz Moscheles's English edition of Schindler's biography, Hach was knowledgeable enough to question the biographer's description of a specific situation, based on an underlying poetic idea, associated with Beethoven's Piano Sonata op. 14, no. 2. He declared that it detracted from the "spirituality" of the music.

Regarding performance, Hach emphasized that clarity must be maintained regardless of the specific tempo marking. Beethoven's works did not call for brilliant finger technique, Hach believed; they would lose their effectivenesss if played with the "modern rapidity" of the era's piano virtuosi.

An influential essay that Hach commended, copiously quoted, and commented upon in six issues was the English critic Henry F. Chorley's lengthy "The Pianoforte," which had first appeared in *The London and Westminster Review*. In his five-part classification of composers and their keyboard works, Chorley placed Beethoven's sonatas in a fourth era representative of "the school of genius," which availed itself of all former schools but worked up its "own distinct and original conceptions."[42] Chorley sought to convey the wide range characteristic of Beethoven's instrumental music to offset reports of it as "merely stern, dark, and gloomy."

Like A. B. Marx and William Gardiner, Chorley also championed the composer's late works when they were still widely misunderstood. He alluded to the recent success in England of performances of the Ninth Symphony, earlier considered a "chaotic puzzle," as an encouraging anticipation of a time when other works of that period, like the Piano Sonata op. 106, would be as much appreciated for their subtleties as were the early sonatas. Hach's reprinting of Chorley's and similar favorable reports of music unknown to American readers contributed to preparing the way for the works' eventual acceptance.

Although Hach did not neglect Beethoven's vocal pieces, he frequently underscored the importance of their instrumental components, as did Dwight in his own comments. In the German critic's informed discussion (recommended by Dwight) concerning Beethoven's "Adelaïde," Hach explained that its English conversion to "Rosalie" by Charles Horn had destroyed the original unity of words and music. Urging singers to return to Matthison's German poetry, Hach stressed that the intrinsic nature of the instrumental material was coequal in conception to the vocal line with text: "In Beethoven's music the accompaniment is always independent and rather cooperating with the voice than merely assisting or supporting it."[43]

Regarding Beethoven's *Fidelio,* Hach printed a translation of Georg Friedrich Treitschke's description of his modifications to the libretto by Joseph Sonnleithner.[44] In ways large and small, the editor instructed his readers about Beethoven. In one case, he remonstrated that, due to lack of careful supervision before a performance by the orchestra of the Boston Academy, a serious distortion had occurred in the Overture to *Fidelio:* an orchestral passage written for two clarinets, in response to two horns, had been played by only one clarinet.[45] He warned that adequate musical realizations and attention to the composer's intentions were not possible unless all appropriate instrumental forces participated.

Hach also offered literary channels through which new ways of thinking about instrumental music could be considered. An extract from Henry Panofka's fictional *Journal of an Artist* included a translated section entitled "Beethoven's Sonata in A Minor." It interpreted very narrowly Jean Paul Richter's view of music as "the language of the heart," a favorite formulation of Dwight's that he could have known independently through the work of Richter or other German Romantic writers. In this instance, the literary idea conveyed the uniting bond achieved through the intimate communion of the violin and piano during the performance of Beethoven's sonata.[46]

E. T. A. Hoffmann's name appeared as author of three witty and imaginative essays or stories about music that were translated into English for Hach's journal. None addressed symphonic issues directly; they were the well-known "Poet and the Composer," "Thoughts on the High Value of Music," and "The Cadenza."[47]

One discussion with significant aesthetic and stylistic implications treated the concept of musical Romanticism. It appeared in *The Musical Magazine* in a translated excerpt as "On the Romantic in Music."[48] The unidentified source, for which Hach supplied only the author's name, was [Karl] August Kahlert's *Tonleben. Novellen und vermischte Aufsätze;* the book's second section, "Beitrage zur Aesthetik der Tonkunst," included the study "Die Bedeutung des Romantischen in der Musik."[49] Kahlert (1807–1864), a professor of philosophy at the University of Breslau, prolific contributor to the leading German music journals, and friend of Robert Schumann, had chosen as his thesis the close ties between religion and the arts. Including as well brief sections on architecture, Hach selected Kahlert's key passages pertaining to music and printed the essay on May 9, 1840. This was the month of Dwight's ordination in Northampton, two months before his article "Concerts of the Past Winter" appeared in *The Dial,* and more than a year before his Harvard address.

Kahlert linked music to the Christian idea of the Deity and proclaimed that it was Romantic because it "had for its end the representation of the Infinite." The evanescence of its sound was analogous to the fleeting nature of man's existence. Kahlert contended that the essence of Romantic art depended "on the endeavor of man to soar above the sphere of his knowledge; it strives to acquaint us with the unattainable, which no intellect can comprehend." Echoing particularly the musical thought of E. T. A. Hoffmann, Kahlert contended that the power of music began where language ended, and he associated Beethoven centrally with this conviction:

> If we call Beethoven the master of all masters, the reason is, that he has exhibited, in the plainest view, that striving after the infinite. Every work of art requires a form, but to go so far above it, without annihilating it, was reserved for Beethoven alone. I place him above S.[ebastian] Bach, because the genius of the latter was more immediately subservient to divine worship; because he did not lose himself like Beethoven, in the magic of sound. I place him above all, because he is independent of words, and lets his inarticulate sounds speak freely for themselves.

Kahlert acknowledged Hoffmann as his earlier authority in stressing that instrumental music was "the most romantic of all arts" and that Beethoven was "the mightiest in instrumental music." Rejecting as a misunderstanding of the term "Romantic" any usage connecting it primarily to a "new effect," Kahlert declared that Romanticism constituted the "inmost essence of music, that it was the mark which distinguished all modern art from the ancient." Freed from the confining limits of text, instrumental music could achieve full independence in the modern era. Kahlert reached a twofold conclusion: "Music is a product of Christianity; instrumental music [is] a product of the German spirit."[50]

This was another important Romantic document appearing three decades after E. T. A. Hoffmann's, and it addressed several of the same musical issues. In 1840, Hach and Dwight shared views that coincided with Kahlert's, as well as Hoffmann's and A. B. Marx's, on two issues: that Beethoven's instrumental music aspired toward the Infinite beyond the realm of the Understanding, and that musical expressivity, in an inner sense, differed from music associated with a "new effect."

In view of the presence of Kahlert's study in Hach's journal as well as Dwight's knowledge of essays by other prominent German authors, it may be questioned why Dwight never applied the term "Romantic" to Beethoven's instrumental music in the 1840s. Did he associate it primarily with European controversies between "ancients" and "moderns" that did not seem germane to the American musical situation? As I shall discuss in Chapter 10, it was not until 1846 that Dwight used the term "Romantic" in connection with instrumental music. Kahlert's essay is one of several indirect channels by which, through the intermediary of Hach, Dwight became acquainted with Hoffmann's fundamental views in connection with Beethoven's instrumental music. However, as will be noted in Chapter 6, another path proved to be more pertinent.

Kahlert's contrast of J. S. Bach and Beethoven as the outstanding representatives of earlier and recent epochs may have reinforced, for Dwight, A. B. Marx's discussion in the *Universal-Lexicon*. However, Marx had been primarily concerned with textural distinctions, whereas Kahlert emphasized that Beethoven had transcended, without destroying, structural limits to create an instrumental world of magic sounds freed of dependence on words or other associations. In the early 1840s, Dwight lacked the necessary musical experience to attempt any historical organization of musical styles. By 1846, however, he was ready to suggest a historical division based on musical character that contained elements of both essays.

Dwight did not overtly echo Kahlert's nationalist claim that instrumental art music was uniquely "a product of the German spirit." That bias was also affirmed by a compatriot of Kahlert who represented opposite musical tendencies in his conservatism, Gottfried W. Fink. Hach carried a translation of a two-part article by Fink surveying "Music in Germany" in which he proclaimed German preeminence in the symphony, as in other instrumental genres.[51] It appeared in *The Musical Magazine* in 1841, a year before the transmission of Fink's highly significant views on the symphonic genre as part of Hach's own original essay on two of Beethoven's symphonies.

Hach established a legacy that endured beyond his residence in a temporarily adopted land. He stimulated and encouraged the understanding of instrumental art music and gave increased prominence to stringed instruments by delineating their history and traditions as well as through his own performance. Hach encouraged a historical and critical perspective about the music of many composers, and he commented perceptively about Beethoven's little-known instrumental music. If Dwight was grateful to Hach for his early intellectual and professional support, he repaid that debt by building a career in music criticism that promoted many of the objectives enunciated during Hach's own brief years as editor and critic in Boston.

PART TWO

———⟫•◦•⟪———

Responses to
Beethoven's Symphonies in
Orchestral Performance,
1843–1846

E. T. A. Hoffmann, Gottfried W. Fink, Hach, and Dwight's Theory of Criticism Applied to the Symphonic Genre, 1843–1844

D wight was stimulated to write his initial essay considering purely instrumental music after hearing Beethoven's Sixth, Fifth, and Second Symphonies in orchestral performance during 1842. The document is noteworthy in the history of Beethoven's reception in America as a symphonic composer and transitional in Dwight's incipient musical aesthetics and critical discourse.

This chapter traces the hitherto unrecognized connection between the symphonic thought of (Christian) Gottfried Wilhelm Fink, the Leipzig music editor and critic—with his unavowed references to ideas introduced by E. T. A. Hoffmann, the critic who had earlier contributed to the Leipzig *Allgemeine musikalische Zeitung*—and essays written in the United States by H. Theodor Hach as well as by Dwight.

Hoffmann's epochal review of Beethoven's Fifth Symphony, one of the leading critical documents of the early nineteenth century, was published in 1810 in the Leipzig *Allgemeine musikalische Zeitung*. In it, he heralded instrumental music as separate by its nature from the sensory world of the actual:

> Music unlocks for man an unfamiliar world having nothing in
> common with the external material world which surrounds him.

> It is a world where he forgets all feelings which he could define
> for another in order to surrender himself to the inexpressible.[1]

This world of thought found striking resonance in Dwight's 1843 essay "Academy of Music—Beethoven's Symphonies,"[2] in which he, like Hoffmann, prefaced extended comments about the Fifth Symphony with an aesthetic credo that accorded to instrumental music his highest recognition as a special world beyond the linguistic realm. Of music, Dwight wrote:

> It begins where speech leaves off. When we have fairly entered
> its element, it alone is all-sufficing; it explains itself, but it tran-
> scends speech and all this defining whim of the understanding.[3]

Although Hoffmann and Dwight attached preeminent value to instrumental art music for its qualities beyond the definable, there are also significant differences between their positions. Both associated sublimity and yearning with Beethoven's Fifth Symphony, but for Hoffmann it opened an imaginary realm clouded by "terror, . . . pain . . . and endless longing," which he overtly connected to Romanticism;[4] for Dwight, these emotions and premonitions neither prevailed nor led to a use of the term "Romantic." Hoffmann's anxiety-filled vision of the spirit realm and his insistence on "endless longing" through a fascination with unity dominated his experience of this work.[5] Dwight, on the other hand, believed that Beethoven was the "most spiritual" composer, one who brought humanity into higher unity with the Infinite. The American critic and his predecessor, Hach, shared a later dynamic perspective in which the finale of the Fifth Symphony was a joyous zenith overcoming uncertainty and struggle.

Dwight can be connected to Hoffmann's writings on Beethoven's symphonies through the American's knowledge of an important essay by Fink, editor of the Leipzig *Allgemeine musikalische*

Zeitung from 1828 to 1841, as well as through Hach. Access to recent German music literature and criticism aided Dwight's active efforts to learn about symphonic music at a time when a representative work like William S. Porter's *Musical Cyclopedia,* published in 1834 in Boston, carried only a short reference to the genre of the symphony as a three-movement work with a middle minuet and trio.[6]

As I have indicated, by the close of 1838 Dwight had utilized Gustav Schilling's *Universal-Lexicon* while preparing his volume of poetry translations. Dwight's reference to Beethoven's Ninth Symphony in his notes to Schiller's "An die Freude"[7] might have caused him then to consult Fink's lengthy and authoritative entry on the symphonic genre in that encyclopedia. In any case, Dwight would have been apprised or reminded of it when Hach translated sections of Fink's article in his 1842 essay.

When the Boston Academy of Music presented early complete orchestral performances in 1842 of Beethoven's Sixth and Fifth Symphonies, respectively (January 15, February 5 and February 26, March 26), Dwight was able to attend. By then, he was living and teaching at Brook Farm.

These symphonic performances galvanized Hach and Dwight to respond swiftly. Each was a champion of orchestral music and of the Academy's leadership in sponsoring these concerts. Dwight gave an unpublished lecture on March 10, 1842, devoted to "Beethoven's The Pastoral Symphony and the Symphony in C Minor."[8] Hach reacted with an essay devoted to these same works entitled "Beethoven's Symphonies"; he delayed its publication until it could appear on April 24, 1842, in the final issue of *The Musical Magazine.*[9]

For the symphonic framework, Hach translated substantial excerpts from Fink's essay—comprising three and one-half of his own fourteen pages—before introducing commentary about the music. Hach mentioned only Fink's name without supplying the title of the article or its source, but I have identified it as Fink's entry "Symphonie oder Sinfonie" in the *Universal-Lexicon*.[10]

Despite Fink's conservatism, his writings provide a valuable perspective on contemporaneous musical thought.[11] One of these was a rich source of information for the youthful American who was then dedicating himself to the musical field. In the autumn of 1842, James Russell Lowell invited Dwight to contribute an article to the inaugural issue of his periodical, *The Pioneer*. Dwight's "Academy of Music—Beethoven's Symphonies" appeared in January and February 1843, in a distinguished forum celebrating the new and universal in literature and the arts and intended for the "intelligent and reflecting portion of the Reading Public."[12] The essay provides evidence that Dwight was very familiar with Hach's discussion of the Fifth Symphony, which he lauded as having been "traced out in a most ingenious and satisfactory manner through all the modulations of the music,"[13] and that he was also conversant with Fink's ideas.

Besides a discussion of varying descriptions of the symphony and its impact on the listener, Fink's entry also included commentary on its general structure, character, texture, and compositional goals. He insisted on Franz Joseph Haydn's position as creator of a new type of instrumental music, which he called *die grosse Symphonie*, "the grand symphony." Emphasizing the German origins of the genre, while rejecting claims for its French or Italian roots, he referred to Haydn, Mozart, and Beethoven as "our three heroes in this German-created kind of music."[14] This is the formulation that Hach transmitted to American readers in establishing the symphonic canon.

The "grand symphony," according to Fink's nineteenth-century concept, was a lively work representing some general feeling, performed by a mass of instruments, and enjoyed by a vast number of listeners. An original and striking subject of inherent individual character was to be the idea, capable of evolving organically by means of a broad "unity of design together with the greatest variety." Decades earlier, in his review of 1810, E. T. A. Hoffmann had stressed the organic structural unity of design in Beethoven's Fifth Symphony. Fink had quoted directly from Hoffmann's review, but without referring to its author by name, in a previous essay on the symphony appearing in the *Allgemeine musikalische Zeitung* in August 1835. He mentioned that work in his later entry on the symphonic genre in the *Universal-Lexicon;* however, he did not quote from Hoffmann in that influential essay. The prior reference establishes his connection to Hoffmann and clarifies Fink's importance as a pivotal figure in the dissemination in America of the idea of the symphony.[15]

In developing his theory of the symphony, Fink considered the genre from several perspectives. It had been called previously "the opera of the instruments,"[16] although Fink did not identify the author of that statement, and it was like a musical drama. Again, Hoffmann said this first in a review in 1809.[17] He went on to praise the new heights to which Haydn and Mozart had brought instrumental music through the symphony and to declare it the highest in its realm analogous to the position of opera in the vocal sphere. Fink retained this conclusion. Hoffmann had further asserted that, as in a drama, the symphonic genre stimulated the new characteristic activity of all the individual instruments in the symphonic whole in contrast to their old-fashioned and limited use in the concerto grosso.[18] Fink omitted this thought entirely.

Fink then introduced his own preferred comparison of the symphony to a dramatically imbued sentimental novel (*einer dramatisirt gehaltenen Gefühls-Novelle*). According to him, a grand symphony must possess some psychological development of feelings expressed in tones and articulated through the instruments, which were to be carefully grouped by the composer to represent the desired sentiment, just as an author would plan the arrangement and interaction of his characters in literature.[19]

When Fink accounted for the extraordinary impact of Beethoven's symphonies, he again drew on the characterization of 1810 by Hoffmann, who had by then placed the younger composer on the same level with Haydn and Mozart.[20] Hoffmann's supernatural realm of "gigantic shadows" in Beethoven became transmuted into Fink's more explicit images of "magicians and fairies intermingling with our human doings" through Beethoven's instrumental music, which Fink did not connect to Romanticism.[21]

H. Theodor Hach transmitted not only Fink's description but also his principle of "unity combined with the greatest variety" in the grand symphony regarded as the highest, most weighty and richly sonorous type of instrumental music. He conveyed Fink's idea of the symphonic genre as one in which different characters act in diverse situations "round [sic] a principal character and a principal view of life, for one definite purpose."[22] Hach also noted Fink's view that if an external model had stimulated the composer's imagination, it must be brought before the "internal eye" of the listener through tones.

Fink had noted that an issue important to his epoch was whether the composer should build his symphony in association with extramusical verbal material. He framed the question according to the composer's will. However, when Hach paraphrased the thought, he changed the point of view and adopted the listener's perspective; Dwight retained a similar stance in favor of the listener. Thus, in asserting that the keys and character of individual symphonic movements were strongly related to each other, Hach questioned if their connection to the initial musical subject of a grand symphony justified imagining in it "a certain story, a certain poem, a distinct course of ideas." He decided in the affirmative, reinforcing Fink's assertion that the symphony must have "some sentiment, some psychological development of a train of feelings not altogether foreign to the mass; otherwise it would contain but unmeaning tones."[23]

Maintaining that in the Fifth Symphony Beethoven's unity of design and its mounting interest from beginning to end argued for the composer's intention to represent one object, Hach applied to each of the movements the image of "*The Skeptic;* honestly searching after truth, and on whom it flashes at last."[24] Thus, after the strife and doubt of the first movement, the Andante variations represented a prayer for truth, the Scherzo an active striving toward it, and the finale a triumphal hymn joyous in its ultimate rediscovery.[25] This professional musician supported that idea, however, through a musical description of the psychological nature and structural relationships of keys, including the employment of strategically placed dissonant chords and their resolution, thematic connections, and instrumental activity.

Hach and Dwight both believed in the psychological association of mood with individual keys. The two writers relied on the unacknowledged authority of Gustav Schilling's entries for each of the keys, as contained in his *Universal-Lexicon.* When confronted by conflicting interpretations for a key, such as those given in Porter's *Musical Cyclopedia* (which had been based, in turn, on lists of key characteristics in writings by William Gardiner), both chose Schilling's views. They were heavily weighted in tradition through the citation of earlier theoretical descriptions. Hach considered in some detail the aesthetic and critical aspects of key choice, whereas Dwight referred to keys of movements or subjects in brief phrases.

In one example from his discussion of the Fifth Symphony, Hach associated the anxiety and restlessness of the search for the highest truth with the key of C Minor. It was "next to the perfect and pure key of C Major," with which it constantly desired to unite (sharing the same dominant G Major) but which it was never able to reach. He then quoted the following passage by unnamed "best critics" to affirm the particular psychological character of C Minor:

> If we indeed admit that the different keys have a peculiar character, there is not another more appropriate to the expression of a distinct, higher feeling than this. Declaration of love and the plaints of unhappy love speak from its softly blending notes; the longing, the sighing of a loving, deeply feeling, pure soul, finds its most touching representation. In its clearness, and in its pure and gentle dominant of G major, it is full of the most heartfelt longing, an expression of higher, holier love, a sigh of longing to the father of light.[26]

As Rita Steblin has shown, the most famous source of Schilling's discussion of keys was Christian Friedrich Daniel Schubart's *Ideen zu einer Ästhetik der Tonkunst,* written in 1784–85 and published in 1806; Schilling also drew directly from other works, however, including the little-known *Charinomos* of 1828 by Carl Ludwig Seidel.[27] In this manner, conventional associations with keys based on late-eighteenth and earlier-nineteenth-century German theoretical works filtered into American musical magazines and thence to references in less specialized journals featuring literature or current affairs.

Dwight's approach to the Fifth Symphony centrally considered the listener's response. To him, the very act of listening with others to a Beethoven symphony constituted a high social pleasure and a manifestation of how an audience could be uplifted, and connected, through music: "Rarely is there an assembly, where all are so lifted above themselves, and made to forget their selfish partialities . . . as an assembly on whom Beethoven and the orchestra have begun to work."[28] Dwight was genuinely committed to the notion of enlightenment through collective association. He placed central emphasis on the orchestral music of Beethoven as the essential key in promoting a beneficial moral impact on listeners as a group, an idea he reiterated frequently thereafter.

Dwight diverged fundamentally from Fink and from Hach on the application of defined images to symphonic music, leading him to originate his own theory of criticism applicable to it. For this reason, the writing of 1843 is significant in Dwight's intellectual development. It represents a tentative first effort to confront this genre and does not yet attempt a symphonic theory, as would his essays of 1845. However, it enabled him to consider the problem of "meaning" in symphonic music posed by Fink, Hach, and others.

Dwight branded as "quackery" any pretense of associating a definite story with a symphony because that approach led to hearing only with the limited power of the "understanding," without engaging the higher poetic and intuitive faculties. He asserted that instrumental music was music proper and that it transported the listener beyond specific thoughts or visual imagery to change his or her state.

Dwight encouraged the listener to add a technical knowledge of musical principles to the internal spiritual essence of the musical experience. Tempting as it might be to trace a connected story through emotions aroused by the principal subject in the unfolding of a symphony, whose musical characteristics Dwight considered to be unity and logical consecutiveness, he cautioned that a story could never be an interpretation of the music. It was only an "allegorical illustration" in the spirit of the music. On this basis, he moved easily in and out of the imaginative sections of his critical discourse.

Dwight's theory of criticism created a mechanism that permitted the use of allegorical illustration without challenging the capacity of instrumental music itself to evoke the ineffable. Music, being infinite in its meaning, could impart personal revelations to every hearer. He or she would be free to imagine a "fancied resemblance" that would be "entirely in the spirit of the music" and that could share with the music its original conception based on "genuine poetic creation."

> What moved the composer to make a symphony, moves the interpreter to make a poem; out of one and the same spirit, they create in their several ways, and there will be a spiritual correspondence between the two products, so that the impression of the one will not disturb, but only illustrate that of the other.[29]

Dwight sought to resolve the apparent contradiction posed by others, including Hach, who had advanced various but definite literary interpretations of the Fifth Symphony. They had been shaped fundamentally, Dwight suggested, by universally shared experience in "the great life-struggle, the contradiction between the Ideal and the Actual." But Dwight, unlike Hach, did not apply specific imagery to each movement. He perceived in the first Allegro a human conflict with necessity; the Andante was lyric, grave, tender; the Scherzo proposed action *as* ideal in its impetuous restlessness; and the finale was a "glorious *Triumphal March.*" However, he used anthropomorphic language to ascribe dramatic human characteristics to the instruments, as had E. T. A. Hoffmann:[30] the cellos "discourse," the earnest sounds of the bassoon "take up and vary" the theme, and, in the third movement, "How the basses labor and tug in broken efforts; though baffled oft, they carry the point at last."[31]

Among the important sources of Dwight's biographical references are Anton Schindler's life of Beethoven and Bettina Brentano von Arnim's ostensible remembrances of conversations with the composer. In his 1841 English edition of Schindler's biogra-

phy, Ignaz Moscheles had added in a supplement three letters supposedly written by Beethoven to Arnim, of which only one is now
considered genuine,[32] and Arnim's communication (dated May 28,
1810) to Goethe taken from her controversial *Goethe's Correspondence with a Child*. From these materials Dwight extracted sections
that reinforced his belief in Beethoven's spiritual faith in an "infinite, to be attained" and the composer's conviction of a unity in
his symphonies.[33] When confronted with Schindler's skepticism
concerning the reliability of Arnim, and Moscheles's belief in the
authenticity of the correspondence, Dwight cited statements reinforcing his view that if Beethoven had not pronounced these words
he had expressed their spirit in his music.[34]

The American critic's approach to the structure of the first
movement of the C Minor Symphony acknowledged two main divisions within which he described themes, main keys, character,
and rhythmic and instrumental features. Dwight did not, at this
time, refer to exposition, development, recapitulation, or so-called
sonata form, although a writer in Philadelphia briefly mentioned
the first two as early as 1845.[35]

An excerpt from Dwight's essay of 1843 shows his treatment of
the symphony's first and second subjects. By means of the transitional phrase "It is as if," he proceeds from description of the
initial motive and its treatment to fanciful allegorical illustration of
its impact before reconsidering musical materials. He emphasizes
the opening motive's inherently flexible design, which makes it
capable of providing unity, together with the variety introduced by
the "distant mellow horns," which anthropomorphically "take up
the three notes in a higher strain, and fall into another key." Here,
Dwight combines basic musical description and subjective poetic
material corresponding to an auditor's impression of the spirit of
the work, an approach intended to assist readers and listeners in a

milieu in which the "science of music" was just beginning to be acknowledged.

> The subject is announced with startling distinctness at the out-
> set, in three short emphatic repetitions of one note falling upon
> the third below, which is held out some time; and then the same
> phrase echoed, only one degree lower. This grotesque and al-
> most absurd passage, coming in so abruptly, like a mere freak or
> idle dallying with sounds, fills the mind with a strange uncer-
> tainty, as it does the ear; for as yet the note is wanting, which
> determines the key of the piece. Still more is this vague appre-
> hension increased, when on the ground-tone of C minor this
> little phrase, once boldly struck, as if by chance, multiplies itself
> in rapid, soft reiterations, which chase each other round from
> voice to voice throughout the whole band, first climbing the
> heights of the trebles, then again down darting through the un-
> fathomable abyss of bass. It is as if a fearful secret, some truth
> of mightiest moment, startled the stillness where we were se-
> curely walking, and the heavens and the earth and hell were
> sending back the sound thereof from all quarters, "deep calling
> unto deep," and yet no word of explanation. What is it? What
> can all this mean? What a world of earnest, strange, portentous
> voices we set ringing round our heads, when we chanced to
> stumble upon that seemingly unmeaning phrase of the three
> notes! Strange and unendurable suspense, dreading we know
> not what! Comes there no sign of hope? Yes—when the burst of
> mingling echoes has once spent itself, there is a moment's pause,
> and then the distant mellow horns take up the three notes in a
> higher strain, and fall into another key, the warm and confident
> E flat major— and on this basis the *countertheme* is introduced,
> a strain of sweetest love and promise, an unlocking of the springs
> of good affection in the soul, as if to drown all doubt. How vain!
> for still the ground trembles; and even now those three dread
> notes are never silenced; they only sink down into the bass, and
> there, all too audible, though deep and muffled, shake away at
> the foundations, and contradict the upper melodies. These are
> the themes.[36]

Dwight learned from Fink, among others, about compositional aspects of the symphonic genre, and from Hach, among others, about the shaping of critical discourse applicable to Beethoven's symphonies. The findings concerning his knowledge of Fink's essay are supported and enhanced by statements from another of Dwight's essays, "Haydn," published in January 1844 in *The United States Magazine, and Democratic Review*. Describing the importance of Handel and Mozart, as well as Haydn, in two earlier issues in March and November 1843,[37] Dwight associated each of the composers with a particular genre. Handel had treated music predominantly in its religious aspect through the oratorio; Mozart had comprehended it as the language of the passions through opera; and Haydn, together with Beethoven, had introduced the new "boundless *world*, it may be called, of *Instrumental Music.*"

Retaining Fink's evolutionary stance in referring to the increasing independence of instruments in eighteenth-century music, Dwight explained briefly that this orchestral world had developed in earlier stages with Handel and with Corelli in Italy. Even the multimovement form called symphony had been limited initially in its capacity for independent instrumental expressivity. It was Haydn's achievement to compose music that could organize the instruments into "a living whole" by bringing out their individual capacities and combining them effectively. Thus, each instrument would have a characteristic expression that would join with the others in a unified whole.

Dwight described the challenge of symphonic music according to principles enunciated by Fink and, earlier, Hoffmann, although he did not refer to any sources in this presentation. He asserted that the problem of the new symphony was

> to combine the greatest variety into a perfect unity; and, as in nature, to give every part its individuality and separate life, while they so blend and work together, either by harmony or contrast, that one thought shall make itself felt as the soul of the whole. A melody is an individual sentiment; an accompaniment gives it

a back-ground and sets it in bolder relief; but a symphony finds the correspondence of nature to the feeling of the heart, makes all things share our mood and become its language. If it be joy, then, in the intermingling melodies, and crude half-discords brightening into harmonies, and all the coloring and shading of the various qualities of tone of various instruments, we have, as it were, all the joyous sounds of nature responding and sharing our joys. This is the continual feeling which we have with Haydn. In the orchestra, each instrument is a character; has its distinct genius; according as it is subdued or prominent, is the whole complexion of the piece changed. Thus the oboe is pastoral; the bassoon, with its low reedy tones, seems like Pan himself; the double bass is an Atlas sustaining the whole mass; the horns always seem to come from the woods, and from a distance; sometimes, to one who hears music in a mood for picture-making, they seem, with their long mellow notes, like a flood of golden light poured in across the back-ground of a landscape, . . . making all its figures bolder. And there is no end to such imaginings. But one thing is established, that in the symphony each of the twenty parts has a character to sustain, and yet the sentiment of the whole is one. And a true symphony, a deep work of art in that form, will be more or less to the different minds who hear it, in precise proportion to their own depth, just as nature is. Haydn caught the harmony, the grace, the cheerful-ness of nature; and all his music seems an exposition of life in harmony with nature. His symphonies were instantly popular; everybody enjoys them, as we do a refreshing walk or a pleasant conversation; an enjoyment which costs us nothing but a genial spirit and a sense for beauty. There are minds to whom nature is more than beautiful, more than refreshing; for them Beethoven wrote.[38]

Dwight contrasted Haydn's "perfection of *style*" and cheerful, "easily understood" music to the "yearnings and uncontainable rhapsodies" of Beethoven. He implied a distinction between the musical character of Haydn's comprehensible, containable beauty in an eighteenth-century sense and Beethoven's limitless, "uncontainable" response to the sublime in his large and powerful symphonies. These were equated with a newer, nineteenth-century approach. Dwight stressed two features of the symphonic genre: unity achieved from the greatest variety and the characteristic activity of all the instruments as one unit. This emphasis confirms his serious study of Fink's essay, in particular.

In the writings published in 1843 and 1844, Dwight set the foundation for his lifelong interest in the instruments of the symphonic orchestra. He saw them as agents whose independent character and will must be blended to create a unified entity, just as, he believed, people must be free to express their individuality while working to create a unified community. Both essays also clarified and confirmed his position regarding the domain of instrumental music.

> But to aim first to paint a picture, or to tell a story, is to leave the true and glorious function of the art, to make it do what it was never meant to do, and excite the same kind of admiration which a mountebank would by walking on his head. Literal description of objects is not the province of music. Music has all the vagueness of the feelings of which it is the natural language; but through an appeal to the feelings may *suggest* more than words can tell.[39]

Dwight's efforts to describe symphonic music in this period can be compared to a more typical American example of brief generalities. Reference to that subject occurs in I. [Isaac] B. Woodbury's manual, *The Elements of Musical Composition and Thorough-Base [sic]: Together With Rules For Arranging Music For The Full Orchestra and Military Bands.* A teacher of piano in Boston and a church organist, Woodbury was also editor of the Musical Education Society's Collection of Church Music, among other publications. Since the summer of 1841, he had been instructing the elements of music to teachers of music and other registrants in a course of twelve lectures at the National Musical Convention.

In August 1843, two competing Musical Conventions and Class Exercises were held in Boston. One group was directed by Woodbury and Benjamin Franklin Baker, and the other was under the leadership of Lowell Mason and George James Webb. Fifty people attended the Music Teachers' Class led by Woodbury and Baker. They met on August 17, 1843, at the Marlboro Chapel to form a five-person nominating committee, including Woodbury, which was also charged with drafting a constitution. On the next day, they adopted a constitution and unanimously elected J. S. Dwight as president.[40]

Woodbury's manual, issued in 1844, ranged from the presentation of basic information about intervals, chords, modulation, and hints on composition, to a description of instruments (primarily a translation of Friedrich Schneider's work on harmony and composition), to offering general remarks about musical genres. In the final section, Woodbury devoted a paragraph each to the consideration of the symphony, the overture, and the concerto under the heading "Of Concert Music." After noting that this field offered the greatest opportunity to treat instruments individually and together, he then described the symphony:

> The *Symphony* is the highest climax of instrumental music—a combination of several instruments, in which every one appears in more or less rivalship with the other, to participate in the general co-operation for melody and harmony. A brilliant, animated, rich style, grand and vigorous melodies in well-poised alternation with soft and tender thoughts, striking and decisive bases, energetic modulations, the boldest interlacements and imitations of melodies and rhythms, the utmost successive changes, and the most varied union of the instruments, co-operating in the general effect, at one time individually, at another simultaneously—now as principals, now as accompaniment, or reinforcing and filling up the score—such are the characteristic features of the symphony. In order to satisfy these

requisites, great mastery of harmony, and knowledge of all the instruments, will be found to be indispensable.[41]

Woodbury added to this general statement of instrumental activity a contrast between the overture, which often served as introduction to a larger work, and the symphony, which was an "independent, entirely unfettered creation of musical imagination."

It is notable that Woodbury, who claimed to have received private instruction from "the Professors of the Conservatory at Paris and the Academy at London," sought recommendations for his manual toward the close of 1843 from several prominent musical colleagues among whom was John Sullivan Dwight. He received, and printed in the front of his work, the following endorsement:

> Boston, Dec. 13th, 1843
>
> Dear Sir,—I have examined with much pleasure your little work on the "Elements of Musical Composition." It appears to me to comprise all that is essential to a popular manual. Your general method is concise & clear; & the various points are unfolded in a much more simple and intelligible manner than is usual in similar books. Through the whole I meet none of that ambiguity with which musical theories are apt to be encumbered; while on certain points, as the inversions of the Common Chord, the several forms of the Minor Scale, &c., it is particularly complete and satisfactory. I trust it will prove acceptable and useful to many learners.
>
> Very truly yours,
> J. S. Dwight[42]

The incident suggests that in 1843 Dwight was well regarded by professional musicians, especially in Boston. The recommendation itself indicates that he had examined Woodbury's little book with comparative knowledge of other similar works.

Through the publications of 1843 and 1844, Dwight widened

his readership beyond earlier musical, religious, academic, and literary circles to include a general public lacking musical education
but interested in the arts, politics, and public affairs. The essays
delineated the importance of the symphonic genre, with emphasis
on Beethoven's contributions, and enabled him to establish his
own theory of criticism applicable to the symphony through "allegorical illustration."

He combined this approach with initial attempts to explain
basic structural and instrumental aspects of the music. In this process, he intertwined "emotive description" of musical passages with
biographical and autobiographical references.[43] Expansion of these
techniques and devices in his major essays on Beethoven's Fifth,
Sixth, and Seventh Symphonies in 1845 would show Dwight's increased awareness of the musical connection between basic syntactical events within large-scale structures.

CHAPTER SEVEN

Frédéric Kalkbrenner's
Beethoven Transcriptions, 1842–1845;
Symphonies versus Chamber Music,
1844–1845

Two musical developments connected to Dwight's leadership
in the Harvard Musical Association occurred during this period, and both affected his perception of the broad dimensions
and dramatic sweep of Beethoven's symphonies. I propose that
one was his discovery of a collection of all of Beethoven's symphonies arranged for solo piano by Frédéric Kalkbrenner. Archival
evidence supports the contention that Kalkbrenner's transcriptions
were available to Dwight in the small music library maintained by
the Harvard Musical Association, of which he was vice-president
from September 1843 through 1845 and beyond. The other development, which precipitated Dwight's emphatic distinction between symphonic and chamber music genres, also relates to his
participation in the association. Beginning in 1844, it sponsored a
new public series of chamber music concerts.

It was an era in the association's history during which two unsuccessful applications were made to the state legislature for an
act of incorporation. The members considered, but finally rejected,
dissolution. In addition, Harvard University had not yet integrated
the regular study of music into the college curriculum, one of the
association's primary objectives. Its members decided to redirect

their energies toward the wider community outside the university and also to continue their efforts to build a music library. In March 1845, a small group including Dwight attained independent incorporation by the Massachusetts legislature. It permitted the association to own land and property to $10,000 in value and to promote general "education in the science and practice of music," as well as to raise funds for the benefit of indigent members.[1]

By 1845, the Harvard Musical Association had acquired a library of about four hundred books, pamphlets, periodicals, and performance parts; these were kept in a rented room at 365 Washington Street in Boston. This site, like its predecessor on the city's Tremont Row, also served as a central meeting place for its members, practice facility, and Saturday afternoon reading library open to the general public.

Members could borrow works to take back to their residences. A large manuscript group of annual Librarian's Reports, preserved in the Archives of the Harvard Musical Association, documents the growth of the library's collection. Each includes a listing of valuable or rare donations and acquisitions made since the last report; such summaries were occasionally published in local newspapers.

One of the most pertinent of these is Henry W. Pickering's Librarian's Report for 1840–41.[2] At that time, the collection numbered about 190 bound volumes, exclusive of magazines, of which approximately 100 were treatises or biographies and 90 comprised printed music. In addition, the library regularly received 4 (unidentified) English, French, and American music periodicals.

Listed among the works presented to the library in 1840–41 since the last annual meeting on Commencement Day, at which occasion the librarian delivered a report, is the notation of "Beethoven's Symphonies arranged by Kalkbrenner." No other similar volume, score, or parts of Beethoven's symphonies are listed. That

Kalkbrenner's work continued to be highly valued can be deduced from Bernard Roelker's Librarian's Report for 1844–45. After recommending that more music for performance be acquired, he noted that the few items of that kind in the collection, such as "the Symphonies of Beethoven arranged for the pianoforte, are in constant demand."[3]

I propose that Dwight, as teacher of music at Brook Farm, active member and officer of the Harvard Musical Association, and respected writer on music, utilized his borrowing privileges to examine Kalkbrenner's collection at his piano at Brook Farm. It would have been an important resource for his study of Beethoven's symphonies in connection with opportunities to hear them in Boston. Can we be certain what constituted Dwight's texts for the symphonies? Dwight remained silent about his musical sources in this era and left no clear testimony about consulted scores, parts, or arrangements.

However, he occasionally alluded to orchestral works by relating his subjective response as pianist, leaving no doubt in these instances of his viewpoint as music maker and participant as well as listener. Playing orchestral works in piano transcriptions offered Dwight the opportunity for private study before or after attending orchestral rehearsals and concerts or during the writing of a lengthy review-essay about music performed months earlier.

In 1842 and early 1843, Dwight prepared to write his invited essay about Beethoven's Fifth and Second Symphonies for *The Pioneer* by attending rehearsals and performances at the Odeon and by playing the arrangements on the piano. Describing the main subjects and keys in the first movement of the Symphony no. 2 in D, op. 36, he exclaimed:

> The very difficulty of executing a piece of such breadth and energy and rapidity helps out its true expression. Just as your wrists

and fingers, if you try to play it on the piano, begin to give out, the music itself falters and pants exhausted, then gathers itself up by short, broken efforts, to rush forward in a fuller stream. This is exceedingly characteristic of Beethoven. What a determined, headlong energy is in his movements! how his theme goes on, gathering up more and more force and fulness in its movement, piling chord upon chord, climbing, climbing, like accumulated waves, which break and all fall back; then gather themselves again for the onset, and climbing by half-tones through all the chords, burst through, and lo the sea is smooth, and we sail along in the sweetest buoyant measure, triumphing with the theme.[4]

Dwight claimed justly that this account of the Second Symphony only hinted at the "general spirit and tone of the whole, with a few random, unconnected touches of description here and there."[5] However, his experience at the keyboard had made more vivid the communication of Beethoven's characteristic energy. For this writer on music, it was built on sequential passages of increasing dynamics, chromatic motion, and dramatic piling on of insistent chords that pressed forward, then receded, only to initiate another outburst.

He used similar imagery two years later to describe a Beethoven trio performed by musicians, including the pianist John Lange:

Every note told full of meaning; and that peculiar characteristic of Beethoven's movement, that grand, continual, undulating swell, the sound subsiding and again growing to the loudest climax of universal accord, was clearly appreciated and brought out in his [Lange's] whole performance.[6]

In the same month, August 1845, Dwight transferred intact his discussion of the Fifth Symphony from *The Pioneer* of 1843 into an expanded and more complex commentary in *The Harbinger, Devoted to Social and Political Progress.* This distinguished journal was edited by George Ripley, with the assistance of Dwight and Charles A. Dana, initially at Brook Farm.[7] That significant act of transfer reveals Dwight's full confidence in his earlier statement on the Fifth Symphony, which had been the product of considerable effort, and his belief that it continued to reflect fairly the essence of his views. His essay on the Seventh Symphony, appearing two weeks later (and months after the orchestral performances had occurred), also contains musical detail of the kind that he could have gained only from direct musical examination.[8]

What could Dwight have learned about Beethoven's orchestral music with Kalkbrenner as pianistic intermediary? Frédéric [Friedrich Wilhelm Michael] Kalkbrenner, celebrated pianist, pedagogue, and prolific composer, had been born in 1785 near Kassel and educated primarily at the Paris Conservatoire. He had commanded respect internationally both in London (where he lived from 1814 to 1824) and on the Continent, particularly in Paris, his main residence.[9] Kalkbrenner had also studied in Vienna from 1803 to 1806, touring there in 1813 and again in 1824. He and Beethoven were on friendly terms.[10] By the mid-1830s, with his health in decline, Kalkbrenner performed fewer concerts as a new generation of pianists, including Chopin, Liszt, and Thalberg began to dominate public attention. He died in 1849 at Enghiens-les Bains, near Paris.

A publisher's prefatory note to Kalkbrenner's transcriptions states that, although the process of arrangement did not call for creativity, it required such precise knowledge of orchestral resources and of the piano that Kalkbrenner's significant reputation would be enhanced.[11] These arrangements would enable all music lovers to have access to Beethoven's symphonies. According to the publisher, they were superior to Hummel's earlier arrangements in their attempt to give an indication of the gigantic effects of the orchestra. Instead of transcribing Beethoven's weighty passages for unison cellos, bassoons, and double basses by means of single notes, as in Hummel's intentionally easy versions for piano with another instrument, Kalkbrenner had tried to present an idea of them in passages for octaves in both hands. In pointing thus to Kalkbrenner's grand attempt to capture in a pianistic idiom "les plus beaux effets d'Orchestre" ("the most beautiful orchestral effects"), the publisher located the salient characteristic.

Dwight would have experienced through Kalkbrenner an originally orchestral Beethoven transformed by virtuosic pianistic effects that remained generally faithful to the spirit but freely added accents, changed a few dynamics, and altered particular articulations (from staccato dots to accent marks, or separate notes to slurs). These occurred partly to delineate melodic from accompanimental, or less prominent, lines due to the relative limitations of keyboard sonority. Primarily, they highlighted contrasts between parts that would have been composed and heard in the original version as distinctively varied instrumental timbres. Kalkbrenner also suggested fingerings to facilitate performance and added pedal markings.

Despite his valiant efforts, Kalkbrenner could hardly convey the intricate interdependencies of inner lines, although he adequately reflected melodic sections and basic harmonies. Lost in his undifferentiated pianistic renderings were Beethoven's dialoguing alternations between two instrumental families, such as strings and woodwinds. One instance, among many, is the exchange in the first movement of the Fifth Symphony (just after the bridge passage played by bassoon) before the return of the second subject in the latter part of the second division.[12] Dwight did not then call it a recapitulation section.

In Kalkbrenner's arrangements, total effects emerged without the subtlety of individual details that had been intrinsic to the instrumental sonorities of the original. Although he was able to bring out effectively an isolated gesture, such as the solo oboe cadenza introduced in the latter section of the Fifth Symphony's first movement, Kalkbrenner reduced the impact of Beethoven's memorable linking of phrases taken up by different solo instruments in succession.

Similarly, sections that had achieved their power through the vigorous participation of the orchestra in Beethoven's variegated rhythmic layering were inevitably flattened in piano reduction by repetitive use of conventional idiomatic figurations. These constant patterns included the Alberti bass, successive octaves in one or both hands, measured tremolos, scales, and arpeggios. Among many instances, and particularly noticeable in final movements, is Kalkbrenner's obliteration of Beethoven's characteristic juxtaposition of rests with chordal punctuation resounding from woodwinds, brass, and timpani in the closing idea of the Fifth Symphony's first movement (before the coda). However, the harmonies supporting the melodic passage for upper strings are rendered adequately.[13]

Kalkbrenner's transcriptions are relatively effective when most straightforward, as in the first and third movements of Beethoven's Seventh Symphony. Even in these cases, Kalkbrenner has freely connected (through slurs) separately articulated passages and blurred the clarity of some phrases by adding pedal. The composer's rhythmic figures and widely spaced instrumental passages are nicely conveyed, however, through Kalkbrenner's exploration of the full range and resources of the piano keyboard. These transcriptions of the symphonies show his effort to duplicate the registers of the main and important supporting lines, although countermelodies are sometimes omitted. The physical layout of this edition would also have partly reinforced Dwight's assumption that the Ninth Symphony had been composed in two distinct parts. The first three movements are bound separately as volume nine; the fourth movement, with French words, appears as volume ten.

In addition to the possibilities for learning presented by Kalk-brenner's transcriptions, Dwight established a regular connection to chamber music in varied combinations that offered him a differ-ent perspective on the symphonic genre during that period. On October 17, 1844, with Dwight presiding as vice-president, the standing committee of the Harvard Musical Association proposed that the group sponsor an innovative series of public chamber music concerts. These events were designed to renew interest among the members and to generate support in the larger commu-nity. In the first season four concerts were given in 1844, two each in November and December, and four concerts were presented in 1845, two each in January and February.[14]

A sampling of programs for 1844–45 in the archives of the Har-vard Musical Association reveals that these concerts featured string quartets, trios, duets for flute or violin and piano, and instru-mental solos for piano, violin, and flute. Composers represented included Beethoven, Mozart, Haydn, Herz, Kuhlau, Romberg, Kalliwoda, Bellini, Spohr, and Hummel. No more than one work by Beethoven regularly appeared on each program. His Piano Trios in C Minor (op. 1, no. 3) and in E-flat Major (op. 1, no. 1) are listed without opus number, but with tempo indications for the movements. The participation of amateur second-violin and viola players may have led to the decision to program less technically demanding string quartets by Mozart and Haydn rather than Bee-thoven; on the other hand, the hiring of a professional pianist made possible an emphasis on Beethoven's piano trios.

The initial, very successful series took place in the music room of Jonas Chickering's piano warehouse, a decision doubtless facili-tated by his offer of its use to the association without charge. The whole venture can be regarded as marking a real transition in Boston's musical life from the practice of playing chamber music primarily in private home musicales to a sponsored and extended public series welcoming a varied but interested audience. The size of the audience changed commensurately from a highly restricted circle of a few invited friends to a gathering initially numbering as many as 150 people at each concert.

The Harvard Musical Association hired four professional musicians among whom were Leopold Herwig, a violinist active in concerts of the Boston Academy of Music and the Boston Philharmonic Society, pianist John Lange, and H. Theodor Hach, cellist, whose *Musical Magazine* was by then defunct. Hach played a significant role in enunciating the conditions under which he and the other musicians would consent to perform. He set forth the minimal criteria that they deemed appropriate to the public transmission of chamber music. This information establishes a necessary background for the interpretation of Dwight's statements regarding these concerts.

Discovery of Hach's valuable autograph letter written from the Institution for the Blind and dated January 2, 1845, offers insight.[15] Addressing Robert E. Apthorp, lawyer, and treasurer of the Harvard Musical Association as institutional sponsor, Hach penned it on behalf of the professional musicians after the first four concerts and during negotiations for the proposed second series. He and his colleagues sought to clarify two issues included by Apthorp in a previous letter pertaining to the location of the series, the expenses, and the extent of control to be exerted by the players over the programs. Hach began by reviewing the disputed items from Apthorp's correspondence:

> All expences [*sic*] incident to said Concerts (except that of
> room-hire, should we change our room) to be borne by your-
> selves; [Apthorp here refers to the musicians.]

The control of all further arrangements connected with the Concerts of course to remain with us.

Regarding the latter clause, Hach indicated full agreement provided it had not been intended to include the selection of music, a right Hach reserved exclusively for the judgment of his musical colleagues and himself. In this instance, it is notable that the musicians did not seek to challenge the authority of institutional management with the exception of the choice of musical repertory.

The musicians dissented regarding the first clause, however. It threatened to change a location that they had assumed to be stable and that they regarded as eminently suitable for the performance and reception of a specific type of music:

We are unwilling to leave Mr. Chickering's rooms which have proved excellent for the effect of chamber music;— yet we would not object to it provided we are allowed to have a voice in the selection of another room in regard to its fitness for our music.

Hach proposed the formation of a committee consisting of Lange and Herwig, to be joined to one representing the association, whose joint charge would be to engage another room, should the association decide on that course. Stipulating further that the musicians would bear only their own expenses for producing the music (but not others relating to a location change or to concert advertisements and ticket sales), Hach emphasized that the success of the first series assured the musicians' right to claim the confidence of the association. Therefore, it was necessary that "the music itself, be left to our own judgement, and that we are consulted about the place, since the effect of this delicate music is easily marred."

In closing, Hach stressed still a third time the link between this

kind of music for small ensembles and the assurance of circumstances leading to its favorable reception:

> We most heartily thank you for your kind acknowledgement of
> our endeavors, and hope that your Society, which has been the
> means of introducing this most refined music to those most ca-
> pable of learning how to appreciate it, will continue to extend its
> beneficial labors for our beautiful art.

It was the professional performing musicians, through Hach,
who insisted upon the appropriate size of a room, with its matching physical limitation of audience size, rather than primarily the
association or Dwight. Hach feared that the "delicate" effect of
chamber music might be easily spoiled, especially in an experimental situation, if it were not heard in the right environment. It was
Hach, but not initially Dwight, who favored the introduction of
"this most refined music to those most capable of learning how to
appreciate it." Dwight ultimately reflected the musicians' point of
view when he described the concerts later that year in *The Harbinger*. They all shared a prevailing concern to establish a supportive
ambience within which chamber music could survive and flourish
in a regular public series.

It is important to recall Dwight's earlier position, however,
which was fully inclusive and quite opposite to that of Hach. In
1840, Dwight had stated his hope that chamber music could be
performed for a broad audience. He had expressly distanced himself from the attitude of "German professors" who played the "diviner music" as if to themselves. Commenting about the performances of two trios by Beethoven on two mixed programs, he had
noted then that they were

> given in the best style of our young German professors, who
> always play as if they breathed an element which we do not.

These were rare sounds in our concert rooms. The few artists who cultivate this diviner music, seem to keep it to themselves, and to feel that it would be casting pearls before swine to produce it before audiences, which can be enraptured about [the popular ballad singer Henry] Russell. But was not the result in these trials encouraging? There was profound silence in the room, followed by a gleam of pure satisfaction on most faces as we looked round;—or was it only the fancied reflection of our own mood? We think not. Let us have more of this. How can we ever have taste enough to keep musicians warm, if they will risk nothing upon us, and never give us a chance to hear the best?[16]

This is a clear expression of Dwight's unmistakable distaste for the exclusionary attitude of German professional musicians, including Hach. Dwight connected his own interests to those of diverse American listeners, whom he hoped would increasingly welcome expanded trials of chamber music.

Unfortunately Dwight's position of 1840, in which he openly encouraged the performance of chamber music before large audiences, did not prevail. When he addressed the issue again in August 1845 in *The Harbinger,* Dwight tried to put the existing concert situation into perspective by describing major distinctions between chamber music and symphonies. More knowledgeable then about the symphonic genre through his reading and repeated hearings of orchestral performances, he remained persuaded that the weighty symphonic style was suited to vast halls and very large, mixed audiences. The concurrent performances of symphonies by the orchestra of the Boston Academy of Music and of chamber music by the musicians for the Harvard Musical Association stimulated Dwight to describe important differences between them, including musical dimensions, performance practice, and audience reception.

In an essay illustrating his preference for calm summer study of music presented in the preceding winter months, Dwight ascribed importance to the original circumstances of a work's creation, extending that sense of eventfulness to the performance itself:

> If it was an era when Beethoven wrote his symphony, so, too, is it when kindred spirits enough among performing artists can be brought together, and can really get inspired with the thing so as to bring it out in a way that the composer himself would be as delighted to hear, as an Orpheus to meet his lost Eurydice.[17]

He divided his review according to notable events in separate genres as presented by three leading institutions: the chamber music concerts of the Harvard Musical Association; the concerts of the Boston Academy of Music, "whose staple was Beethoven's Symphonies, as usual"; and a performance of an oratorio by the Handel and Haydn Society of Boston.

Dwight expressed appreciation of chamber music for its intimate approach to a union of form and content, in contrast to large-scale instrumental pieces, although both could elevate musical taste. In the passage below, his reference to the taste of "real musicians in Germany" marks his close connection to Hach, among others. The first eight concerts of chamber music had met his expectations of progress. Dwight continues:

> For the first time in our city, a truly musical and constant audience assembled to enjoy music of that form which may be called the quintessence of music. The instrumental "Quartette," [sic] the most refined and intimate of musical pleasures, the purest and favorite form of musical communion, among the real musicians in Germany and everywhere, was a thing almost unknown to our people. Now and then, in the most private way, the elements of a Quartette have been assembled, and perhaps some three or four who could feel entirely with the performers, have had the rare privilege to enjoy with them their exquisite feast. On this occasion, the best musical talent among us was exercised

for the instruction and edification of some hundred and fifty of
the best musical listeners. The result was most successful; a taste
was truly formed for it, which will always call for it again. In the
nature of the case, the audience must be small and select, since
the music is not on a scale sufficiently grand for great halls, nor
must its sphere be disturbed by the presence of incongruous and
unsympathizing elements.

We had the Quartettes and Trios, with piano accompaniments, of Haydn, Mozart, Beethoven, Spohr, Kalliwoda &c.
These great writers have entrusted their most choice ideas to
this form of art. The Quartette of the four stringed instruments
of the violin family is to the full orchestra, what a most perfect
outline engraving is to a painting; the charm is always intrinsic,
in the idea itself, and the perfect correspondence of the form
thereto. No original sin or weakness in that can escape detec-
tion; for all orchestral coloring, all borrowed aid of external accompaniments are wanting. There stands the music in its naked
beauty or deformity. If the theme springs from a genuine inspiration of true feeling, if it be developed and treated in both scientific and instinctive conformity with the laws of art, you have the
highest pleasure music can give, you quaff the very essence of
the thing.

These words, which have been variously interpreted, convey
Dwight's acknowledgment that a particular kind of intimate and
concentrated music had been introduced in constructive circumstances to listeners who were best—not necessarily because of
their wealth or social position but because they either enjoyed art
music, were educable to it, or had an acquaintance with chamber
music. Depending on one's perception of his whole viewpoint, one
can interpret Dwight's emphasis to be on the preparation of the
listeners. He creates a parallel deriving from the use of the word
"best" in connection with the musicians: "On this occasion, the
best musical talent among us was exercised for the instruction and
edification of some hundred and fifty of the best musical listeners." He celebrated the capacity of the event to generate education
and pleasure.

In his central argument, Dwight implied that orchestral music, with its vast instrumental resources, could tolerate "the presence of incongruous and unsympathizing elements," but chamber music could not. The interest obtained from the "external accompaniments," together with the essential stylistic elements of symphonies and other orchestral music, justified their appropriate performance in large halls filled by mixed audiences comprising both experienced and unsophisticated listeners. That is an important point. On the other hand, the small scale and "refined" nature of chamber music called for favorable conditions suited to its flourishing. That the series had sold out with 150 regular listeners was a mark of its success.

Despite Dwight's statement regarding the perfection of chamber music, he referred with pleasure to the "borrowed aid" of large-scale orchestral apparatus, whose coloring could attract broad audiences through reinforcing, complementing, and varying the musical materials in their unfolding. One has the impression that Dwight himself preferred the trappings of a full orchestra, or painting, to the intrinsic "charm" of a string quartet, or "most perfect outline engraving." In establishing their differences, he renewed his convictions about the strong link between symphonic music and its suitability for large audiences.

My interpretation differs notably from the account of Michael Broyles, who discusses the 1845 commentary on the association's chamber music concerts from the viewpoint of a "paradox of a democratic society and elite musical institutions." Linking Dwight's major organizational role in sponsoring the concerts to the limitation of audience size, he describes as a "retraction" the decision to address a "limited circle" rather than the whole population. He generalizes to conclude: "No longer were the elite seeking the common man."[18]

Dwight's statements regarding the Harvard Musical Association's chamber music concerts are not typical of his many writings about the symphonic genre in the mid-1840s. They require clarification in a whole context that takes into account his efforts to differentiate orchestral from chamber music and includes consideration of their circumstances of presentation. He reluctantly shifted his position about chamber works under the impact of the German professional musicians' convictions applied to that kind of music. He fully advocated the continued performance of symphonic, and other orchestral, music before a broad population.

In the essays of 1845, Dwight's language and approach regarding symphonic music continued to accord with his basic position enunciated in 1838 in the *Boston Musical Gazette:* he actively supported opportunities for the widest possible base of citizens to acquire musical education. He hoped, and expected, that some would learn to prefer art music and that one major composer might ultimately emerge.[19] This view retained a focus on the societal and cultural benefits to be derived from making symphonic music accessible to the broad community, with the goal of enabling an informed citizenry to make artistic choices. In this way, Beethoven's symphonies could offer interest to diverse and unsophisticated audiences.

Drawing on the Harvard Musical Association's growing library of books and music, Dwight found in the transcriptions by Kalkbrenner one way of supplementing his attendance at rehearsals and performances with active musical study. Their "orchestral" piano effects presented to this amateur pianist demanding and exhilarating challenges emphasizing the scope and dramatic power of Beethoven's symphonies. From another perspective, the association's early chamber music concerts presented to this teacher and writer on music vivid illustrations of the instrumental and characteristic distinctions between the symphonic and chamber music genres. Both developments contributed to Dwight's musical learning in a quintessentially nineteenth-century manner.

CHAPTER EIGHT

———————≫•◦•≪———————

Fourierist Aspects of
Dwight's Major Essays,
1844–1845

Two related convictions shaped Dwight's thought in these
years: music, as art, held a privileged position in his age;
music, as science and art, could be a key to knowledge of the self,
of Nature, and of God. These concepts nourished his attachment
to Beethoven's symphonic music, affected his judgments of other
works, and inspired a vital engagement in a movement calling for
universal harmony through the reform of society. In 1844 and
1845, his connections to Albert Brisbane (1809–1890), leading
American exponent of the social theory known as Fourierism after
its French founder, Charles Fourier (1772–1837), and his translations of Fourier's writings strengthened Dwight's views about the
importance of art music as a harbinger of a better future in
America.

Scholars have disagreed about the extent to which Dwight's
writings reflect principles of Associationism, the communitarian
movement in the United States based partly on Fourierist ideas.
Dwight's major publication outlet beginning in 1845 was *The Harbinger,* the official Associationist organ. This highly influential
weekly reform periodical reached well beyond its estimated two
thousand readers through articles pirated in other journals or

spread through private circulation. Irving Lowens has attributed the remarkable success of its music department largely to the fact that Dwight did not use its columns to "propagandize for Associationism," remaining instead a practical reviewer who "left out the theorizing."[1] However, Charles Crowe, George Ripley's leading modern biographer, has asserted that "Ripley's associates followed his lead in subordinating the arts to Fourierist theory."[2] A position between these two is accurate: Dwight's knowledge of Fourierism, through his own direct translations, and particularly in its American version expounded by Brisbane, informed his essays to varying degrees without submerging musical values. Further, a recognition of those connections considerably clarifies Dwight's thought in relation to Beethoven's symphonies.

I propose four categories, together with at least one example of each, according to which Dwight's writings of these two years may be divided: primarily Associationist documents; writings on music containing considerable reference to Fourierist ideology; musical accounts in which it may be traced to some degree; and pieces about music in which there is very little or none. I shall consider briefly distinctions between Fourier's and Brisbane's perspectives, as well as Brisbane's role as intermediary, before assessing their impact on Dwight's musical discourse.

Fourier was an eccentric, solitary, and largely self-educated French radical author. Although he had produced voluminous additional manuscripts, his doctrines were disseminated in three published works: *Théorie des Quatre Mouvements* (1808), *Théorie de l'Unité Universelle* (1822; first issued as *Traité de l'Association Domestique-Agricole, ou Attraction Industrielle*), and *Nouveau Monde industriel* (1829).[3] Confiscation of Fourier's property during the French Revolution had provided the background for his attacks against the abuses of his society and of civilization, which he regarded as mercenary, fraudulent, and exploitative of workers.

Denying the efficacy of previous philosophical views through "l'éc-art absolu," absolute doubt of the past, he railed against the chaos of a fragmented civilization.[4]

Fourier recommended substituting for it a utopian society made possible through the cooperative efforts of individuals in an era of "Compound Association." Poverty, unemployment, and unhappiness resulted not from the flaws of human beings, who were instinctively good and perfectible, but rather from the evils inherent in civilization. These would no longer exist in a re-created ideal realm called "Harmony," in which human work could be made attractive and productive.

Fourier's emphasis was on social, rather than political, reform. It could be accomplished by the building of communities, or phalanxes, around the world based on the recognition of the integral human needs of love and work. Fourier proposed that there were twelve fundamental "passions," or basic drives, motivating human efforts. These comprised five "sensitive," or sensual, passions (sight, sound, smell, taste, touch); four "affective," or social, passions (friendship, love, familism or the parental instinct, ambition); and three "distributive," or directing, passions (tendency to emulative rivalry ["cabalist"], need for alternating, "periodic" variety ["butterfly"], and desire to synthesize pleasures appealing to the senses and the soul ["composite"]). These would interact in ideal Harmony to produce personal and societal benefits ranging from satisfying individual lives to the efficient organization of industry and the elimination of plagues and war.

Brisbane adapted this elaborate system in his American version on the basis of private lessons with Fourier in Paris and extensive study of his notes and unpublished manuscripts following Fourier's death. Brisbane's cosmopolitan study and extensive international travel enabled him to meet many of the era's leading figures. These included Victor Cousin (whose philosophy lectures he followed at the Sorbonne); Hegel (whose philosophy lectures he studied in Berlin with the help of the philosopher Karl Ludwig Michelet); Goethe; Mendelssohn; Liszt; Heinrich Heine; and Bettina Brentano von Arnim.[5] He took pleasure in the German fondness for music and poetry, but his personal musical preferences centered on Italian opera, notably the works of Vincenzo Bellini.

Brisbane believed in the importance of the social redemption of collective humanity, which included his recognition of the association of men and women in more equal roles. He attended Saint-Simonian meetings in Paris and was sympathetic to the group's general aim of alleviating human misery; among other objections, however, he opposed the demands of its leaders for absolute control. While he was in Berlin, a friend sent Brisbane one of Fourier's books. From that time, the American studied Fourier's objectives of dignifying the labor of the masses through "attractive industry" and increasing their opportunities through universal education. Brisbane agreed with the French thinker's stress on the establishment of more moral institutions and on the essentially positive nature of human passions. He was also very interested in Fourier's belief that only in music, among all areas, had humans realized "harmony" both in "scientific" (technical) and in artistic senses.[6]

When Brisbane set forth his interpretation of Fourierist doctrine in *Social Destiny of Man* in 1840, he viewed the United States as the natural location for experiments founded on beliefs in social justice, universal opportunity, and human perfectibility.[7] He omitted Fourier's controversial notions regarding love and marriage, as well as his extravagant cosmological speculations, and trimmed his detailed tables and complicated terminology. His presentation was a simplified and more morally conservative version of Fourier's views regarding humanity's high social destiny to discover the Divine code by which to achieve "universal unity."

Instead of the conflict and competition of opposing, isolated interests that had led to discord in civilization, humanity could attain order by bringing the varied spheres of industry into harmonious interaction. The term "industry" divided human activities according to domestic occupations, agriculture, manufactures, commerce, education, sciences, and fine arts.[8] Carl J. Guarneri has observed that Brisbane organized *Social Destiny of Man* around a critique of civilization's concept of "individualism": it promoted selfish competitive values as opposed to the fraternity encouraged in cooperative association. Therefore, while the concept of "individuality" included legitimate self-expression, individualism as an ideology was to be avoided.[9]

Brisbane delineated the practical advantages of a community model of agricultural association. Its inhabitants, fewer in number than Fourier required in his grandiose plan, would retain unity of interest in all operations because they would be paid for their labor, hold shares, and own property. Family and individual living arrangements would be separate and private, but all could dine together in the main building, or phalanstery. The settlement would also include a community kitchen for efficient food preparation, public meeting rooms, and farming implements held in common.

Life in a phalanx would be organized so that individuals could choose occupations that were pleasing to them; there would be a variety of tasks, a division of labor, and frequent changes of daily occupation to stimulate and maintain interest. The educational system would remove the disadvantages of civilization's neglect of body and soul by attending to "compound" mental and physical needs as well as "integral" activity organized for the range of human faculties.[10]

It was Brisbane's suggestive work that George Ripley read, discussed with Transcendentalist colleagues, and reviewed for *The Dial* in 1840 before establishing Brook Farm along similar lines.[11]

Ripley believed that Fourier led modern thinkers concerned with practical social evils and ways of removing them, but that the general principles of his thought were separable from details suited to French adaptation. Ripley was very interested in Fourier's system of "combined and organized industry" stressing "the cooperative principle."

John S. Dwight, then in Northampton, Massachusetts, heard from his friend Samuel Osgood that the Ripleys were reading Brisbane's book but were at first unconvinced of its applicability to their needs. After expressing his belief that they "eschew Brisbane's dictum," Osgood continued with the hope that "we shall soon see their projected Utopia realised."[12] Dwight and Osgood remained concerned and actively interested in the new colony in West Roxbury. Osgood forecast one of its main difficulties as he expressed wishes for the success of Brook Farm in another letter to Dwight some months later: "Heaven help them, and save their zeal from being evaporated by the hot summer suns, that are to shine down upon their toils."[13]

Ripley ultimately adapted aspects of Brisbane's vision in a more free arrangement, joining with it his Transcendentalist belief in fraternal values and a liberal Christian hope of improving society. Ripley's original objectives for Brook Farm projected a small model society built initially around agriculture, but fostering the unity of intellectual and manual labor to attain common objectives. Each person could grow through the choice of work adapted to individual talents. Basing his community on a belief in the innate goodness of human beings (in accord with Fourier's similar views), Ripley brought together families from the middle and working classes striving to achieve the integral education of mind and body. His farm depended on cooperative labor, and its participants worked more enthusiastically as owners of divided joint-stock shares.

These elements were in place years before Brook Farm's official adoption of Fourierism in 1844.[14] According to Guarneri and Crowe, Brook Farm had already adapted a blend of ideas that made natural, rather than artificial, its systematic transition to Fourierism. That controversial shift occurred in order to reverse a financial crisis brought about by a shortage of capital and poor crops resulting from stony soil. It introduced greater organizational efficiency and a diversification of operations bringing in mixed industry. Accompanying these were the institution of a wage structure based on differential, rather than equal, wages and a decision to build a large central phalanstery.

Ripley, Dwight, and their colleagues participated actively as leaders, writers, and lecturers in the New England Fourier Society from 1844 to 1846. Ripley was its president, and Dwight was a member of the executive committee. On the national level, the various American experimental communities (of which about one-half of the fifty-five were officially Fourierist between 1842 and 1849) gathered under the more general banner of Associationism.[15]

Dwight and Brisbane increased their professional contacts in late 1844 and 1845. This bore important ramifications for Dwight's activities as lecturer in 1846, as will be considered in Chapter 9. Brisbane had previously established an influential column (1842–43) in Horace Greeley's *New-York Tribune;* he had also written on Association for *The United States Magazine, and Democratic Review* and had completed another book about it in 1843.[16] He had then returned to Paris for continued examination of Fourier's manuscripts and for more intensive musical study to further his understanding of Fourier's analogy between the harmonies of universal unity and the theory of music.

Brisbane took three daily lessons for about eight months starting in April 1844, primarily in sight-singing and ear-training ac-

cording to the Galin-Paris-Chevé method.[17] This was a modifica-
tion of a system of number, or figure, notation first proposed in
1742 by Jean-Jacques Rousseau.[18] Rousseau had originally intended it as a new notational system substituting numbers, instead
of syllables, for notes; favoring simplicity, he advocated learning
how to write music using fewer signs. (In his system, for example,
the figure "4," with an ascending line crossing it from left to right,
would be equivalent to a "fa" sharped.)

In the nineteeth-century Galin-Paris-Chevé method, Nanine
Paris Chevé, Brisbane's main teacher, taught Rousseau's system
only as an approach to standard notation. She pronounced Brisbane to have a "poor ear," according to his recollection, but he
was satisfied, nonetheless. He also gained new appreciation of the
practical problems of musical performance under the guidance of
Émile Chevé.

Brisbane's visits to Brook Farm increased upon his return from
Paris in the late fall of 1844. On one occasion in early 1845 he
stayed for a month as he, Ripley, Dwight, and a few others planned
strategy to make Brook Farm America's most important phalanx.
The same small group of leaders undertook to investigate aspects
of Fourier's writings. Dwight revised Brook Farm's constitution
according to Fourierist principles, completing it in early 1845.

In January 1845, Dwight took charge of the entire school program at Brook Farm (which comprised primary through college-
preparatory levels), succeeding Ripley's sister, Marianne Ripley, as
director of education. That summer, Brisbane conducted a series
of "scientific classes" at Brook Farm on Fourier's teachings.[19] One
result of all this consultation was a decision to broaden the scope
of Brisbane's paper, The Phalanx, and move it from New York to
Brook Farm. With George Ripley as its new chief editor, it was
renamed The Harbinger in token of its symbolic progressive mis-
sion. Its first issue appeared in June 1845.

Throughout this productive and busy period, as Dwight moved to the forefront of Fourierist organizational activity in New England, he continued to teach in the school, direct education, write, translate, lecture, assist Ripley with editorial duties, and farm. In addition, he served as vice-president of the Harvard Musical Association. Given the importance of music in the programs of Fourier and Brisbane, Dwight attempted, when possible, to integrate aspects of Fourierist thinking in essays on musical subjects.

The first of the four categories into which I divide Dwight's writings includes avowedly Associationist documents not primarily related to music. This broad classification shows the larger framework of Dwight's mental activity during the period in which he wrote his important early essays about Beethoven's symphonies. On February 29, 1844, in the year before he became educational director, Dwight delivered to the New England Fourier Society in Boston *A Lecture on Association, in its Connection with Education,* which was published immediately thereafter.[20] The system of education described in the latter part of the lecture was "essentially that adopted at Brook Farm," according to a note following a lecture published with it.[21] I shall briefly describe it before assessing the first section, which is significant for its revelation of Dwight's deepest convictions attached loosely to Fourierist rhetoric.

Fourier's doctrine of "universal unity" provided the theoretical basis for Dwight's educational philosophy, which centered on individual development achieved by means of harmonious relations with others in groups.[22] Boldly attacking "transcendental" extremism that exaggerated "self-ism," he affirmed the importance of self-culture in an associative setting that encouraged free development in groups rather than through the imposition of authoritarian discipline. He suggested a plan based on "influences, exercises, and studies" corresponding to infancy, youth, and the late teen years. Infants would experience the influential benefits of charac-

ter development, outward nature, art, and organization in a pleasing environment provided by caregivers, including, but not limited
to, parents. Dwight defended the importance of music in the community as an inspirational, moral, and aesthetic presence.

In the "period of pupilage" extending from ages six to sixteen,
youngsters would devote their mornings to physical labor in
"groups and series," frequently changing tasks according to inclinations, and their afternoons to intellectual exercises. These stimulated the perceptive faculties (singing, drawing, dance), together
with thought and memory (reading, writing, languages, geography,
science, history). At first, they would consist primarily of oral description and concrete group exercises taught by different teachers
according to the subject. Faster learners would continue advanced
"studies" in private, smaller classes. In the "period of probation,"
people aged sixteen to twenty would assume greater responsibili-
ties in community association and might broaden their learning
with foreign travel. In fact, however, the older students often attended colleges after their preparation at the well-regarded Brook
Farm school.

The vast literature about Brook Farm includes interesting reminiscences and memoirs attesting to the excellent educational benefits and success of this program. Music organized by Dwight
played a significant role in numerous daily casual, convivial, and
festive events in the community. The affection of the young people
for him appears to have been genuine and reciprocated. The accounts do not give details regarding the repertory and conduct of
Dwight's instruction at piano, vocal, or theory lessons.[23]

The earlier part of Dwight's lecture on education considered
the issue of individual sin as isolated and competitive selfishness
encouraged by civilization. His hope for improvement in society,
which he considered then in transition, was based on the joining of
individuality (not the ideology of individualism) with universality.

These must be regarded, he believed, as mutually reconcilable rather than opposite elements. Striking a confident and assured tone, Dwight posited three realms—material, social, and ideal—instead of his more typical division into a real (material) and an ideal (spiritual) universe. Organized, rather than isolated, industry planned according to the natural tendencies ("passional attractions") of people would furnish the key to the integral development of humanity.

Dwight recommended a search for unity combining the perception of truth (science) with the love of fellow human beings. He invoked briefly a liberal Christian hope of "a kingdom of heaven on earth" together with a Transcendentalist concern for the ennoblement of all work. These combined with a Fourierist proposal hailing the rewards of "attractive industry": associated labor could foster greater connections to all human and spiritual realms.

Characteristically, Dwight found a felicitous metaphor for these aims in music, specifically in the symphonic genre:

> Each note in the great world-symphony is a whole, a unit in itself, and must assert its individuality, insisting on its own peculiar sound, at the same time that it reverently dedicates itself and helps fulfil beyond itself the harmony of the whole. Apply this to society. Each member is a unit by himelf, an individual; and yet he belongs to humanity. In living for the whole he lives most effectually to himself; for it takes all humanity to complete him, to set him in his own only place, and so surround him as to illustrate and bring out his peculiar beauty. He is not himself except in true relations with the whole. Yet he must not *lose* himself in the whole; he must preserve his individuality.[24]

Thus in universal unity, each part "only lives in the whole," just as each member is most true in being rightly related to "the harmony of the whole." Humans could attain unity of relations in material, social, and ideal spheres through the appropriate use of their tendencies (or passions). Integral industry would be achieved only when all humans experienced the joy of joining in the universal love of all things to "cultivate the earth *as one*."

Dwight incorporated these themes in columns for *The Harbinger,* some of which were Associationist articles unconnected to music. An instance is his "Individuality in Association," which elaborates on the necessity of individual contribution to the collective destiny of humanity.[25] This piece also offers a gloss on the Fourierist dictum "Attractions proportional to Destinies" by explaining that an individual engages most readily in that work performed voluntarily and according to his or her ideal aim.

For my second proposed category, Dwight's writings on music with considerable reference to Fourierist ideology, I choose two examples from *The Harbinger.* As primary reviewer and as editor of its music department, Dwight inaugurated his position with a column on music that revived old ideas and established new critical principles incorporated within an Associationist framework. Rejoicing that the United States was beginning to evince interest in music as an art and a "language of the soul," he explained his interest in music from abroad as part of the "material and spiritual" exchange of nations preparing the way "for all to become One."[26]

This universal vision was inherent in his musical preferences and in his hopes for America. Describing humanity's journey toward the fulfillment of "its glorious destiny" in unity and harmony, Dwight praised the earnest pursuit of the highest creative accomplishment as "artistic." Music was an expression of the greatest social movement to occur in America, "the common gathering place of all nations." The inward unity of people would take place in society as a whole through the indispensable acceptance of music as a natural language of sentiment. He enunciated the Fourierist view, echoed also by Brisbane, that the scale of musical tones was analogous to the scale of human passions as an expression of the correspondence between material and spiritual laws. Music held the key to "knowledge of ourselves, of Nature and of God."

Dwight asserted a double set of critical objectives, one musical and the other of larger perspective. He proposed to consider musical works by diverse composers and performances:

> To guide public taste in its selection, to inspire artists in their performance, and above all to exhort the musician to a high sense of the dignity of his profession, and teach others to respect it, too, shall be our aim in criticism.

These musical efforts dominated, but they coexisted with other aims that were less systematically carried out during the four years of *The Harbinger's* existence:

> Three things we shall have in view: (1.) the criticism of music as an Art; (2.) the interpretation of it as an expression of the life of the age; and (3.) the development of its correspondence as a Science with other sciences, and especially with the Science of the coming Social Order, and the transition through which we are passing towards it.[27]

Another instance of musical discourse with extended Fourierist reference is the essay describing the Harvard Musical Association's chamber music concerts (which I discussed above without its Fourierist sections). After commenting on the experience of chamber music, Dwight described three of his favorite composers—Haydn, Mozart, and Beethoven—in terms that can be associated with E. T. A. Hoffmann's characterizations of 1810 (through Fink and others). They are here encased in an ingenious new Fourierist structure that illuminates Dwight's ability to clothe his strong inner convictions in appropriately tailored outer garb. To overlook references of this kind or to dismiss them as mere Fourierist propaganda is to obviate their significance in Dwight's mental development.

He chose four composers and characterized each according to Fourier's classification, and Brisbane's interpretation, of the four social ("affective") passions in human nature. Universal friendship is linked to Handel; love is associated with the "tender, mystical" Mozart; paternity, or the family bond, is connected to the "sunny, genial" Haydn inhabiting the actual realm of domestic joys; and ambition is the passional drive linked to Beethoven as "strong, inspiring, . . . full of new longings, born of new triumphs." Dwight's main point was that these social passions did not permit human isolation but variously brought the soul into "living unity" with the source. He described ambition as a positive, aspiring tendency that found delight in "eternal order . . . , which reverences all things and persons in their place, confounds no everlasting and true distinctions, and is ambitious only to find its place, that it may feel the whole harmony of which it is an humble, though indispensable note, not for selfish distinction for distinction's sake."[28]

Having carefully redefined the essence of ambition in an opposite sense from the world's "vile inversion," Dwight went on to explain that it was illustrated by Beethoven's idealizing tendency symbolic of the coming amelioration of society:

> Beethoven is the aspiring Promethean spirit, struggling for release from monotony and falseness, sick of the actual, subduing every sincere sadness by heroic triumphs in art, which are like tears brightening into joys of most rapturous, inspired visions of a coming Era, which shall consummate the Unity of all things.

This florid rhetoric blends the Transcendentalist and Fourierist values from the second quarter of the nineteenth century that were integral to Dwight's engagement with Beethoven.

My third category of the critic's writings comprises musical accounts in which Fourierist beliefs are manifested to some extent. When he transferred his first thoughts about Beethoven's Fifth Symphony from *The Pioneer* of 1843 into *The Harbinger* of 1845, Dwight prefaced the older material with new reflections. By then, he had become committed to a central "unitary" vision which underscored his faith that many Americans, not just a privileged few, were capable of responding to the orchestral Beethoven.

Expressing satisfaction that the Boston Academy of Music had attempted to educate, create, and maintain a "high standard" of taste for works by "the great masters," he noted that the "imperfectly executed" results had approximated "studies" rather than finished performances. Still, Beethoven was "really known to many; and some of the symphonies have been studied and repeated till the orchestra have really got to feel them, and cooperate as one in the production of them."[29] In the Fourierist sense, this process was an exact example of many working together harmoniously through a "combined order." Both musicians and public had grown and benefited.

At a fundamental level, Dwight contended, Beethoven's music was not too difficult or advanced for the contemporaneous level of performance and culture. To the contrary, he argued, Americans had a need, a capacity, and an inclination that would assure its successful reception:

> The truth is, Beethoven's is the music of this age; it gives voice to the imprisoned soul and aspiration of this age. Spiritually and essentially, it can be better comprehended by unmusical Americans in Boston now, than it could in Vienna when it was born. It was prophetic of the great world-movement that now stirs so many hearts.

To comprehend it, preparation of the soul was more necessary than musical refinement. To his fundamentally democratic and

Transcendentalist beliefs regarding the intuitive capacity of humans to approach art music, Dwight joined his Fourierist-derived educational theories and hopes for the reform of society. If American souls stirred instinctively to Beethoven's orchestral music, then the ears would follow:

> [I]t will open our ears for us through our souls; it will inspire us, since it came from that which in the depths of our hearts most interests us. The child will study what it loves; and we apprehend it is our destiny in this age and in this land to love Beethoven.

A musical culture he considered to be in its period of pupilage could follow "attractions proportional to destinies" to attain naturally, and by inclination, an appreciation of the symphonies in their essence. Dwight's previous statement on Beethoven's Fifth Symphony thus appeared in an expanded new framework.

His first essay on Beethoven's Seventh Symphony also includes some pertinent Fourierist allusions. Appearing in *The Harbinger* only two weeks after the account of the Fifth Symphony just discussed, it was also a summer reflection written months after the actual performances. Less lengthy and less dependent on anecdotal biographical information, it attempted to be more musically specific. Dwight admitted that "having no verbal key from the composer, we shall not dare to offer any fanciful interpretation of our own."[30] One discerns in the background an image of Beethoven, the lonely prophet whose inner sense aspired earnestly "to express the cooperation of all things," but this "striving for the infinite" is translated more directly into musical terms.

Dwight conveyed dual delight in perceiving the symphony's musical continuity, achieved in all movements through the pervasive power of the tonic tone, A, together with a metaphysical unity:

The key note with which it begins and ends, is A major. There is a wonderful continuousness in it. Something strikes you at first, which is heard to the end. Neither the sombre Andante, nor the wild Scherzo, nor the again triumphant Finale, can drive it out of your mind. That A is heard all through. In the Andante, it is still the key-note, though in the minor mood; in the Presto, it is present as the Third of the key-note F; and even there, upon the background of F, it continues to make itself the prominent figure, and the whole passage ends in a loud, long unison on A. The key then changes to D major, while the rapid tempo yields to the slower, statelier movement of that most sublime, full, celestial strain, . . . awakening at the same time, a sense of awe and an inward consciousness of power and of a great destiny, a grand unitary sentiment. . . . [I]n this wonderful passage, also, the A is prolonged in trumpet tones, the *Dominant* in more than the technical sense to the whole strain in D. The Presto revelry in F is renewed; is again arrested by the commencing chords of that grand Chant; and the key-note of F barely saves itself at the close, by a few swift helter-skelter leaps of modulation. The *Finale Allegretto* again returns, of course, to the fundamental of A.

In each movement Dwight also perceived an organizational unity of rhythmic structure, as well as key, which evinced itself as "one short rhythmical phrase [that] marshals the procession of the full-ranked harmonies." His language characterizes musical events, but there is a familiar subtext. In the first movement, after the majestic introduction, the theme enters:

It is the same monotonous phrase, of a single measure starting in a galloping dactylic rhythm, and drawing everything after the lead. It gives the impression of a uniform, determined movement through the whole universe of being. One restless energy, one unquenchable, but dignified and self-controlling emulation, urges all things onward, kindles itself anew in every nature, till all are enlisted in one glorious, active dedication of themselves to unity. Nothing parts with its own individual features, yet all accept the impetus divine, and haste to swell the rapid, orderly procession. The little monotonous phrase not only wakes up its

own natural harmonies, but traverses all manner of keys, and
presses the most daring discords, willingly or unwillingly, to
chime in with it, and follow whithersoever it leads.

After considering the second movement lengthily from several
vantage points and noting that Beethoven's scherzo movements
replaced the "old Minuet and Trio," Dwight connected the four
movements of the symphonic genre on the Beethovenian model.
It was dynamically organized and conveyed a generalized character. The movements contrasted in tempos and moods within a
theoretical framework. No specific extrinsic situation applied to
the whole:

> The artistical structure of a Symphony, the distribution of its
> various movements, (commencing with the Allegro, then the An-
> dante, then the Scherzo, and then the Finale,) is not arbitrary,
> but has a certain metaphysical completeness. The first dis-
> courses, as it were, to the Intellect; lays down a certain proposi-
> tion and unfolds it. The Andante is the climax of the whole, and
> reproduces what before was Thought, as Feeling. The playful
> Scherzo is the alternation of fancy; and the Finale, rapid, ener-
> getic, and triumphant usually, has in it more of the Will, and
> embodies Thought in Action.[31]

To this statement Dwight attached a Fourierist declaration extending his analogy of Beethoven with the social passion of purified ambition. That composer would inspire humanity with the
vision of a better future achieved through cooperative social destiny. He represented the seventh note (or leading tone) striving
mightily to bring about the ultimate resolution of the octave in all
its harmonious perfection:

> The music of Beethoven, we have said it more than once, is a
> presentiment of coming social harmony, a great hearts' [sic] con-
> fession of its faith, one of the nearest and clearest echoes of the

approaching footsteps of the good genius of Humanity. He is the seventh note in the scale, the note which cries for the completion of the octave, the note whose correspondence is the passion of the soul for Order, the purified ambition, which no longer inverted and seeking only self-aggrandizement, contemplates a glorious hierarchy of all humanity, in which each, feeling his true place, and filling it, and felt in it, may in one act help to complete and enjoy the universal accord, and thus, in the only conceivable manner, satisfy the craving of each single soul to embrace the Infinite at once.

In this epoch, Dwight could briefly join his societal hopes for the future to his intrinsic musical preferences.

Characteristically, the essays written in the summer did not elaborate on details of performance. However, during the concert season, Dwight ventured impressionistic comments about a recent performance still fresh in his memory. After rehearing the Seventh Symphony performed by the orchestra of the Academy some months later that autumn, he noted strengthening additions to the double basses that lent greater "solidity and dignity," while improving the balance from its previously "top-heavy" quality. Dwight preferred string prominence in symphonic performance to create a sound that he identified as "more an orchestra, and less a band."[32]

Finally, the fourth category pertaining to Dwight's essays comprises musical accounts that contain very little, or no, trace of Fourierist reference. In this group I place the most straightforward symphonic discussion of this period, one associated, ironically, with Beethoven's Sixth Symphony. Dwight had first discussed it in an unpublished lecture of March 1842 in Boston, and much of the poetic and nontechnical material in a published essay of 1845 may derive from that presentation. It consists of earlier views juxtaposed with new musical formulations.

Beethoven's Sixth Symphony was being rehearsed by the orchestra of the Academy late in October 1845 when Dwight chose to write about it in *The Harbinger.*[33] Amid biographical, autobiographical, and literary allusions, he made a serious attempt to convey technical detail regarding symphonic form. Treating the "thunderstorm" movement merely as an insertion, Dwight mistakenly described a basic four-movement structure in connection with this unconventionally organized work and insisted on its "mechanical form."

Despite these substantial flaws, he presents a brief general sketch of symphonic structure in first movements. In this instance, it is not possible to substantiate directly Dwight's access to a particular source. However, such a source may be inferred from internal documentary language. The names of prominent theorists of the symphony in the nineteenth century—Anton Reicha, A. B. Marx, and Carl Czerny—do not appear in the book lists of acquisitions by the library of the Harvard Musical Association before 1845. Gustav Schilling's entry on "sonata" in the *Universal-Lexicon* is not specific regarding structure. According to publication dates, nevertheless, Dwight could have been acquainted with either the second volume of Marx's *Die Lehre von der musikalischen Komposition,* which appeared in 1838, or with Czerny's translation of Reicha's *Vollständiges Lehrbuch der musikalischen Composition,* which was published in 1832.

The descriptions by Marx and by Reicha-Czerny differ considerably from each other, but both are much more detailed than is Dwight, especially in the area of harmonic activity. In addition, they use the term "sonata form," to which Dwight does not allude at this date. All recognize the importance of structure in the first movements of symphonies. All describe the gradual modulation out of the principal (tonic) key to the fifth, or dominant, key in major-key structures and the usual repetition of the first of two parts in symphonic first movements. Dwight emphasizes that this occurs for structural reasons and to enable the listener to absorb

the thematic materials before they are transformed by the composer's "science" in the second part.

Similarities in Dwight's essay to Marx's brief discussion include
an emphasis on the initial motives, or themes, and their "working
up" (Dwight's phrase) through germinal growth toward the organic unity of the whole. However, Marx allows for the possibility,
among others, of introducing an entirely new subject in the second
part of the first movement ("oder einem kurzen neuen Satze"),[34]
while Dwight insists that there is to be "always novelty, but no new
subject" in the "second division."

More striking is Dwight's first use of the term "middle subject"
to designate the second subject, or thematic group, with its extension (or continuation) toward new cadential material closing the
first part of an initial movement. That reference suggests his recent
acquaintance with Reicha-Czerny who, unlike Marx, describe in
almost four paragraphs the modulatory entry out of the first subject into the new key of a "Mittelsatz (Mittelgesang)." Compositional skill is required to balance, treat, and lead the middle subject toward new yet appropriate material.[35] Dwight's short
discussion is also similar to the Reicha-Czerny treatise in its greater
emphasis on a binary concept for the structural division of the
movement.

Dwight described first-movement form (which he referred to as
"symphonic") in the following passage, adding brief comments
about the remaining movements:

> In the Symphony it is the first movement only which is strictly
> Symphonic. This is commonly an Allegro, consisting of two divi-
> sions. The former contains all the simple themes or *motivi,* and
> is always repeated. The latter is the working up of these themes
> into all manner of transformations and combinations; and it is
> here that the skill and science of the artist are put in requisition;
> his problem being to stick to his text, and never repeat himself,

to develope [sic] the *motivi* of the first division into inexhaustible novelties. Attend well, then, to the first division of the *Allegro,* (which for that very reason is always repeated,) and you have the key to the whole labyrinth of harmonies into which it introduces you. It begins always with the main theme or tune of the piece, then modulates gradually into the fifth of the key, which gives an answering melody, the *counter-theme,* or *middle subject,* then through a somewhat lengthened cadence, often enriched with several new melodies, returns into the first *theme,* modulates as before into the *counter-theme,* and winds away through the same lengthened cadence, not to return again, but to pass into a new world of endless transformations, into the *second division,* where forms are varied and multiplied without end; but in every one you still recognize the old features of the first themes: always novelty, but no new subjects. Such is the skeleton of the Allegro, or first movement of a Symphony; which is always in the *Symphonic* form. Then follows the slow and thoughtful Andante or Adagio, which is commonly in the Rondo form; that is, an air repeated three or four times, only each time with a more florid accompaniment. Awhile it dallies in the graceful, playful form of the Minuet and Trio, or fantastic Scherzo; and then it gives full reins, and lets excited fancy spend itself in the rapid, wild Finale.[36]

Dwight similarly concentrated on the thematic and tonal nature of the first part of the first movement in his account of Beethoven's Sixth Symphony. He wrote little about the musical substance of other movements, contenting himself with characterizing their meters or accompaniment patterns. He noted the welcome reminiscence of the Andante at the close of the "thunderstorm" movement. But it was the melodic material of the first movement as germinal core of an entire work that dominated Dwight's musical and poetic efforts. Locating four subjects in the first part of the Sixth Symphony's first movement, he characterized them at length and with particular attention to the interchange of phrases between the instruments. This is a brief excerpt from his discussion of the second subject:

Thus, when a snatch of melody lights like a sunbeam on the topmost notes of the flutes and oboes, thence glides down through the violins, the seconds, the tenors [violas], the deep full violoncellos, till finally the double basses convey it down to depths inaudible, the musical hearer, who can scarce contain his pleasure, may be excused if he try to make his neighbor *see* it, by telling him to imagine himself stretched upon a grassy slope in a summer afternoon, dreaming of all. . . . Those acquainted with the technical structure of a Symphony, will best recognize the passage which we mean, if we call it the *countertheme,* or *middle subject* of the first division of the *Allegro.*

I have noted Dwight's interest since 1835 in William Gardiner's capacity to describe instrumental activity. There is one reference in this essay to Gardiner's remark that "the ground-tone of the all-pervading hum in the open air" is marked by an F-natural, the tonic key of this symphony. Otherwise, Dwight refutes strongly the premise of the author of *The Music of Nature:* "We feel that this Symphony answers the whole question about the *descriptive* or *imitative* powers of music." His summary of that issue may have sharpened his resistance toward other kinds of instrumental music of an overtly "programmatic" nature by enunciating a standard according to Beethoven's Sixth Symphony.

Dwight sharpened an earlier contrast between Haydn, who had painted "the actual merely," and Beethoven, who had reached beyond the external world to make of it a "mirror of the soul" in communing with "the *spirit* of nature." Convinced that all in nature corresponded to something in the human soul, Dwight lauded Beethoven's capacity to sing the poetic experience, the *feeling* of nature, through melody. Regarding this piece as an aspect of Beethoven's "sunny side" in his "most comprehensible style," the American critic echoed faintly E. T. A. Hoffmann's perception, nonetheless, of a "foreboding of the mysterious and almost supernatural character" of the composer.

There is virtually no direct Fourierist emphasis in this essay, but one oblique reference suggests Dwight's fundamental values reinforced by Fourierist beliefs. It occurs in the discussion of this symphony's first subject considered as source for all that follows in a Beethovenian first movement:

> Beautiful is the way in which this air is introduced. At first a mere snatch of it, just a phrase of a couple of bars, from a single instrument, as if some wandering zephyr sung [sic] it as it passed by; then a long hold upon the last note, as if surprised and wondering what will become of this. Anon it is answered in another quarter; kindred phrases blend with it; different instruments repeat it with fuller harmonies; it melts away in the distance, and, when we think it gone, it comes up again from the deep basses; it resounds in full octaves from the whole band; it fills out all things; it *is* the tune of Nature! Out of this simple air all the rest follows of course; all the successive melodies and modulations flow out of it and return back into it by the same necessity by which all the parts of a landscape seem to date from and illustrate every single part; "we are all *one,* though many," they seem to say.[37]

In sum, Dwight included Fourierist references in writings on Beethoven's symphonic music in 1844 and 1845 because they were part of his mental outlook. Although he rarely utilized outright propaganda or elaborate Fourierist terminology, he often enriched his musical essays with musical metaphors based on Associationist beliefs. These were particularly apt in describing Beethoven's symphonies, which Dwight presented as epitomes of "universal unity" in structural and metaphysical senses. He applied to his criticism those positive and dynamic principles that resonated with his fundamental philosophy. In that era, Dwight hoped that social reform could be accomplished through universal cooperation in a "world-symphony." He believed that an orchestral performance of a symphony by the prophetic Beethoven not only uplifted listeners in collective bonding but also represented the joining of fellow musicians engaged in a practical and symbolic demonstration of fraternal harmony.

———————➤•◦•◄———————

CHAPTER NINE

Dwight in New York:
Beethoven in the Lecture Plan, 1845–1846;
The First American Performance of
the Ninth Symphony, 1846

Two major events caused Dwight to travel to New York in March and again in May of 1846: the opportunity to present invited lectures on music in that city, a goal unfulfilled since 1841, and a desire to hear the first performance in the United States of Beethoven's Symphony no. 9 in D Minor, op. 125, as the focus of a trip undertaken on behalf of Brook Farm. These occasions culminated an era of high idealism that was opened by Dwight's translation of Schiller's "An die Freude" and that was intensified on hearing it as part of Beethoven's Ninth Symphony. During 1846, Dwight increased his translations of varied writings by Fourier for *The Harbinger* and continued his multiple activities as an Associationist. In March of that year his efforts acquired greater urgency: Brook Farm's survival was threatened by a disastrous fire that destroyed the nearly completed phalanstery shortly before the beginning of the critic's planned lectures in New York.

The significance of Dwight's organization of the lecture series of 1846 can be better appreciated after contrasting it with his plan for a set of talks delivered in Boston in 1842. Neither course was ever published, but newspaper advertisements, letters, and Dwight's articles leading to the lectures of 1846 establish a basis for understanding the evolution of his thought regarding Beethoven's position in the history of music.

Correspondence reveals that Dwight had initiated the idea of giving lectures in New York as early as the fall of 1841. He appealed for assistance to his former Harvard classmate and friend, the Reverend Henry W. Bellows. A sympathetic reply from Bellows, dated October 5, 1841, indicated that he would try to help him, but nothing came of this attempt.[1] In February and March of 1842, after moving to Brook Farm, Dwight delivered a set of eight lectures in Boston.

Sparsely worded advertisements in the *Boston Daily Evening Transcript* show that the 1842 lectures were organized with attention to genres, as well as to biographical and artistic concerns, but without particular reference to historical sequence.[2] Announced as weekly musical lectures "on the Life and Genius of some of the great Musical Composers, and on the style and departments of music which they represent," they were presented in the "Saloon" of the Odeon, the concert hall in which the Boston Academy had performed the initial orchestral concerts featuring Beethoven's symphonies. All of Dwight's talks were held on Thursday evenings at 7:30, except for the first two, held at 7 o'clock. Tickets for the course, at two dollars, could be purchased easily at designated music and book stores. The dates and subjects of the 1842 series were

February 3	Handel
February 10	Handel's "Messiah"
February 17	Mozart
February 24	Haydn
March 10	Beethoven; the Pastoral Symphony and the Symphony in C Minor
March 17	Beethoven
March 24	The Pianists
March 31	Sebastian Bach

The announcement of the seventh lecture did not list the subject. It appeared in a letter to the editor from "one of the audience," who expressed regret at the sparse crowd as well as the pleasure and benefit he had obtained from attending. The writer hoped that more people would come to the remaining lectures to encourage a repetition during the following winter and to prevent the lecturer from seeking an audience in another city. This letter, written by one who shared Dwight's belief in music as "the fine art of greatest promise in our times," praised him as "a lecturer of refined taste, familiar with good music as far as any one can be in this country, and with the best foreign works upon the subject."

In that series, Dwight led with two lectures about a composer and a favorite work familiar to the audience through performances by the Boston Handel and Haydn Society. He placed the two lectures on Beethoven at a point after which he and the audience would have had the opportunity to hear the Sixth and Fifth Symphonies in orchestral performances in January and February. It is notable that Dwight included then, as well as later, a lecture devoted to virtuosi, in this instance pianists. Their visits to Boston and other American sites had become important features of concert life.

On November 17, 1842, while preparing his essay for *The Pioneer,* Dwight wrote again to his New York friend to renew his earlier proposition to give lectures there. He candidly admitted his need of income, proposed most of the same subjects as in the Boston series already given that year, and asserted his purpose to "prepare people with little knowledge to hear great music more understandingly." Dwight ascribed considerable importance to the project:

> A year ago we spoke of the possibility of finding an audience for my musical lectures in N. York. What do you think of it *now*? I

am in great need of some income in that way, since I can no
longer preach. I should like to give a course of *four* or *six* lectures, pretty early in the winter, on the lives & musical styles of
some of my heroes such as Handel, Mozart, Haydn, Beethoven,
the "pianists" &c.—They are not scientific in their character,
but calculated to awaken an interest in those men, to make the
musical character appreciated, & to prepare people with little
knowledge to hear great music more understandingly. Could you
do anything to get me an audience?[3]

The letter continued with specific detail about others who might
be contacted. Dwight requested that Bellows procure a list of people who would support the enterprise in order to combine this
substantial "business" in New York with an offer from the Mer-
cantile Library Association of Newark, New Jersey, to deliver one
lecture.

Bellows's cordial reply included a promise to try on Dwight's
behalf and an invitation for him to stay at his home during a visit,
together with practical information about expenses. A lecture
room would cost a minimum of seventy-five dollars for six nights,
tickets for a course would be two dollars each, and an audience of
at least fifty persons would be necessary to assure the investment.
He had mentioned Dwight as a lecturer to directors of literary
associations in New York. Bellows's doubts about the possibility
of a successful outcome can be deduced from his statement that
"[i]t may be that more interest would be manifested in a course of
Music lectures than I know of."[4] Another letter indicated that
there was as yet no news about the lectures.[5] Once again, the venture did not come to fruition.

Given this background, Dwight should have welcomed an invitation from Albert Brisbane three years later to present a series of
lectures in New York, yet he needed to be convinced before agree-
ing to the project. This time, he would be obliged to fulfill some-

one else's conditions. A month before Brisbane extended the offer, Dwight had published an essay in *The Harbinger* that may have encouraged Brisbane to ask Dwight's cooperation in his venture.

Dwight had authored a predominantly positive article, "Fourier's Writings," in which he acknowledged that these works had constituted "a most significant era in our reading, and our whole thought must ever own their influence."[6] Fourier had manifested personal idiosyncracies, Dwight asserted, but his writings were universal in scope. That he had spoken "*of* the passions rather than *from* the passions" and given little evidence of personal feeling for beauty suggested to Dwight that Fourier lacked the poetic imagination to explore "the inward life" of characters. However, his classifications and observations possessed grandeur regarding human destiny in the scale of beings.

Among Fourier's main principles, Dwight praised the "law of the series" as the guide to the unity of all things. Two illustrations of a perfect series were the scale of musical tones, drawn from the material realm, and the scale of the passions, from the spiritual side of being. Fourier's approach was intricate. Briefly, the simplest series unfolded into three, forming the three notes of the musical triad (or common chord) corresponding to the three classes of the passions (sensitive, affective, and intellectual or distributive). The series at the next level presented seven, as in the seven varied pitches of the diatonic scale analogous to the seven passions (affective and distributive, omitting those relating to the material world). At a further level, the series presented twelve, furnishing the complete chromatic scale in music and all twelve passions. Dwight found reinforcement in Fourier's system for his own intuitive beliefs: knowledge of music could be a key to knowledge of all else in the universe. Despite the seemingly "inflexible external-

ity" of his approach, the American critic prized Fourier's fundamental search "to resolve nature and the soul into one system."[7]

In December 1845, one month later, Brisbane penned three
flattering letters inviting and exhorting Dwight to present lectures
that would highlight, among other subjects, the musical aspect of
Fourier's system. The first explained the circumstances but also
reveals that, through Brisbane, Dwight gained access to the work
of Jérôme-Joseph de Momigny (1762–1842), a leading theorist of
the early nineteenth century, and also became familiar with the
Galin-Paris-Chevé method of sight-singing.

Brisbane explained that George Foster, a musician and writer,
had learned the "Chevé method" and wanted to teach it to a class
in New York. He had asked, and received assurance of, Brisbane's
assistance in preparing the lessons and advertising the event. To
give the Chevé system weight and add "genuine scientific importance" to the undertaking, Brisbane asked Dwight to participate:

> I want three or four lectures from you on the genius and science
> of Music, which will give a deeper insight into the subject than
> it now possesses. I should want one lecture upon the philosophy
> of the Gamut, and the character of the 7 fundamental notes
> composing it. Nothing in reality is known on this point, and I
> think that we can tell the world something new. You could take
> all that *Momigny* says, that is good, besides your own reflections,
> and I am quite sure that I have discovered something that you
> could work up admirably.
>
> Another lecture might be on the philosophy and aesthetic
> [*sic*] of Music as a whole, and others on such subjects as you
> judge proper, . . . such as intonation, measure, rythm [*sic*], mod-
> ulation. My idea is that you could give the people a deeper theo-
> retical view of the Art and philosophy of Music than any man in
> the World. You of course would have nothing to do with the
> practical part of giving the lessons. Foster must take care of all
> that. We want some real and sterling scientific views at the begin-
> ning to give a genuine value, and a high character to the subject,

and understanding. Reflect and let me know whether you would like to come under those circumstances. You would probably give these lectures before a select and invited audience. I cannot say that I am *fully* and *entirely* decided upon going strongly into the matter, but if you could come in, I think I should, and hence I make the inquiry of you whether you can come. Your answers one way or the other will speedily settle the matter. If you decide not to come, send me Momigny in the Harbinger package. I want also the theory of accords by Chevé (it is not called however by that name), a little lithographical book of a dozen pages, 8 vo. If you have it not among those musical exercises written in figures, it may be in my box in the attic of the P. House. . . .

    If you come in, . . . your position will be that of an *Oracle*[,] *of a real teacher.* If you could not come, would you prepare these lectures on the above subjects and let us have them?[8]

Dwight declined. Lacking his response, it is impossible to know his stated reason. However, four days after receiving his reply, Brisbane wrote back that Dwight had misunderstood the nature of the project. He, Brisbane, had never expected to make a public presentation. Did Dwight feel disinclined to accept his suggestions or to be associated in a musical enterprise with an amateur who had studied music only briefly? Brisbane offered a clarification:

    I did not intend to appear in it in any way or be known in it. The only stage on which I intend to play is that of a Social Reform, and I never intend to be taken out of that element.

    If Foster could get [Elam] Ives or some good man to unite with him, organize a large class, and then be sustained by some scientific explanations from you, which would be given as public lectures, but connected with this movement, it would, I believe succeed. You may be certain that I would not undertake anything so foreign to my natural affinities.[9]

This explanation appears to have persuaded Dwight and led to his acceptance.

Brisbane then sent an excruciatingly detailed third letter asking Dwight to explain in a lecture the "philosophy of the gamut" according to Fourier's law analyzing "the division of every unity into its comprehensive elements." Amid extensive verbiage, he restated his belief: if an analysis of the "unity or the whole of sound into the various notes" could be explained philosophically, it would provide a guide for the "division of all other unities." Brisbane urged Dwight to "think of all this, and if *Momigny* says anything of value incorporate it. Keep the work if you wish to use it."[10]

Brisbane had long been interested in understanding the relationship between the "harmonies" of the passions and those of the material world. He accepted and promoted the Fourierist idea that the sense of hearing naturally led people toward pleasing, rather than displeasing, vibrations. This sensitive passion, therefore, could be "a true guide in its sphere." Just as it led rightly to apt musical harmonies, the other eleven passions were also capable of fitting, rather than discordant, action. It was a human responsibility to discover and apply the regulating laws behind them to bring about universal order and happiness.[11]

Brisbane's recent study of elementary theory, ear-training, and sight-reading in Paris had increased his interest in the musical aspect and apparently led to his acquaintance with an unspecified work by Momigny. The incomplete and casual references to Momigny in the first and third letters imply that Brisbane had brought with him and shown, or at least discussed with Dwight, Momigny's book during one of his earlier visits to Brook Farm in 1844 or 1845. Brisbane may have been responsible for bringing Momigny's work to Dwight's attention, but, respecting Dwight's musical judgment, left it to him to decide how it might be incorporated in the proposed lectures.

The work in question might be Momigny's *Cours Complet d'Harmonie et de Composition* or his *La Seule Vraie Théorie de la*

Musique, a theory book addressed to both beginners and more advanced students. It includes basic information about scales and intervals, as well as double counterpoint, fugues, and composition with text.[12] In either case, Dwight would have noticed a pedagogical emphasis on unity and variety.

In Momigny's *Cours Complet d'Harmonie et de Composition,* he would have found useful a later-eighteenth-century view of music as a natural language suited to convey sentiments along with a specific classification of consonances and dissonances. Could Dwight have known of Momigny's description of the octave as "the most perfect consonance" because of its unity?[13] That might explain his new emphasis beginning in August 1845 on Beethoven as "the seventh note in the scale, the note which cries for the completion of the octave, the note whose correspondence is the passion of the soul for Order."[14] There is no evidence in Dwight's essays of this period that he incorporated the more original aspects of Momigny's melodic theory.

These are the circumstances leading to the series of lectures delivered by Dwight at the New York Society Library in March 1846. According to advertisements in *The New-York Daily Tribune,* the four lectures were scheduled to be delivered on Wednesday, March 11; Monday, March 16; Thursday, March 19; and Saturday, March 21, at 7:30 in the evening.[15] They were half the number given in the Boston series and had to be compressed within the span of two weeks, since Dwight could not remain in New York for a longer period. The crisis at Brook Farm had increased his need to return there as soon as possible.

A "general notice" announced the proposed subjects of the course:

> Mr. John S. Dwight, of Boston, will commence a course of Lectures on Music at the Society Library on Wednesday evening,

March 11th, at 7½ o'clock. The Course will consist of Four Lectures:

The First—Music in its most general character as an expression of feeling, and especially of the Religious Sentiment.

Second—On the more *Scientific phase of Music,* with Sebastian Bach as the worthiest representative.

Third—On the *Expressive Era* in Music, which succeeded the Scientific and Scholastic, with illustrations from Handel, Mozart, Beethoven, &c.

Fourth—The Third Phase in the *historic development of the Art*— namely, the Modern Music of *Effect*—The Virtuosos, Prodigies, &c.[16]

A column dated March 16 supplies the additional information that Dwight "admirably analyzed and commented upon" Mozart's Mass in C Major in his opening lecture.[17]

The first talk was introductory and dealt with the general character of music, with particular reference to the "religious sentiment" in the Mass. The others were shaped according to three eras based primarily on Dwight's perception of their general musical character: the "scientific and scholastic"; the "expressive" succeeding it, with Beethoven listed among others; and the "modern music of *effect*." The last depended largely on a performer's impact achieved through the brilliant display of technical prowess and emphasized the nature of a solo instrument. This organization of lectures strove for greater sophistication in a more compressed format than the one underlying Dwight's previous lectures of 1842.

In this series, Bach, about whose actual music Dwight knew comparatively little, culminated a first phase of complexity represented by his "learned" fugues. In this connection, one recalls A. B. Marx's emphasis on Bach's polyphonic texture as an important stylistic determinant differentiating his music from Beethoven's. Dwight's inclusion of Handel in the second, "expressive" era conveys his subjective response to *Messiah,* primarily, as an exceptional instance of perceived universality. That second phase was broad and included vocal works with text as well as entirely instrumental music. Beginning in 1845, he utilized broadly characteristic classifications according to the categories of "science" (representing learned or complex music, especially fugues), "expression," and "effect."

Dwight was independent in formulating a musical plan based on composers and their works rather than accepting Brisbane's recommendations for a format, including a whole lecture on the "philosophy of the gamut." However, a report of the second lecture indicates that Dwight made an effort to oblige him somewhat: "The novel and instructive views evolved by Mr. Dwight of the unity and correspondence of Music with the passions of Man and with the whole Universe, were well calculated to enchain the attention of his audience."[18]

Before considering the development of Dwight's thought through earlier writings prefiguring the new organization of the New York lectures, with particular reference to Beethoven's position, a brief sampling of press reactions and correspondence will offer a contemporaneous perspective. The most hostile response to the lectures was printed by the semiweekly *Gazette and Times,* which had originally asserted that Dwight's "refined taste, metaphysical perception, extensive attainments and moral sensibility, admirably fit him to illustrate the principles and influence of music." After the series, however, the reporter professed disappointment:

> [T]he views which he advocated had nothing to do with music; except so far as he chose to drag them together by main force, little or no information was given upon the subject, and the lec-

turer spent his time and that of his audience upon ingenious and labored contrivances, or conceits as another journal well calls them, which have nothing to do with music as a science, an art, or as an excitement or relief of the passions and affections. He took certain well known facts in nature which furnish very excellent illustrations to writers upon the arts, and shew [*sic*] a pleasing similarity in some of their primary elements, and made these the main object, the gist of all his lectures, and endeavored to make them the most important part of music.

We think the Courier has given him to [*sic*] much credit for musical knowledge and taste; he seemed to evince no more than should be found in any well educated amateur of good taste.[19]

The most favorable notices appeared, predictably, in Greeley's *New-York Daily Tribune,* a radical paper highly sympathetic to Transcendentalist aims and fully dedicated to the Associationist cause of social reform. It extended exaggerated praise without entering into substantive detail, as in the following brief excerpt, which appeared after the first lecture: "The beautiful thoughts with which it peopled our brain—the fervid enthusiasm it awakened in our heart—the sublime prospects of immortal truth it opened to the mental vision—are among the things never to be forgotten."

The *Tribune* also published the comment of the New York correspondent of an unnamed Philadelphia paper:

Such a fresh, sparkling, enthusiastic discourse on music it has never before been my good fortune to listen to. Mr. Dwight is no mere critic, no dry *dillettante* [*sic*], expending oceans of words upon rehashed common-places. He is a poet, endowed with all the finer instincts and correlative affinities which belong to that character in its highest development.[20]

Whether curiosity or publicity accounted for it, Dwight's audience increased noticeably for the second lecture. Among those attending were

many of the most distinguished ladies and gentlemen of our intellectual circles. The lecturer, although having to treat almost
exclusively of the abstract theoretical, or scientific part of Music,
betrayed such a perfect knowledge and profound appreciation
of his intricate and most difficult subject—so utterly abandoned
himself to the wondrous fascination of the divinest of the Arts—
that he carried his audience with him, and powerfully excited
their enthusiasm over what, in another's mouth, would have
been but a catalogue of dry details.

The *Tribune* found the third of the "invaluable expositions of
music" to be "glorious":

Such sparkling, profound, beaming, refreshing criticism it is sel-
dom our good fortune to imbibe. Indeed these Lectures on
music are in every sense most excellently perfect.[21]

Dwight's friends and colleagues at Brook Farm soon heard of
his success. Sophia Ripley, for one, wrote to him supportively:

And so my estimate of your lectures was not one of my exaggera-
tions after all! Tributes to the merits of the first one are coming
in upon us, & yet I cannot think the audience, unaccustomed to
your mode of expression, to your somewhat associative dialect
can have gone into the depths of the thought. . . . I wish you
could have seen the group in the reading room last evg [*sic*] after
supper, the tall ones stooping over, & the short ones standing
tiptoe to read the notice of you in the Tribune.

Her letter also reflected their mutual concerns about whether to
make new property arrangements for Brook Farm while trying to
save the school, *The Harbinger,* and the domestic industry.[22]

On the day of the second lecture, Dwight wrote at length to
George Ripley with assurances of some success in having secured
financial support for the endangered Brook Farm from Greeley

and other Associationist friends in New York. Almost in passing he noted:

> At the first Lecture there were about 120 persons present. . . .
> The impression was far better than I had hoped—I believe it
> gave universal satisfaction to those who heard, although I extem-
> porized Association at the end of it.

The uncertain weather had caused postponement of the second lecture, which was delivered on Monday, March 16; on Saturday "a large number of people went to the hall to be disappointed—but it all serves to give wider notice."

Dwight wanted particularly to convey his activity on behalf of their community to its founder. To an individual who doubted that Brook Farm could remain at its location, Dwight had been firm: "I convinced him, I think, that it is indispensable for us to go on, and go on *where we are,* for some years more at least." He expressed pleasure in seeing old friends and meeting new ones, enjoying Beethoven and Mendelssohn through the private performances of Frederick Rackemann. Above all, he "held forth" to anyone who would listen concerning the history, condition, and prospects of Brook Farm. Dwight reassured Ripley that "I talk association everywhere. Everybody questions me, and I have removed prejudices from a good many minds." He also confessed delight at the parties, music, walks, "gastrosophic adventures," and hosts of visitors crowding his time in New York.[23]

George Ripley responded graciously, referring to newspaper accounts of Dwight's success and assuring him that he was constantly missed. No decision had been taken regarding the future course of the farm. In its precarious circumstances, the residents agreed about the desirability of retaining every branch of the industry but differed as to the means. Ripley had one concrete suggestion: to encourage subscriptions for *The Harbinger* from friends in New York and ask what they thought of "making a direct application for subscribers on the strength of its musical merits."[24] This was another indication of the esteem in which the Ripleys held their colleague.

Dwight had been strengthening his preference for the "expressive" Beethoven, while also acknowledging, since 1840, his accommodation to "the modern music of effect" composed or performed by brilliant virtuosi. To review his writings as he juxtaposed these two areas is to note how the rich concert experiences of the intervening years led him to expand and reinforce his fundamental position when designating the second and third phases in the lecture series of 1846. The citations will illustrate Dwight's consistently mixed reception of virtuosi and their repertory from 1840 to 1846. This is a conclusion not in agreement with Michael Broyles's view that "[i]f we look back to the beginning of the 1840s, we find that Dwight's position toward the virtuoso was considerably different from what it had become by 1845."[25]

When Dwight praised the artistry of Rackemann and Kossowski in 1840 for introducing "the new school of Piano Forte playing," he stressed their addition of rich meaning to the "peculiar soul" of the piano through exploration of its brilliant idiomatic usage in repertory and performance. He had discovered pathos in Chopin's nocturnes, individuality in works by Adolf Henselt, massive constructive power in music by Sigismund Thalberg, and original genius in the *Galope* [*sic*] *Chromatique* of Franz Liszt. Dwight favored Liszt as a "devout admirer of Beethoven."

One of the striking features of the new style that Dwight had identified was the placement of a melody in the middle register with florid material surrounding it from above and below. It had signaled a welcome extension of the full range of the instrument, which became "quite an orchestra in itself." One recalls Dwight's enjoyment of these compositions "for what they are, without complaining that they are not something else." He had balanced that enthusiasm by admitting his preference to hear "true classic works, not written for the sake of displaying the Piano Forte, but for the sake of music. The pianists of the day show too much of ambition, too little of inspiration, of true art-feeling, in their playing and their choice of subjects."[26]

When he reconsidered the issue in 1845 at the height of his Fourierist activity, he approached it from the perspective gained in listening particularly to Beethoven's symphonies in orchestral performance. On hearing the famed violinist Ole Bull, he was enthusiastic about the abundant original melodies in his compositions but faulted their aimless lack of unity. That was his most important critical criterion when judging works. Bull's improvisations had been well received, and there was much to enjoy deeply in his performances. However, Dwight believed generally that solo virtuosi suffered from the tendency of the age in their exhibition of restless individual prowess.

As I have pointed out, Dwight considered "intense individualism" to be a musical sign of a disaffected, transitional period. As in society competition and individualism could perfect "elements which are hereafter to form harmony," similarly, in music, "this solo-playing is wonderfully developing the powers of the individual instrument. When shall we have them all combined in a true unitary concert?" The need to be individually prominent, rather than to work for a common goal, impeded genuine musical effort: "When unity shall be the law of all society, there will be orchestras of genius."[27]

As in the past, he could enjoy particular solo performances. However, Dwight's musical and social values, together with his preferences for full instrumental sound, recognized in orchestral blending of musical instruments a metaphor for a new social order of justice through human collaboration. He retained these associations with orchestral music long after the Fourierist stimulus had waned.

In August 1845, Dwight elaborated on his earlier distinction between the "new school" and the "great Classic Compositions" by juxtaposing references to virtuoso pianists with comment about John Lange's keyboard performance in a trio by Beethoven:

> We have had among us pianists, perhaps, who were greater proficients in the difficult wonders of the new school; but for the rendering of the great Classic Compositions with feeling, force and truth, to say nothing of all the minor elegancies of a finely finished style, we never have had his equal. Especially to the works of Beethoven we have never heard such justice done. Every note told full of meaning.[28]

Although in this instance an orchestral medium was not at issue, Dwight associated Beethoven's music with expressive musicianship rather than proficiency in executing technical feats.

Dwight approached the subject from another perspective in discussing Beethoven's Overture to *Egmont,* op. 84, a work that had made a powerful impact on him in a piano arrangement before he heard it in orchestral performance. Judging it to have been ineptly played, he thought that a disappointed public had been unable to appreciate the grandeur of its conception. Believing the chief problem to have been that it was "played altogether too fast," Dwight remarked that this was "the common mistake with all our orchestras, especially when they undertake Beethoven. . . . There is a certain repose about great things which will not let itself be run away with." Therefore, orchestral and solo music required independent treatment according to the differences in performance medium.

Dwight underscored the "great effects" inherent in orchestral music, effects that could only be simulated in music for a solo instrument. Great orchestral pieces should be performed with recognition of their breadth: each person in the orchestra should "feel" all the other parts, not just play his part in isolated fashion, and even music of fast character should not be performed too rapidly. Appropriate performance of works like the *Egmont* overture could be achieved by a subtler approach of "quickening thought,—not fiddlebows and elbows—by a judicious poetic development of his theme." The principle was that contrasts in orchestral performance needed to be intrinsically connected to the musicianly treatment of thematic material, giving due regard to the weight of the massed sections of the orchestra. That was Dwight's orchestral conception.

In the performance of solo music, however, great effects needed to be represented because they were not inherent in the pieces. While it was also true that the "musical chronometer," the measuring of time, had increased performance speeds due to the "feverish spirit of the age" and the "fashion of solo-playing," Dwight's enunciation of a difference in the approach to performance based on media and genres should not be overlooked. It was impossible for the piano to "represent a whole orchestra," despite the attractive possibilities of quick successive strokes, rapid filigree, swift passages, arpeggios, and tremolos inserted between the melody notes. These devices provided amazing "breadth of tone" but left the ear "little space" between the notes.

In the course of articulating these differences, Dwight acknowledged, almost in spite of his preferences, the legitimacy of virtuoso music. This he accomplished largely by justifying it in connection with Beethoven:

> Is not Beethoven the source whence many an arrowy mountain
> stream, like Liszt, and many a shining mill-fall, like Thalberg,

and many a jet-d'eau of Ole Bull's and Paganini's, to say nothing
of numberless canals, derive their waters? Let them rush to glory
as they will; but when they lead us to their spring, their master,
we would see it well up calmly, strongly as its own force impels,
as it would if they were not.[29]

Dwight's discourse in this era reflects only occasional outbursts
of pique. One must examine a broad group of the writings in order
to avoid ascribing undue importance to lapses that were unrepre-
sentative at this time. An extreme in vituperative exaggeration (a
tendency that became more pronounced in later years) occurred
in his suggestion that the Boston Academy could help to "prepare
the ears" for Beethoven's orchestral music by performing less technically challenging works by earlier composers:

> They were great masters who paved the way for Beethoven; from
> Bach to Haydn there was a line of influences enriching the soil
> from which such a genius was to spring. But if we did not have
> Beethoven, would it be Bach and Haydn that would be given us
> to prepare ourselves withal? Anything but that; the most modern
> of the moderns, all the opera trash of the day, all the dazzling
> superficialities of solo-players, and those who write "for ef-
> fect,"—these would be given us.[30]

However, on hearing Ole Bull play again later in 1845, Dwight
expressed continuing admiration for his genius and fascinating
qualities, even as he castigated the sphere of "Virtuoso-dom" for
its temptation to ambition rather than deep creation. Reputations
of such prodigies were rapidly eclipsed in contrast to the "solid,
eternal foundations" of Mozart's or Beethoven's fame. Still,
Dwight acknowledged that Bull had aroused the enthusiasm of
"this wide-spread and diversified people" with his violin playing as
few could have done and, for that, thanks were due him.[31]

When Dwight set forth in 1845 his considered views regarding

"The Virtuoso Age in Music," he was careful to outline both negative and positive features. Any of his regular readers would have been aware of his preferences for Beethoven, Mozart, Handel, and others, but Dwight also acknowledged that the "new school" (his designation since 1840, now expanded to include violinists) was significant in his musical era. In two successive and lengthy pieces in *The Harbinger,* he examined the issue independently and with reference to particular composers. In briefest summary, Beethoven and a few others were "expressive," from his vantage point, because of their genuine, artistic capacities to conceive a "beautiful whole." The soul and mind of the listener were permanently strengthened by the effort to understand the sentiment and conception of the composer through the music itself.

In the work of the modern "mechanical finger-school," the emphasis was on the performer, then on the particular nature of his or her instrument, and finally on the piece of music. The soloist might become the center of egocentric exhibition, during which the listener would be momentarily dazzled by "effect," skillful display, and difficulty conquered instead of an aspiration to acquire a higher understanding of the music. Dwight believed, rather, that the spirit of the complete organic entity should encourage respect for its humblest as well as its most difficult parts: "It is not beneath one's dignity, surely, to help perform 'the Messiah' or a Symphony by Beethoven, though one's part be ever so easy, ever so little prominent."[32]

Yet Dwight also found much to praise in music by the virtuosi of his day. They had produced good music that would outlive fashion and extend artistic boundaries through instrumental conceptions heightening the public's sensitivity to new qualities of tone and rhythm. Their music had also expanded the powers of their instruments. He lauded four exemplars, three of whom he had praised in similar terms more briefly in 1840—Liszt, Chopin, and

Thalberg, with Paganini now added. If one ceased to be amazed by the extraordinary effects, one could begin to distinguish styles and enjoy their novel works "not as mere feats of execution, but as intellectual creations."

Dwight drew upon biographical and journalistic accounts in his comments about each. He connected Liszt with Bach, as well as with Beethoven in his musical education and preferences. In enthusiastic narrative, Dwight explained how each had uniquely contributed to musical and instrumental excellence. He concluded that "on the whole, therefore, and in the long run, art must be the gainer by this prevailing passion for the difficult and wonderful in music. It cannot be injured, in the end, by the improvement of its *mecanique* [*sic*]." The American critic had fairly accounted for recent developments, although he cherished the continuing hope that people would come "to know how to prize and seek a thing in proportion to the depth and purity of mind which inspired it,—to love best the music which contains most thought."[33]

That Dwight was still capable of being virtually overwhelmed in the actual presence of a dynamic virtuoso can be seen in the case of Leopold De Meyer's visit to Boston. Dwight began with an expected assertion that the "deepest in music," Bach and Beethoven, had not had the triumphal international success of cosmopolitans like De Meyer because "they were too deeply engaged." Having demarcated clearly his continuing commitment to "the older faith in music," the critic then assured the reader of his determination to cast aside resistance with the aid of "reflection, as well as by a certain catholicity of nature." In an autobiographical tone of confession, Dwight described an experience in which he and other musical "cognoscenti" invited to De Meyer's rooms were soon rendered "children with delight."

Hearing De Meyer play a potpourri, including a transcription of Rossini's Overture to *William Tell,* a fantasy on a drinking song from *Lucrezia Borgia,* the inevitable Yankee theme and variations on "National Airs," the virtuoso's own *Marche Marocaine,* and improvisations on a fugue subject, Dwight was moved to exclaim:

> Criticism was put to flight; the resisting gentlemen were taken off their feet, and there seemed a general impulse to fling their arms about each others' [*sic*] necks, as in Schiller's Hymn to Joy. Joy, indeed, was the sentiment of it; besides that, it had little other; it was the perfect gratification of the senses, and seemed to do one a physical good. No one stopped to consider that it was not the deepest sphere of musical expression; to regret any other sentiment would have been sheer pedantry.

Dwight fully relished this event. He invested it with greater importance by interpreting the transformation of cold, conventional colleagues into enthusiastic admirers bonded by "joyous intimacy" as a Schillerian jubilee.

Although offering no critical comment, Dwight sought to prevent misunderstanding. As in the past, he considered this musical celebration in relation to his composer of preference:

> We attempt no criticism; we venture no conjectures as to how De Meyer may compare with Liszt or Thalberg; we care not to settle his rank as a composer or performer. Whatever his sphere may be, he exerts the power of genius *in* that sphere, and therefore must be in harmony with true genius in all spheres. . . . That his music is a genuine thing, and that his skill quite distances all that *we* have heard, is true and undeniable. . . . We are thankful for the prodigy, but faithful yet to our Beethoven.[34]

That Dwight should have connected his joyous, spontaneous appreciation of De Meyer's artistry with Schiller's ode is comprehensible. In addition to his continuing attachment to the main sentiments of the revised poem, he was astonished by the virtuoso's impact on his listeners and willing to respond positively to excellence as a communicating force. Dwight was delighted by the excitement of De Meyer's performance rather than by his pieces. Although grateful for opportunities to test his abiding commitment to Beethoven's music, his enthusiasm for virtuosi of De Meyer's caliber, at the sheer physical level of the senses, assured him of a capacity to be open-minded.

Dwight acknowledged that this brilliant instrumental music had value and reflected external aspects of his modern era. It could also lead listeners toward an acquaintance with the "classic music" that he considered "of a higher order."[35] In essence, then, Dwight placed Beethoven in the lecture plan of 1846 no longer primarily as "modern" in contrast to earlier composers. He was, rather, designated "expressive" and "classic" in relation to a more recently acknowledged and fully legitimate "modern music of effect."

It was with considerable pleasure that Dwight anticipated attending the first performance in America of Beethoven's Ninth Symphony. It was to be held at Castle Garden in New York on May 20, 1846, two months after his lectures in that city. On this trip, at a meeting with New York Associationists at Brisbane's home, Ripley would present a plan to preserve those portions of Brook Farm that could sustain continuing operations.[36]

There were problems locally and nationally, for the United States had declared war against Mexico one week before the concert. Dwight was deeply opposed to the Mexican War, as to all wars, and believed that his country needed to turn away from that conflict. Four days before the event billed as a Grand Festival Concert, he alluded to the coming first performance of the Ninth Symphony as a sign of "the musical awakening in our country." Might it not help to bring about that larger combined order in society toward which he and his Associationist colleagues had been working?

The New York Philharmonic Society had made known that the

purposes of this special concert were to improve musical taste and to raise funds for the construction of a large concert hall. For these specific reasons, ticket prices had been increased to the high cost of two dollars each and the members of the orchestra had contributed their earnings. Dwight expected that the building of the proposed edifice in New York would lead to a greater public willingness to support resident musicians, frequent opportunities to hear art music, and the introduction of music festivals similar to those held in Germany and England.

In May 1846, Dwight knew that only a small segment of the American public had heard any of Beethoven's music, but he looked forward to its significant impact. Among the influences of great minds, he declared, some were as yet like "smaller circles, setting out, and only felt by a few, but destined to encircle the whole ocean of Humanity, ere their influence is exhausted. Of this latter class is the music of Beethoven."

Announcing the forthcoming festival concert to his readers in *The Harbinger,* Dwight reminded them of salient biographical material drawn from Schindler's work. He also described the general large-scale structure of the Ninth Symphony as consisting of only two parts. The first opened with the "strange rustling of barren fifths," which he considered to convey an "emptiness or chaos." The second consisted of the choral finale, which Dwight interpreted as the musical reflection of the ultimate "consummation of man's social destiny."[37] A dynamic but generalized framework was thus suggested to encompass the whole.

There followed a long citation from an unidentified source. In fact, it was a "self-borrowing": Dwight was quoting directly his own commentary on Schiller's "An die Freude" written before the close of 1838 in his notes to the *Select Minor Poems,* in which he had excerpted A. B. Marx's discussion of the Ninth Symphony from his essay on Beethoven in the *Universal-Lexicon.* Although

Dwight had enriched his musical learning and experience considerably in the intervening years, he continued to place confidence
in the German critic's musical judgments.

Through Dwight and Marx, American readers who had benefited from opportunities to hear other symphonies by Beethoven
as complete orchestral works could associate the "boundless
yearning to embrace the whole" with that composer's selection of
Schiller's poem as a symbol of their common artistic search to
unite all humankind. It is remarkable that Dwight did not choose
to alter a word of his previous commentary. He remained steadfast
in applying a Transcendentalist and Fourierist perspective to the
conviction that Beethoven was the composer who best exemplified
an inner mental-spiritual capacity enabling him to conceive a
"beautiful whole."

In the days and weeks before the performance, the New York
press announced the details. The secretary of the Philharmonic
Society invited all competent vocalists and string players to participate if they could attend all rehearsals as well as the performance.
The "grand orchestra" was scheduled to meet independently several times, as was the chorus, before the single combined dress
rehearsal.[38] Dwight was present on that occasion, which began on
the day of the concert at 8:30 in the morning at Castle Garden.

All contemporaneous accounts, including Dwight's, estimated
the large and fashionable audience at the evening performance to
have numbered about two thousand people. However, a notation
found at the New-York Historical Society in the manuscript "Original Day Book" of Castle Garden under the date May 20 reads
"Philharmonic Society—about 1200 present."[39] Henry C. Watson,
the music critic of *The Albion,* had written program notes for the
event. However, with the Mexican War dominating the news, his
paper, like the other press, gave the festival concert very little notice. Performances were reported to have been "highly satisfac-

tory," and it was hoped that the proceeds had been sufficient to allow the Philharmonic Society to begin construction of its proposed concert hall.[40]

The Ninth Symphony had been placed after the intermission. The first half of the concert, under Ureli Corelli Hill's direction, had consisted of three overtures (by Weber and Mozart), a concerto (for piano in G Minor by Mendelssohn), and three arias (by Donizetti and Verdi). As the musicians performed Beethoven's difficult and demanding symphony under the guidance of their conductor, the English musician George C. Loder, some in the audience left the hall. This fact attracted press attention.

Among those dismayed by the discourtesy was a writer for the *Gazette and Times,* who commented that Beethoven's work was vast in ideas and design and, at times, incomprehensible. He was better able to chronicle the circumstances and chastised the "breach of politeness." Asserting that this practice had been observed at other concerts, however, the reviewer remarked that the conductor should have "stopped the performance till all had left who wished to do so, as he has done before." He also recommended, as had others, that the Philharmonic Society repeat this festival concert at the customary ticket price of fifty cents, instead of two dollars, in order to fill the cavernous spaces of Castle Garden.[41]

The American première of the Ninth Symphony in 1846 and its first public London performance in 1825 shared several characteristics. Public incomprehension and adverse critical commentary regarding the unusual duration of the work were exacerbated in both instances by placement of the symphony in the last part of long, varied programs. The initial performance in each country also encountered obstacles caused by inadequate rehearsal time. However, the provision of multiple independent choral and orchestral rehearsals in New York had attempted to avoid the difficulties inherent in the Philharmonic Society of London's early custom permitting only one rehearsal for each concert.[42]

Those additional precautions may have been suggested for the first American performance by Loder, who was its conductor as well as the vice-president of the Philharmonic Society of New York. They illustrate the experience he had gained after a series of successful performances of the Ninth Symphony beginning in 1837 in London. After it had received varying responses in that city between 1825 and 1837, English opinion of the piece turned in its favor after April 17, 1837, according to David Benjamin Levy. This was partly a consequence of performances mounted under the dual musical direction of Ignaz Moscheles as conductor and George C. Loder as leader, or first violin–concertmaster.

Loder, who hailed from Bath, occupied the position of leader in at least six documented performances of Beethoven's last symphony conducted by Moscheles between 1837 and 1843 in varied situations and locales, including the Drury Lane Theatre and the Hanover Square Rooms. These concerts marked a decisive era during which the "Choral" Symphony won acceptance and acclaim in London.[43] Therefore, when Loder acquired his excellent reputation as a conductor in New York a few years later and undertook to direct the symphony for the first time in the United States, he provided a genuine link to the performance traditions that Moscheles and he had established previously in London.

When Dwight described the outstanding musical event at Castle Garden, he wrote a characteristically discursive essay appearing more than three weeks later in *The Harbinger*. The delay had been occasioned by his eventual return trip to Boston from New York, but also by his social-reform activities. One week after the concert, on May 27, the American Union of Associationists was formed with Horace Greeley as its president. Dwight and George Ripley accepted positions as two of the four directors located at Brook

Farm; three others, including Brisbane, were based in New York. The new group's avowed aims included disseminating the principles of "Associative Unity" throughout the country and preparing for a reorganization of towns, whose main objective would now be "perfect Justice."[44]

Dwight's essay differed markedly in scope and aim from the brief notices in the daily press. Many of his readers in Boston could not have been present at the first performance; that city would wait seven more years before hearing the Ninth Symphony.[45] In this situation, he attempted to provide an account of the social and musical atmosphere as well as his first impressions of the work itself. Dwight cast the symphony, and the larger ambience in which he had heard it, in the framework of a struggle between the forces of darkness and light in which light had prevailed and his highest faith in Beethoven had been confirmed.

On his way to Castle Garden, it had been necessary to pass a crowd of fifty thousand gathered in a New York City park for a war rally called by President James Polk. That had been the anguishing context for Dwight's denunciation of all wars and this particular battle, instead of which he proposed art as a progressive force for peace and progress. He asserted his gratitude at having left the "oppressive element" to enter the "circle of light and beauty where Beethoven and Mozart were to hold forth." The dual nature of his praise of art was consistent with his earlier views: it could be heralded in terms of aesthetics, quoting John Keats's "A thing of beauty is a joy forever," and of morality, when "Hours spent with multitudes enjoying the grand works of music, are hours of which conscience never accuses us."[46]

Dwight conveyed in picturesque detail the appearance of Castle Garden, with the staging arranged to accommodate about one hundred instrumentalists and approximately twice that number of singers flanking them on either side. In the vast circular hall, only a portion of the seats had been filled for the performance, and the music had been blurred by bad acoustics: "Only an angel suspended in the dome could catch all the sounds." Dwight expressed pleasure in having attended the final open rehearsal, despite its musical inadequacies and the bustling occasioned by the erection of the groundwork by the busy musicians, who were obliged to double as carpenters.

During that time, he had tried to become familiar with the music's main themes to aid his comprehension. Having been impressed by the precision and quality of the New York players as they performed familiar overtures (especially that to Mozart's *Die Zauberflöte*) in the first half of the program, he judged that Beethoven's work contained "frightful difficulties," a perception implying that its unusual musical and technical challenges had not been mastered in this first performance.

Dwight alluded briefly to exaggerated reports expressing the extremes of awe or doubt about Beethoven's capacities at the time of the Ninth Symphony's creation. Dismissing them, he judged the piece to be a culmination of "the essence of all his other symphonies" in its artistic striving and exclaimed at the "stupendous grandeur" with which the work was built. Dwight's conception of the whole is likely to have been affected, on his retrospective reflection, by the words of the recitative effecting the transition between the symphony's instrumental and vocal portions—"O Freunde, nicht diese Töne! / Sondern lasst uns angenehmere anstimmen, und freudenvollere" ("O friends, not these sounds! / But let us strike up something more pleasant, and full of joy").

He heard the greatest sadness in the first movement, which, he acknowledged, also contained gigantic power. Although the image of struggle inevitably presented itself to him, Dwight contrasted the "tragedy of individual destiny," epitomized by the earlier movements of the Fifth Symphony, to the Ninth Symphony's vision of collective human struggle between discord and ultimate harmony. Amid the perceptible changes and surprises, he noted the predominance of the same basic sentiment in the "singular" Scherzo and in the "profoundly beautiful and consoling Adagio, with its two alternating movements."

At the opening of the Finale, which he interpreted as the structural "second part" of the symphony, Dwight perceived and noted the brief thematic recollections of the earlier movements. However, it is possible that he had been able to anticipate their reappearance on the basis of his knowledge of A. B. Marx's description of this movement. Dwight also identified the distinctive nature and connective function of the important cello recitative. At no point in this review, however, did he signal as problematic Beethoven's introduction of voices or their impact on the symphonic genre. Significantly, he did assert that Beethoven had accomplished the essential transition thematically through the instruments that prefigure the vocal material. Dwight described this section as follows:

> The second part of the Symphony commences with an impatient burst, followed by short reminiscences of all the themes which went before. Each is restlessly taken up and tried and hastily dismissed, as if the instruments were vainly striving to find the key that should unlock and give true utterance to the deep thought with which they inwardly labored. Then the violoncellos commence a broken recitative melody, as if they would sing; which is answered in fragments by other instruments, and finally resounded by the whole orchestra. And thus the vocal parts are strangely sketched out beforehand by the instruments, in a manner that raises expectations to the highest pitch.[47]

For Dwight, there was no question that Beethoven's work was to be connected in meaning to Schiller's ode. He gave no indication of his views regarding the composer's selective use of the poem but reiterated the emphasis with which he had greeted it in his earliest commentary, that of "human brotherhood." Dwight recognized in Beethoven's work a powerful affirmation deriving from what Maynard Solomon has called "the most universal paradigm of fraternity in world culture."[48]

To that primary concept Dwight joined the Fourierist hope of a "triumph of the grand unitary sentiment," along with his more recent image of Beethoven's music understood as the "impatient Seventh note" striving toward the octave symbolic of a glorious societal resolution. He also referred dispassionately to the promise of the Gospel, which people had until then revered only with their eyes and ears, and juxtaposed with it the deeper inner necessity that they all work together toward a better world, symbolized through Beethoven's "boundless yearning" to embrace a harmonious whole. Dwight's vision of the Ninth Symphony celebrated eventual reconciliation, after struggle, through collective cooperation, but it was contingent on the important premise that the "deeper soul" of his age would begin "to understand itself."

> This is the chorus of Humanity; the fond embrace and kiss of the millions, in a high festival in honor of the Good Spirit. How it confirmed the thought suggested by the opening movement, and resolved into full light and joy and beauty the oppressive feeling with which those sad strains so well harmonized! It is the music of the high hour of Human Brotherhood; the triumph of the grand unitary sentiment, into which all the passions and interests of all human hearts are destined finally to blend. No words can describe the grandeur with which all this is worked up, till it becomes perfectly stupendous towards the close. . . . As this age begins to understand itself, and appreciate its own tendencies, will the music of Beethoven be enjoyed and felt. For it is the music of this age, (not of the superficial outside character of the times, best reflected in the brilliant sensuous creations of a Rossini, or of a Leopold de Meyer, full as his music is of animal excitement, war and conquest,) but of the deeper soul of

the age which is even now being born. To the struggling impatient Seventh note Beethoven has been more than once compared; it cries out to be resolved into the crowning octave, the completion of the melodic circle. Just so his boundless yearning and aspiring tell of a glorious "resolution" such as men have heard promised in that Gospel which they revere, but hitherto have heard only with their ears, and read only with their eyes.

We went away physically exhausted by the excitement of listening to so great a work, but unspeakably confirmed in all our highest faith. . . . The battle will be clearly fought out between the powers of darkness and of Light: but we trust our own hearts and God's word, and the Symphony, that Light will prevail, that Society will be saved, and, conforming itself at length to the Laws of the Divine Order, will become Society indeed, instead of that mere mockery of the word, that poor confused assemblage of isolated and antagonistic interests, which it is and has been.[49]

Dwight's first encounter with the Ninth Symphony in orchestral performance crowned an epoch in which he identified his most cherished ideals for humanity with Beethoven's symphonic music.

CHAPTER TEN

————— ❖ —————

Conclusion:
Dwight's Symphonic Beethoven Standard, 1846

In one decade, Dwight moved from the outer circle of Transcendentalists, at a time of uncertainty about his career plans, to active leadership as an Associationist with the goal of forging a new kind of reflective music criticism. His humanistic outlook in that era focused on an ideal of societal reform through cooperation, which was joined to a musical one emphasizing the values inherent in the building of a sense of community. The application of these views resulted in Dwight's vision of music as the "great reformer"[1] helping human beings to recognize their shared destiny and the advantages of joining together to achieve harmony in musical, social, and individual senses.

In Beethoven's symphonies Dwight discovered works that he associated with his artistic and societal hopes for the future; these, in turn, stimulated his important early critical essays. That he regarded them as significant can be judged not only from frequent reiterations of particular points in subsequent reviews but also from specific recommendations in 1847 and in 1849 that readers consult his essays of 1845 in the first volume of *The Harbinger* for extended commentary about the Fifth and Seventh Symphonies.[2]

I have noted that a constructive and independent conception emerging from his larger vision was a view of the orchestra as a cooperating enterprise acknowledged at musical and metaphysical levels. It grew out of his belief in the matching goals of unity in an orchestra's performance and democracy in matters musical or political.

Dwight's ideas on this subject can be better understood in contrast to the strongly differing perspective of William Wetmore Story, a friend and fellow member of the Harvard Musical Association who later gained prominence as an expatriate sculptor. Unlike Dwight, Story expressed no interest in acquiring a "scientific" knowledge of musical principles, and he responded superficially to instrumental music as an embodiment of imaginative fancy. In 1846, he contributed a musical column to *The Harbinger* in the absence of Dwight, who was then presenting his series of lectures in New York.

Story maintained that a good conductor could not obtain an organized performance from an orchestra unless he were a despot. To the disservice of both, Story made a false analogy between a democracy and an orchestra that was not performing well: "It has all the faults incident to a *democratic* orchestra, when the leader is only one of the people. In fact, an orchestra should be a complete despotism, and the leader should be an unflinching despot."[3]

That conception opposes Dwight's positive evaluation of the qualities desirable in a good orchestra leader and, by extension, those most suited to a leader in a democracy. Dwight's criteria can be further gleaned from a contrast between two Boston orchestras whose diverse performance levels he attributed primarily to differences in leadership. It was not sufficient to have "science, and good taste, and character which all respect" without also possessing "that tact, that magnetism, that singular power of inspiring

others to co-operation." Dwight's goal was cooperation, not despotism.

The successful leader had "magnetic control of his orchestral
forces; he is felt in every thing; he is both law and impulse to them
all; and they love to serve him; and this is the absolute condition
of good music."[4] The willing spirit of the musicians produced a
"unity and beauty as of many made one," just as all the independent instruments contributed and blended to achieve a unified
orchestral sonority. This and other passages relating to orchestral
music yield vital interpretative insights at material, social, and in-
tellectual/spiritual levels.

In the orchestra, as in education and society at large, Dwight
fostered the reconciliation of enhanced individuality with the at-
tainment of shared objectives in the human community. To him,
orchestral performances of Beethoven's works in the concert hall
could uplift large gatherings of people through the symphonic joining of inner spiritual values and coherent musical structures.
Dwight's affirmation of their "classic" stature referred not to a
historical era but to their embodiment of enduring artistic standards, together with their capacity to unite individuals in mutual
sympathies.

The critic played a potential role in society consistent with these
ideals. Based on his discoveries particularly of German, English,
and French music literature and criticism, Dwight developed a
high regard for the responsible music critic who could act as an
interpreter to the public. He judged the critic's position next to
that of the creative artist because of the central importance he
attached to explaining or evaluating works of art. The task of guiding the public required that intellect dominate over feeling, although both were vital. Therefore, Dwight affirmed that the critic's
subjective responses must be placed in a larger framework provid-

ing information and stimulating the readers' comprehension of the issues.

In a review-essay written in late 1846 while struggling with others to preserve his Associationist ideals, Dwight stressed active participation in fulfilling cooperative enterprises rather than the isolated juridic function. However, as I have indicated, he highly valued criticism, whether musical or literary, as an essential activity to be honored and validated as it had not been until then in American arts and letters.

> While we believe that it is greatest to work in and with Humanity, to *be* a part, rather than to know the whole, we acknowledge the obligation of humanity to those who see and weigh and interpret, as well as those who create. Criticism has its place, though only few have found it.

Dwight praised a respected literary classification of critics by Margaret Fuller, dating from 1840 and republished in 1846, as "most justly and satisfactorily defined." According to this three-part scheme, "subjective" critics judged everything according to a limited individual standard. "Apprehensive" critics went beyond their own concerns to enter into the existence of a work. "Comprehensive" critics were able additionally to understand the author's design, judge the skill with which it had been accomplished, and "know how to put that aim in its place, and how to estimate its relations. And this the critic can only do who perceives the analogies of the universe."

Dwight admired Fuller's observations from "A Short Essay on Critics" to the extent of asserting: "Nothing can be truer. We would gladly quote the whole of this Essay, had we room." Striving characteristically to reconcile aesthetic and moral perspectives, he broadened the scope of his commentary beyond the work under review. To Dwight, criticism possessed "a character only second to that of creative art and poetry themselves, that of being their interpreter, of expounding what is beautiful and true, and exposing what is false."[5]

As a critic, Dwight utilized in his early Beethoven essays varying mixtures of biographical, autobiographical, and emotive musical discussion, but he attempted increasingly to incorporate basic technical description about structures. Limited references to poetic-imaginative content of a generalized, characteristic nature were linked to musical detail through his device of "allegorical illustration." Dwight's positive reception of the symphonies did not lead him to proselytize. Instead, he adopted an educative tone regarding structural and aesthetic aspects of the symphonies considered as independent, large-scale orchestral compositions.

However, Dwight's establishment of criteria by which Beethoven's symphonies would be recognized as the highest exemplars of expressive instrumental music also impeded his capacity to evaluate divergent new instrumental approaches in their own right. In the second half of 1846, his judgments began to show signs of this difficulty, which became increasingly pronounced in later years. An example of the problem illuminates the principle underlying his critical dilemma and also affords rare insight into Dwight's conception of musical Romanticism. It explains why he had firmly resisted calling Beethoven's symphonies Romantic.

In a celebrated view of 1846 that incurred the displeasure of the composer Anthony Philip Heinrich, Dwight contrasted his instrumental pieces to Beethoven's works and offered a glimpse into the critical basis of his conclusions. Granting that Heinrich's large-scale compositions were rich in ideas, Dwight discerned in them a lack of "poetic or dramatic unity." "Unitary design" had been sacrificed to "beautiful details." Emphasizing that music lost its essential nature when connected with extrinsic specificity, an argument he had reiterated since 1836, Dwight cautioned that a composer should not attempt to depict external images through tones. On that basis and for the first time, Dwight deemed "romantic" Heinrich's attempt to convey in purely instrumental terms the "picturesque and marvellous." They were vivid fictive elements that were not in accord with the essentially abstract Beethovenian symphonic model conceived by Dwight.

> In efforts to describe things, to paint pictures to the hearer's imagination, music leaves its natural channels, and forfeits that true unity which would come from the simple development of itself from within *as music*. Beethoven had no *programme* to his symphonies, intended no description, with the single exception of the *Pastorale* [*sic*]; yet, how full of meaning are they! Mr. Heinrich belongs to the romantic class, who wish to attach a story to every thing they do. Mere outward scenes and histories seem to have occupied the mind of the composer too much.[6]

Dwight regretted Heinrich's effort to portray musically events such as the "Indian War Council" and the "Advance of the Americans" in his *Tecumseh, or The Battle of the Thames,* although he lauded that composer's enthusiasm for American ideals. Orchestral music might include picturesque elements if written "from the sentiment" experienced instead of "trying to compose tone-narratives and tableaux of them."

Recalling assertions he had made in disagreeing with William Gardiner, Dwight applied to this new instrumental situation his principle that imitation and depiction were not the "true end" of music. A series of connected historical events might constitute a good story, but when translated into musical passages they did not cohere into musical unity. Therefore, Dwight used a narrow definition to identify musical Romanticism with the marvelous, either in an opera such as Carl Maria von Weber's *Der Freischütz* or in instrumental music associated with an overtly extrinsic depictive element.

The American critic contended instead that symphonic music should develop its own musical materials and impart only a generalized inner sentiment of the soul. As I have noted, Dwight maintained that its unity was built according to a structural organic principle of composition emanating from initial material developed coherently through the characteristic activity of instruments working together. In 1846, concerned but not yet pessimistic, Dwight still believed in the widespread eventual recognition of the aesthetic and moral significance of Beethoven's symphonies as emblems of a new era. He interpreted them as fundamentally expressive of the composer's artistic grappling with the central struggle "between light and darkness" that "has a meaning for the soul and makes us greater while we listen."[7]

Dwight's response to the symphonic Beethoven, which he chose to identify as the opposite of musical Romanticism, nonetheless introduced to Americans a new Romantic outlook that made an asset of symphonic music's capacity to transcend the limits of specific words or images. Shaped by a diversity of nineteenth-century European approaches, Dwight's criticism affirms, in its own way, the high importance of a purely abstract instrumental medium by describing musical characteristics and by recognizing precisely as an attribute its "vagueness of meaning."[8] In America, he fostered the Romantic idea according to which, in the words of Edward A. Lippman, "the realm of music seems to take on a mysterious and self-contained character that stands in opposition to the world of everyday experience."[9] At the same time, however, Dwight shared with nineteenth-century European critics a perception of Beethoven's music as generalized "reflection of human experience."[10]

He sought to naturalize the symphonic Beethoven by introducing into public discourse in the United States the unfamiliar idea of the artist as composer, rather than poet or painter, who could inspire and dignify his audience. He connected Beethoven's symphonies with a movement toward the future amelioration of society, a link that he asserted before Fourierism pervaded his thought but one that he strengthened under its impact. Nevertheless, Dwight chose Beethoven's symphonies as exemplars primarily because of their higher unity of structural and ethical qualities.

Dwight established a new, if still rudimentary, formalist attentiveness to the basic syntactical relationships in Beethoven's symphonic structures. He combined it with a resolutely limited interpretational approach hailing their heroic character, massive power, and bold rhythmic energy. Lacking intensive knowledge of symphonic traditions preceding Beethoven, this American critic heard his works not as disruptive but rather as "modern" and then as "expressive" and "classic." Stressing the importance of motivic-thematic and tonal coherence in the architecture of first movements, he described symphonic movements as belonging to a dynamic cycle.

Dwight introduced into musical discourse in America valuable insights about the nature of the symphonic genre. He delineated its distinctive musical criteria of weight, mass, sonority, and kinds of thematic material appropriate for development in the structure. Emphasizing the characteristic cooperation of diverse instruments in the symphonic genre, he described it as uniquely separate both from the distinguishing features of chamber music and from the different traits producing the "effect" of brilliant music for solo instruments.

Building on his considerable knowledge of European musical sources, this American critic placed a symphonic repertory new to the United States within a social framework. He regarded it as central to his pragmatic educative goal of encouraging informed listeners. In the process of "preparing people with little knowledge to hear great music more understandingly," John S. Dwight contributed significantly in America to public comprehension of Beethoven's symphonies and to the establishment of a substantive critical tradition.

Notes

INTRODUCTION

1. John S. Dwight, ed., *Dwight's Journal of Music, A Paper of Art and Literature* (Boston, 1852–1881; repr., New York and London: Johnson Reprint, 1968).

2. Alexander Wheelock Thayer, *Ludwig van Beethovens Leben,* trans. and ed. Hermann Deiters, 1st ed. in 3 vols. (Berlin: F. Schneider, 1866; Weber, 1872, 1879). See Elliot Forbes, rev. and ed., *Thayer's Life of Beethoven* (Princeton: Princeton University Press, 1967). See also Michael Ochs, "A. W. Thayer, the Diarist, and the Late Mr. Brown: A Bibliography of Writings in *Dwight's Journal of Music,*" in *Beethoven Essays: Studies in Honor of Elliot Forbes,* ed. Lewis Lockwood and Phyllis Benjamin (Cambridge, Mass.: Harvard University Department of Music, 1984; distributed by Harvard University Press), 78–95, and Christopher Hatch, "The Education of A. W. Thayer," *Musical Quarterly* 42 (1956): 355–65.

3. Marcia Wilson Lebow, "A Systematic Examination of the *Journal of Music and Art* Edited by John Sullivan Dwight: 1852–1881, Boston, Massachusetts" (Ph.D. diss., University of California, Los Angeles, 1970), 311–20.

4. Richard Crawford calls attention to the importance of studying musical learning in nineteenth-century America through a perspective attuned to that era's contextual concerns. See Crawford, "Musical Learning in Nineteenth-Century America," *American Music* 1 (1983): 1–11.

5. See Arnold Schmitz, *Das romantische Beethovenbild* (1927; repr., Darmstadt: Wissenschaftliche Buchgesellschaft, 1978); Jean Boyer, *Le 'Romantisme' de Beethoven: Contribution à l'Étude de la Formation d'une Légende*

181

(Paris: H. Didier, 1938); Leo Schrade, *Beethoven in France: The Growth of an Idea* (1942; repr., New York: Da Capo Press, 1978).

6. Peter Anthony Bloom, "Critical Reaction to Beethoven in France: François-Joseph Fétis," *Revue belge de musicologie* 26–27 (1972–73): 67–83; Robin Wallace, *Beethoven's Critics: Aesthetic Dilemmas and Resolutions during the Composer's Lifetime* (Cambridge: Cambridge University Press, 1986).

7. See, for example, Hans Heinrich Eggebrecht, *Zur Geschichte der Beethoven-Rezeption: Beethoven 1970* (Mainz: Akademie der Wissenschaften und der Literatur, 1972); studies of "Beethoven à Paris," *Revue Internationale de Musique Française* 22 (1987): 7–70; Stefan Kunze, gen. ed., with Theodor Schmid, Andreas Traub, and Gerda Burkhard, *Ludwig van Beethoven: Die Werke im Spiegel seiner Zeit; Gesammelte Konzertberichte und Rezensionen bis 1830* (Laaber: Laaber-Verlag, 1987); James H. Johnson, "Beethoven and the Birth of Romantic Musical Experience in France," *Nineteenth-Century Music* 15 (1991): 23–35.

8. William S. Newman, "The Beethoven Mystique in Romantic Art, Literature, and Music," *Musical Quarterly* 69 (1983): 354–87.

9. Alessandra Comini, *The Changing Image of Beethoven: A Study in Mythmaking* (New York: Rizzoli, 1987).

10. Before 1841, except for isolated and occasional instances, Beethoven's symphonies, as full orchestral compositions, were largely unknown to the American public. See H. Earle Johnson, *First Performances in America to 1900: Works with Orchestra* (Detroit: Information Coordinators, 1979), 28–45; and Anne Hui-Hua Chan, "Beethoven in the United States to 1865" (Ph.D. diss., University of North Carolina, 1976), 97–103.

11. Chan, "Beethoven in the United States," 86–87, 213. See also Nicholas Temperley, "Beethoven in London Concert Life, 1800–1850," *Music Review* 21 (1960): 207–14.

12. Wilson Coker, *Music and Meaning: A Theoretical Introduction to Musical Aesthetics* (New York: Free Press; London: Collier-Macmillan, 1972), 8–9.

13. Johan Huizinga, *Homo Ludens: A Study of the Play-Element in Culture*, trans. prepared partly from the author's English trans. (New York: Roy Publishers, 1950; repr., Boston: Beacon Press, 1955), 164, 202.

CHAPTER ONE

1. Charles Crowe, *George Ripley: Transcendentalist and Utopian Socialist* (Athens: University of Georgia Press, 1967), 104, and 68, 71, 112–20, 165–

66. Other helpful general treatments of Transcendentalism can be found in Brian M. Barbour, ed., *American Transcendentalism: An Anthology of Criticism* (Notre Dame and London: University of Notre Dame Press, 1973); Paul F. Boller, Jr., *American Transcendentalism, 1830–1860: An Intellectual Inquiry* (New York: G. P. Putnam's Sons, 1974); Lawrence Buell, *Literary Transcendentalism: Style and Vision in the American Renaissance* (Ithaca and London: Cornell University Press, 1973); Perry Miller, ed., *The Transcendentalists: An Anthology* (Cambridge, Mass.: Harvard University Press, 1967); Russel Blaine Nye, *Society and Culture in America, 1830–1860,* The New American Nation Series, vol. 3 (New York: Harper and Row, 1974), esp. 329–30; and René Wellek, "The Minor Transcendentalists and German Philosophy," *New England Quarterly* 15 (1942): 652–80.

2. William Foster Apthorp, "John Sullivan Dwight," *Boston Evening Transcript* (September 5, 1893); repr. in Apthorp, *Musicians and Music-Lovers and Other Essays,* 5th ed. (New York: Charles Scribner's Sons, 1908; repr., Freeport, N.Y.: Books for Libraries Press, 1972), 277–86.

3. George Willis Cooke, *John Sullivan Dwight: Brook-Farmer, Editor, and Critic of Music; A Biography* (Boston: Small, Maynard, 1898; repr., New York: Da Capo Press, 1969).

4. Lindsay Swift, *Brook Farm: Its Members, Scholars, and Visitors* (1900; repr., New York: Corinth Books, 1961).

5. Eleanor Robinette Dobson, "Dwight, John Sullivan," in *Dictionary of American Biography,* ed. Allen Johnson and Dumas Malone (New York: Charles Scribner's Sons, 1930), 5:567–68.

6. Edward Waters, "John Sullivan Dwight: First American Critic of Music," *Musical Quarterly* 21 (1935): 69–88.

7. See an early example in M. A. De Wolfe Howe, *Boston: The Place and the People* (New York: Macmillan, 1903), 245, and a more recent one in E. Digby Baltzell, *Puritan Boston and Quaker Philadelphia: Two Protestant Ethics and the Spirit of Class Authority and Leadership* (New York: Free Press; London: Collier-Macmillan, 1979), 287.

8. J. Wesley Thomas, "John Sullivan Dwight: A Translator of German Romanticism," *American Literature: A Journal of Literary History, Criticism, and Bibliography* 21 (1949–50): 427–41, esp. 438, 441. See other views of Dwight's connections to German literature in Stanley M. Vogel, *German Literary Influences on the American Transcendentalists* (New Haven: Yale University Press, 1955), 143–49, and Henry A. Pochmann, *German Culture in America: Philosophical and Literary Influences, 1600–1900* (Madison: University of Wisconsin Press, 1957), 449–51, 769 nn. 357–59, and 770 nn. 360–63. Vogel considers Dwight's contributions in "belletristic forms of German

culture" important but believes his translations, although accurate, possessed neither grace nor charm. In a passing reference to his leadership in advocating "German music," Vogel pronounces Dwight to have been "a virtuoso on the piano and flute" (148). Pochmann considers many of Dwight's translations to have been among the "best translations ever made" of the shorter poems of Goethe and Schiller. In other respects, Pochmann relies heavily on Cooke for musical quotations and discussion.

9. Walter L. Fertig, "John Sullivan Dwight, Transcendentalist and Literary Amateur of Music" (Ph.D. diss., University of Maryland, 1952).

10. Walter L. Fertig, "Dwight, John Sullivan," in *The New Grove Dictionary of American Music,* ed. H. Wiley Hitchcock and Stanley Sadie (London: Macmillan; New York: Grove's Dictionaries of Music, 1986), 1:667–68.

11. Fertig, "John Sullivan Dwight, Transcendentalist," 39 n. 74, 88, and 171.

12. Irving Lowens, "Writings about Music in the Periodicals of American Transcendentalism (1835–1850)," *Journal of the American Musicological Society* 10 (1957): 71–85.

13. Ora Frishberg Saloman, "Dwight and Perkins on Wagner: A Controversy Within the American Cultivated Tradition, 1852–1854," in *Music and Civilization: Essays in Honor of Paul Henry Lang,* ed. Edmond Strainchamps and Maria Rika Maniates, in collab. with Christopher Hatch (New York: W. W. Norton, 1984), 78–92.

14. Christopher Hatch, "Music for America: A Critical Controversy of the 1850's," *American Quarterly* 14 (1962): 578–86; Betty E. Chmaj, "Fry versus Dwight: American Music's Debate over Nationality," *American Music* 3 (1985): 63–84.

15. Daniel Edgar Rider, "The Musical Thought and Activities of the New England Transcendentalists" (Ph.D. diss., University of Minnesota, 1964), 156–218.

16. Joel Myerson, *The New England Transcendentalists and the "Dial": A History of the Magazine and Its Contributors* (Rutherford, N.J.: Fairleigh Dickinson University Press; London: Associated University Presses, 1980), 145–49; William G. Heath, "John Sullivan Dwight," in *The Transcendentalists: A Review of Research and Criticism,* ed. Joel Myerson (New York: Modern Language Association of America, 1984), 131–34.

17. William Anson Call, "A Study of the Transcendental Aesthetic Theories of John S. Dwight and Charles E. Ives and the Relationship of These Theories to Their Respective Work as Music Critic and Composer" (D.M.A. diss., University of Illinois at Urbana-Champaign, 1971); J. Peter Burkholder, *Charles Ives: The Ideas Behind the Music* (New Haven and London:

Yale University Press, 1985), 20–32, esp. 28–29. Burkholder describes Dwight as a "musical conservative" who opposed the "moderns"; Dwight's aesthetic view of the spiritual value of music corresponded more "in rhetoric than in reality" to that of Ives, according to Burkholder.

18. See particularly Lebow, "A Systematic Examination."

19. Chan, "Beethoven in the United States," 23–25, 38–49, 62–71.

20. Irving Sablosky, *What They Heard: Music in America, 1852–1881, from the Pages of "Dwight's Journal of Music"* (Baton Rouge and London: Louisiana State University Press, 1986).

21. Sterling F. Delano, *"The Harbinger" and New England Transcendentalism: A Portrait of Associationism in America* (Rutherford, N.J.: Fairleigh Dickinson University Press; London: Associated University Presses, 1983), 125–47.

22. Ora Frishberg Saloman, "American Writers on Beethoven, 1838–1849: Dwight, Fuller, Cranch, Story," *American Music* 8 (1990): 12–28.

23. Ora Frishberg Saloman, "Fink, Hach, and Dwight's Beethoven in 1843–44," *Musical Quarterly* 76 (1992): 488–501; Saloman, "Continental and English Foundations of J. S. Dwight's Early American Criticism of Beethoven's Ninth Symphony," *Journal of the Royal Musical Association* 119 part 2 (1994): 251–67.

24. Michael Broyles, *"Music of the Highest Class": Elitism and Populism in Antebellum Boston* (New Haven and London: Yale University Press, 1992).

25. Carl J. Guarneri, *The Utopian Alternative: Fourierism in Nineteenth-Century America* (Ithaca and London: Cornell University Press, 1991), 280–81.

CHAPTER TWO

1. John S. Dwight, "The Pierian Sodality and Earlier Musical Clubs of Harvard College. By John S. Dwight. Reminiscences of an Ex-Pierian. (Samuel Jennison). From the Harvard Book, 1875," 1–5, Harvard Musical Association Library, Boston.

2. "Records of the Arionic Sodality—Cambridge 1813," bound manuscript, unpaginated [93–94], Harvard Musical Association Library, Boston.

3. Ibid., [95]. Much of this entry also appears in Arthur W. Hepner, *Pro Bono Artium Musicarum: The Harvard Musical Association, 1837–1987* ([Boston]: Harvard Musical Association, 1987), 3–13, esp. 6–7. See also Walter Raymond Spalding, *Music at Harvard: A Historical Review of Men and Events*

(New York: Coward-McCann, 1935; repr., New York: Da Capo Press, 1977), 39–77, which includes Dwight's remembrance of the Pierian Sodality in "College Music," *Dwight's Journal of Music* (June 19, 1858), beginning on 75.

4. Dwight, "The Pierian Sodality," 5.

5. Myerson, *The New England Transcendentalists,* 145.

6. Cornelius C. Felton, autograph letter signed, April 25, 1832, Ms. E.4.1 no. 3, Dwight Papers, Rare Book Room, Boston Public Library; Josiah Quincy, autograph letter signed, April 26, 1832, Ms. E.4.1 no. 2, Dwight Papers, Rare Book Room, Boston Public Library; and Charles Follen, autograph letter signed, July 17, 1832, Ms. E.4.1 no. 4, Dwight Papers, Rare Book Room, Boston Public Library.

7. Samuel Osgood, autograph letter signed to John Sullivan Dwight, February 24, 1834, Ms. E.4.1 no. 6, Dwight Papers, Rare Book Room, Boston Public Library.

8. Charles Timothy Brooks, autograph letter signed to John Sullivan Dwight, March 12, 1834, Autograph File, Houghton Library, Harvard University.

9. Charles Timothy Brooks, autograph letter signed to John Sullivan Dwight, May 26, 1834, Autograph File, Houghton Library, Harvard University.

10. [Friedrich] Schiller, "Hymn to Joy," trans. D. [Dwight], *The New-England Magazine* 8 (May 1835): 380–81.

11. Henry W. Bellows, autograph letter signed to John Sullivan Dwight, October 25, 1836, Ms. E.4.1 no. 10, Dwight Papers, Rare Book Room, Boston Public Library.

12. John S. Dwight, trans. with notes, *Select Minor Poems, Translated from the German of Goethe and Schiller* (Boston: Hilliard, Gray, and Company, 1839). Despite its publication date, the book became available in December 1838. Page numbers cited follow the published edition.

The editor's manuscript, dated "Boston 1839," bears an inscription to a friend in his hand referring to "these dry leaves from the old tree (1839!)." Ms. G.38.25, Dwight Papers, Rare Book Room, Boston Public Library.

13. John S. Dwight, autograph letter signed to James F. Clarke, March 10, 1837, Ms. E.4.1 no. 12, Dwight Papers, Rare Book Room, Boston Public Library. Two other letters, from contributors Margaret Fuller and Charles Timothy Brooks, show the work in progress in May 1837. Fuller admits she has not yet completed the translation of poems originally undertaken and mentions mutual friends (including the Ripleys and Jane Tuckerman, sister of Dwight's Harvard friend John Francis Tuckerman) through whom they

exchanged work materials: S. M. Fuller, autograph letter signed to J. S. Dwight, May 31, 1837, Ms. E.4.1 no. 15, Dwight Papers, Rare Book Room, Boston Public Library. The letter from Brooks, then a minister in Newport, Rhode Island, promises his help and notes another matter of mutual interest about Lowell Mason, professor at the Boston Academy of Music and compiler of volumes of sacred music: "That pile of Mason's Music still lies *au fond de mon* trunk— I hear he is gone to Europe": Charles Timothy Brooks, autograph letter signed to John S. Dwight, May 11, 1837, Autograph File, Houghton Library, Harvard University.

14. Dwight, *Select Minor Poems,* 203–6, and Notes to the Translations from Schiller, B, 435–37.

15. Ibid., A, 427–35, esp. 428. Schiller himself considered it a bad poem; see Maynard Solomon, "Beethoven and Schiller," in *Beethoven Essays* (Cambridge, Mass., and London: Harvard University Press, 1988), 209. For a modern literary appraisal of the first version of that poem, see Hermann J. Weigand, "Schiller: Transfiguration of a Titan," in *A Schiller Symposium: In Observance of the Bicentenary of Schiller's Birth,* ed. A. Leslie Willson (Department of Germanic Languages, University of Texas at Austin, 1960), 85–132. See also Nicholas Cook, *Beethoven: Symphony No. 9* (Cambridge: Cambridge University Press, 1993), esp. 106–9.

16. Dwight, *Select Minor Poems,* 207–23, and A, 429.

17. M. H. Abrams, *Natural Supernaturalism: Tradition and Revolution in Romantic Literature* (New York: W. W. Norton, 1971), 172–312, esp. 215–16.

18. Dwight, *Select Minor Poems,* A, 434–35. See [Thomas Carlyle], *The Life of Friedrich Schiller: Comprehending an Examination of His Works* (London: Taylor and Hessey, 1825), 303–4. Dwight could have used either the first English edition or a Boston edition made from it by Carter, Hendee, and Company in 1833. See also Friedrich Schiller, *On the Aesthetic Education of Man, in a Series of Letters,* ed. and trans. Elizabeth M. Wilkinson and Leonard A. Willoughby (Oxford: Clarendon Press, 1967), esp. Letter 9, 56–59.

19. See the use of the term "aesthetic utopianism" and the important discussion in Solomon, "Beethoven and Schiller," 205–15, esp. 214. Art must restore not merely the memory of a lost innocence but also envision particularly a future Elysium whose joyous state could transcend the alienations of the present in civilization. See also Lawrence Kramer, *Music as Cultural Practice, 1800–1900* (Berkeley and Los Angeles: University of California Press, 1990), 22–30.

20. Dwight, *Select Minor Poems,* A, 429; [Carlyle], *The Life of Friedrich*

Schiller, 174–82, esp. 181–82. For helpful background on Carlyle, see A. Abbott Ikeler, *Puritan Temper and Transcendental Faith: Carlyle's Literary Vision* (Columbus: Ohio State University Press, 1972), and Julian Symons, *Thomas Carlyle: The Life and Ideas of a Prophet* (Freeport, N.Y.: Books for Libraries Press, 1952).

21. Dwight, *Select Minor Poems,* A, 432–34; [Carlyle], *The Life of Friedrich Schiller,* 139–41.

22. [Carlyle], *The Life of Friedrich Schiller,* 301–2.

23. [J. S. Dwight], *Report Made at a Meeting of the Honorary and Immediate Members of the Pierian Sodality, in Harvard University, Cambridge, August 30th, 1837, with a Record of the Meeting* (Cambridge, Mass.: Folsom, Wells, and Thurston, 1837), 6–7; repr. in *Boston Musical Gazette* (June 27 and July 11, 1838), 33–34, 42. Dwight asserted his authorship of that report in 1852, according to a five-page manuscript in his hand that he titled "H.M.A." (Harvard Musical Association Library, Boston). It is described on an outer cover as a "Brief Historical Sketch by J. S. Dwight, 1852." Dwight wrote: "Resolved to invite all old members to meet on Commencement (Aug. 30, '37) when Report of a Committee (by J.S.D.) was presented enlarging on the idea [of a General Association of Past and Present Pierians] & suggesting objects" (1).

24. Dwight, *Select Minor Poems,* translator's preface, x.

25. Ibid., x–xi.

26. J. S. D., "Art. VI.—*William Tell; a Drama, in five Acts.* From the German of Schiller. Providence: B. Cranston & Co., 1838. 12 mo. pp. 120," *The Christian Examiner* (January 1839): 385–91, esp. 390.

27. Dwight, *Select Minor Poems,* translator's preface, xi.

CHAPTER THREE

1. Dwight, *Select Minor Poems,* B, 435–37.

2. See Birgitte Moyer, "Marx, Adolf Bernhard," in *The New Grove Dictionary of Music and Musicians,* ed. Stanley Sadie (London: Macmillan, 1980), 11:739–41. See also Wallace, *Beethoven's Critics,* 45–64.

3. ABM. (Adolf Bernhard Marx), "Beethoven, Ludwig von," in *Encyclopädie der gesammten musikalischen Wissenschaften, oder Universal-Lexicon der Tonkunst,* ed. Gustav Schilling (Stuttgart: Franz Heinrich Kühler, 1835–1838), 1:513–20.

4. Ibid., 1:519–20. Portions that Dwight omitted from his translated ex-

cerpt are placed in brackets here. "Wie im äussern Leben er sich fruchtlos nach dem süssbefriedenden Familienbande sehnt [und sein herz mit väterlichem Antheil an übelgerathenen Verwandten täuscht und gern immer wieder zur Täuschung zurückkehrt,] so wendet er in seiner Kunst mit Sehnsucht Erinnerung und Wünsche der Liebe hin zu den Menschen, so wächst ihm das Verlangen nach Menschen-Musik, nach Gesang, und führt ihn auf den Gipfel seines Schaffens. Die neunte Sinfonie, mit Chor, wird geschrieben. [Schon einmal, in seiner "Fantasie mit Orchester und Chor," hatte er spielend die Bahn vom Clavier zum Orchester und Verein von Gesang und Instrumentale sich vorgezeichnet,—um von da erst in die tieferen Kreise seiner Instrumentenwelt zu dringen.] Jetzt fasst er im höchsten künstlerischen Selbstbekenntniss alle Resultate seines Lebens zusammen. Riesengewaltig beschwört er die riesigen Mächte des vollsten, bewegtesten Orchesters; sie müssen, dürfen ihn umscherzen,—und ihr tief—aufjährender Sturm, wie der leichte Tanz ihres Scherzes, trägt nur sein Verlangen, dass sich in zarteste Sehnsucht, in den wehmüthigsten, schmelzendentsagenden Abschied löst. Das alles kann nicht ferner genügen. Es zertrümmert; und die Instrumente selbst ergreifen (in Recitativform) die Weise menschlichen Gesanges. Noch einmal wehen traumhaft alle jene Gestalten vorüber, menschliche Stimmen ergreifen jenes Recitativ, und sie führen zu Schillers Freudengesang, Ihm ein Bundeslied aller Menschen. Nichts kann rührender seyn, nichts lässt uns so tief schauen in seine Brust, als wie erst Bässe, dann Sänger das "Freude schöner Götterfunken" so einfältig, so volksmässig anstimmen, so hingegeben in das sanfte Verlangen und Lieben, das nur Menschen, Menschen! sucht, nur der Gemeinschaft mit Menschen bedarf, und nichts höheres mehr kennt und will."

5. Dwight, *Select Minor Poems,* B, 436–37. There are no substantive changes in the manuscript, B, 459–61.

6. Marx's connection of the poem to Beethoven's symphony was clear in 1835, but he changed his view about that relationship in 1859; see Ruth A. Solie, "Beethoven as Secular Humanist: Ideology and the Ninth Symphony in Nineteenth-Century Criticism," in *Explorations in Music, the Arts, and Ideas: Essays in Honor of Leonard B. Meyer,* ed. Eugene Narmour and Ruth A. Solie (Stuyvesant, N.Y.: Pendragon Press, 1988), 33, 40.

7. ABM. (Marx), "Beethoven," 1:516–17.

8. Ibid., 518.

9. Mark Evan Bonds, *Wordless Rhetoric: Musical Form and the Metaphor of the Oration* (Cambridge, Mass. and London: Harvard University Press, 1991), 169–70. See also John Neubauer, *The Emancipation of Music from Language: Departure from Mimesis in Eighteenth-Century Aesthetics* (New Haven: Yale University Press, 1986).

10. ABM. (Marx), "Beethoven," 1:519.

11. Scott Burnham, "Criticism, Faith, and the *Idee:* A. B. Marx's Early Reception of Beethoven," *Nineteenth-Century Music* 13 (1990): 183–92, esp. 192. I thank Scott Burnham for kindly providing a copy of the manuscript before its publication.

12. Ibid., 184.

13. J. S. D. (John Sullivan Dwight), "Music, as a Branch of Popular Education," *Boston Musical Gazette: A Semi-Monthly Journal Devoted to the Science of Music* 1 (May 16, 1838): 9–10.

14. [John S. Dwight], "On Music," autograph manuscript, Ms. fC.1.7 v.3, Dwight Papers, Rare Book Room, Boston Public Library, esp. 14–15. This caption appears on the back of the manuscript, which carries as headings the titles of two works to be reviewed. For the published excerpt of this manuscript, see [J. S. Dwight], "Sacred Music," *The American Monthly Magazine* (November 1836): 447–57.

15. J. S. D., "Music, as a Branch," 10.

16. [John S. Dwight], *Report,* 6–8.

17. J. S. D., "Music, as a Branch," 10. Dwight's use of the phrase "Let the million be musical at all" may allude to the musical activities of Joseph Mainzer, a German music teacher whose free singing classes for large groups of artisans in Paris had become well known between 1835 and the publication in 1841 of his textbook, *Singing for the Million.* For example, Henry F. Chorley favorably describes Mainzer's success in *The Athenaeum: Journal of English and Foreign Literature, Science, and the Fine Arts* no. 527 (December 2, 1837): 881. Chorley notes that "this gentleman's success should encourage all who wish to diffuse a musical taste among the humbler orders." See also Bernarr Rainbow, "Mainzer, Joseph," in *The New Grove Dictionary of Music and Musicians,* ed. Stanley Sadie (London: Macmillan, 1980), 11:539–40.

CHAPTER FOUR

1. See Jonathan Wilshere, "Gardiner, William," in *The New Grove Dictionary of Music and Musicians,* ed. Stanley Sadie (London: Macmillan, 1980), 7:164.

2. Donald W. MacArdle, as cited in Temperley, "Beethoven in London Concert Life," 211.

3. Lowell Mason, comp., *The Boston Handel and Haydn Society Collection of Church Music* (Boston: Richardson and Lord, 1822; repr., with introduction by H. Wiley Hitchcock, New York: Da Capo Press, 1973).

4. William Gardiner, comp., *Sacred Melodies, from Haydn, Mozart and Beethoven, Adapted to the best English Poets, and Appropriated to the use of the British Church* (London: Clementi, [1812, 1815]).

5. Mason, *Boston Handel and Haydn Society,* iii–v.

6. Carol A. Pemberton, *Lowell Mason: His Life and Work* (Ann Arbor, Mich.: UMI Research Press, 1985).

7. [John S. Dwight], "On Music," 4–5.

8. Ibid., 13–15.

9. Stendhal [Marie-Henri Beyle], *The Life of Haydn, in a Series of Letters written at Vienna; Followed by The Life of Mozart, with Observations on Metastasio, and on the Present State of Music in France and Italy,* trans. [Robert Brewin] from the French of L. A. C. Bombet, with Notes by the Author of *The Sacred Melodies* [William Gardiner] (London: John Murray, 1817), 247–48. The Haydn text was drawn from Giuseppe Carpani's biography, *Le Haydine, ovvero Lettere sulla vita e le opere del celebre maestro Giuseppe Haydn* (Milan, 1812); the biography of Mozart was indebted to Friedrich von Schlichtegroll's "Mozarts Leben" published in *Nekrolog auf das Jahr Siebzehn Hundert Einundneunzig* (Gotha, 1792). An edition of Stendhal's work was published in Providence, Rhode Island, by Miller and Hutchens, and Samuel Avery, in 1820; see 161. All further references are to the first edition of 1817. In his annotation about "the chaos," William Gardiner referred to his own paper, previously published in *The Monthly Magazine* (March 1, 1811).

10. For this and the. following quotation, see [John S. Dwight], "On Music," 17–19. The quotations also appear in the published excerpt in *The American Monthly Magazine* (November 1836): 450. An excerpt from Gardiner's material appears in Nicholas Temperley, *Haydn: "The Creation"* (Cambridge: Cambridge University Press, 1991), 93–94.

11. G. [Gardiner], notes to Stendhal, *The Life of Haydn,* 3.

12. Ibid., 115–16.

13. [E. T. A. Hoffmann], "Recension" [Review of Beethoven's Symphony no. 5 in C Minor], *Allgemeine musikalische Zeitung* 12 (July 4 and 11, 1810): 630–42, 652–59, esp. 632–33.

14. G. [Gardiner], notes to Stendhal, *The Life of Haydn,* 63–65.

15. Ibid., 106–7.

16. Ibid., 205–7.

17. Stendhal, *The Life of Haydn,* 122–23, 236–46. See J.[ean] J.[acques] Rousseau, "Imitation," in *Dictionnaire de Musique* (Paris: la veuve Duchesne, 1768), 253–54: "Il [le musicien] ne représentera pas directement ces choses, mais il excitera dans l'ame [*sic*] les mêmes mouvemens [*sic*] qu'on éprouve en les voyant." ["The composer will not represent these things directly, but

he will excite in the soul the same emotions that are experienced on seeing them."—Trans. mine.]

18. William Gardiner, *The Music of Nature; or, An Attempt to Prove that What is Passionate and Pleasing in the Art of Singing, Speaking, and Performing Upon Musical Instruments, Is Derived From the Sounds of the Animated World* (London: Longman, Orme, Brown, & Longman, 1832; repr., Boston: J. H. Wilkins & R. B. Carter, 1838).

19. Dwight, *Select Minor Poems*, D, 463.

20. J. S. D. [John S. Dwight], "Art. II.—*The Music of Nature; or, An Attempt to prove that what is passionate and pleasing in the Art of Singing, Speaking, and Performing upon Musical Instruments, is derived from the Sounds of the Animated World. With curious and interesting Illustrations. By William Gardiner. Boston: J. H. Wilkins & R. B. Carter. 1837. [sic] 8vo. pp. 505.*," *The Christian Examiner and General Review* 25 (September 1838–January 1839): 23–36.

21. J. S. D., "Review of Gardiner's *Music of Nature* By Rev. J. S. Dwight. [From the *Christian Examiner*]," *Boston Musical Gazette: A Semi-Monthly Journal Devoted to the Science of Music* 1 (September 19, 1838): 81–82 and (October 3, 1838): 89–90.

22. Gardiner, *The Music of Nature*, 229.

23. Ibid., 398–403, esp. 399.

24. J. S. D. [John S. Dwight], "On the Proper Character of Poetry and Music for Public Worship," *The Christian Examiner and General Review* 21 (November 1836): 254–63, esp. 261–62.

25. J. S. D. [Dwight], "Art. II—*The Music of Nature*," 25–26.

26. Ibid., 30–32, 34.

27. Ibid., 23–24.

28. Ibid., 35–36.

29. Ibid., 26.

CHAPTER FIVE

1. [H. Theodor Hach and T. B. Hayward], eds., *The Musical Magazine; or Repository of Musical Science, Literature, and Intelligence* (Boston: Otis, Broaders and Company, 1839; Boston: George P. Reed, 1840, 1842). All references are to the three-volume set located at the Music Division, Library of Congress, Washington, D.C.

2. For further details about their connections in Germany, see Michael

Broyles, ed., *A Yankee Musician in Europe: The 1837 Journals of Lowell Mason* (Ann Arbor, Mich. and London: UMI Research Press, 1990), 31, 46, 58, 60, 61, 177, and 223 n. 15.

3. Pemberton, *Lowell Mason,* 69–70.

4. H. Theodor Hach, autograph letter signed to R. E. Apthorp, January 2, 1845, Harvard Musical Association Library, Boston. I shall discuss this important document in Chapter 7. Before Hach returned with his family to Germany in 1846, the Perkins Institution thanked him for his "valuable services" and expressed its "high regard for him as a man and a teacher" in the *Fourteenth Annual Report of The Trustees of the Perkins Institution and Massachusetts Asylum For the Blind, to the Corporation* (Cambridge, [Mass.], 1846), 22.

5. Thomas Carlyle, autograph letter signed to John Sullivan Dwight, March 14, 1839, Amy Lowell Autograph Collection, Houghton Library, Harvard University.

6. Hach and Hayward, "Prospectus," *The Musical Magazine* 1 (January 5, 1839): 2–3.

7. Hach, "Prospectus," *The Musical Magazine* 3 (January 9, 1841): 1.

8. [Hach and Hayward], "New Musical Publications. *The Life of Haydn . . . ,*" *The Musical Magazine* 1 (June 8, 1839): 189–90.

9. Myerson, *The New England Transcendentalists,* 148.

10. D. [Dwight], "The Religion of Beauty," *The Dial* 1 (July 1840): 17–22.

11. D. [Dwight], "Ideals of Every-Day Life, I and II," *The Dial* 1 (January and April 1841): 307–11, 446–61.

12. George Ripley, autograph letter signed to John S. Dwight, July 7, 1840, Ms. E.4.1 no. 24, Dwight Papers, Rare Book Room, Boston Public Library.

13. [Hach and Hayward], "Review. *The Life of Haydn . . . ,*" *The Musical Magazine* 1 (August 31, 1839): 287.

14. D. [Dwight], "The Concerts of the Past Winter," *The Dial* 1 (July 1840): 128.

15. J. F. T. [John Francis Tuckerman], "Art. III.—*Biographie Universelle des Musiciens,* par F. J. Fétis.—Paris, 1835. Art. *Beethoven,*" *The Boston Quarterly Review* 11 (July 1840): 332–57, esp. 353–54. It referred to François-Joseph Fétis, "Beethoven (Louis van)," in *Biographie Universelle des Musiciens et Bibliographie Générale de la Musique* (Brussels: Leroux, 1835), 2:100–112.

16. D. [Dwight], "Concerts of the Past Winter," 129–31.

17. Ibid., 132–33.

18. Ibid., 131.

19. Ibid., 134.

20. [Hach], "Handel and Haydn. The Messiah and The Creation. *Dial,*" in *The Musical Magazine* 2 (August 1, 1840): 256.

21. [Hach], "The Messiah and The Creation. (From *The Dial*)," in *The Musical Magazine* 2 (August 15, 1840): 263–65.

22. Hach, "Prospectus," *The Musical Magazine* 3 (January 9, 1841): 1.

23. [Hach], "Advancement of Music," *The Musical Magazine* 3 (January 9, 1841): 19–23.

24. George Ripley, *The Claims of the Age on the Work of the Evangelist. A Sermon Preached at the Ordination of Mr. John Sullivan Dwight, As Pastor of the Second Congregational Church in Northampton, May 20, 1840* (Boston: Weeks, Jordan, and Company, 1840), 15–20, 25.

25. William Ellery Channing, *Charge* (Boston: [Weeks, Jordan, and Company], 1840), 30–31, 34, 41.

26. Sophia Ripley, autograph letter signed to John S. Dwight, May 6, [1841], Ms. E.4.1 no. 34, Dwight Papers, Rare Book Room, Boston Public Library. The reference is probably to the earliest Boston performance (April 3, 1841) of three movements of Beethoven's Fifth Symphony by the orchestra of the Boston Academy of Music. The third movement was excluded. See Johnson, *First Performances in America,* 36.

27. As late as June 25, 1841, two months before the date of the proposed event, archival records show that Rev. Henry Ware, Jr., was chosen to speak, with George S. Hillard as his substitute, but neither was able to accept; see manuscript "Records of the Board of Directors of the General Association of Members of the Pierian Sodality," Harvard Musical Association Library, Boston, 10.

28. Fertig, "John Sullivan Dwight, Transcendentalist," 48.

29. John S. Dwight, "Address, Delivered Before the Harvard Musical Association, August 25th, 1841," in [Hach], *The Musical Magazine* 3 (August 28, 1841): 257–72.

30. Ibid., 258–62, 264–65.

31. [Hach and Hayward], "The Late Musical Season," *The Musical Magazine* 1 (July 20, 1839): 236.

32. [Hach], "Ninth Annual Report of the Boston Academy of Music—1841," *The Musical Magazine* 3 (August 28, 1841): 273–74.

33. [Hach], "Concerts," *The Musical Magazine* 2 (January 4, 1840): 16; see also [Hach], "Proceedings of the Musical Convention of 1840," *The Musical Magazine* 3 (April 10, 1841): 125–26, and [Hach], "Music Performed in the Boston Academy of Music's Concerts, During the Past Winter," ibid. (May 8, 1841): 135.

34. [Hach], "Lectures on Music," *The Musical Magazine* 2 (July 18, 1840): 239–40.

35. Otto Kinkeldey, "Beginnings of Beethoven in America," *Musical Quarterly* 13 (1927): 217–48, esp. 232.

36. [Hach and Hayward], "Miscellaneous Gleanings, From The Musical Library," *The Musical Magazine* 1 (May 25, 1839): 174–75. The entire document appeared in translation for the first time in America in *The Parlour Review* 1 (1838). Drawn originally from *The Harmonicon* (January 1828), it was included in a reprinted article on Beethoven taken from George Hogarth's *Musical History, Biography, and Criticism* (London: J. W. Parker, 1835), according to Chan, "Beethoven in the United States," 32–33.

37. Excerpts from Franz Gerhard Wegeler and Ferdinand Ries, *Biographische Notizen über Ludwig van Beethoven* (Coblenz: K. Bädeker, 1838), contained in H. F. C. [Henry F. Chorley], "Review. The London and Westminster Review. April–July 1839. Article III. The Pianoforte," in [Hach and Hayward], *The Musical Magazine* 1 (August 17, 1839): 263–65 and (September 14, 1839): 293–96.

38. Excerpt from [Bettina Brentano von Arnim], *Goethes Briefwechsel mit einem Kinde* (Berlin: F. Dümmler, 1835), translated, in part, [Arnim], *Goethe's Correspondence with a Child* (London: Longman, Orme, Brown, Green, and Longman, 1839), cited in H. F. C. [Henry F. Chorley], "Review," in [Hach and Hayward], *The Musical Magazine* 1 (September 14, 1839): 296–97.

39. Fétis, "Beethoven, (Louis van)," 2:100–112, in [Hach], "Biography. Beethoven," *The Musical Magazine* 2 (September 12, 1840): 289–96; (October 10, 1840): 321–28; and (October 24, 1840): 356–60.

40. [Hach], "The Art of Music in Our Periodical Literature," *The Musical Magazine* 3 (November 6, 1841): 345–50. Fuller's essay, "Lives of the Great Composers, Haydn, Mozart, Handel, Bach, Beethoven," appears in *The Dial* 2 (October 1841): 148–203. For further information about Fuller's views, see Ora Frishberg Saloman, "Margaret Fuller on Beethoven in America, 1839–1846," *Journal of Musicology* 10 (1992): 89–105, and Saloman, "Margaret Fuller on Musical Life in Boston and New York, 1841–1846," *American Music* 6 (1988): 428–41.

41. [Hach], "The Art of Music," *The Musical Magazine* 3 (October 23, 1841): 333–34. See also [Anton Felix Schindler], *The Life of Beethoven, Including His Correspondence with His Friends, Numerous Characteristic Traits, and Remarks on His Musical Works,* ed. Ignace [Ignaz] Moscheles (London: Henry Colburn, 1841), 1:18–20; 2:85–86, 123.

42. See particularly H. F. C. [Henry F. Chorley], "Review," in [Hach and Hayward], *The Musical Magazine* 1 (July 20, 1839): 235 and (September 14, 1839): 297–98.

43. [Hach], "Concerts," *The Musical Magazine* 2 (March 28, 1840): 110–11. See also Kinkeldey, "Beginnings of Beethoven in America," 231–32.

44. [Hach], "Fidelio," *The Musical Magazine* 3 (November 20, 1841): 357–61.

45. [Hach,] "Concerts," *The Musical Magazine* 2 (February 20, 1841): 64.

46. H[enry] Panofka, "Beethoven's Sonata in A Minor. Extract from the Journal of an Artist," in [Hach and Hayward], *The Musical Magazine* 1 (February 2, 1839): 35–38 and (February 16, 1839): 49–52.

47. E. T. A. Hoffmann, "The Cadenza," in [Hach], *The Musical Magazine* 1 (August 31, 1839): 280–84, (September 14, 1839): 298–301, (September 28, 1839): 313–18, (October 12, 1839): 328–30, and (October 26, 1839): 342–45; E. T. A. Hoffmann, "The Poet and the Composer," in [Hach], *The Musical Magazine* 2 (July 4, 1840): 209–14, (July 18, 1840): 225–31, and (August 1, 1840): 241–47; and E. T. A. Hoffmann, "Thoughts on the High Value of Music," in [Hach] *The Musical Magazine* 3 (March 6, 1841): 65–70.

48. [Karl] Aug.[ust] Kahlert, "On the Romantic in Music," in [Hach], *The Musical Magazine* 2 (May 9, 1840): 149–53.

49. [Karl] August Kahlert, *Tonleben. Novellen und vermischte Aufsätze* (Breslau: Georg Philipp Aderholz, 1838), 199–212. See also Wolfgang Boetticher, "Kahlert, Karl August Thimotheus," in *Die Musik in Geschichte und Gegenwart,* ed. Friedrich Blume (Kassel and Basel: Bärenreiter, 1958), 7:cols. 425–27.

50. Kahlert, "On the Romantic in Music," 150–52; Kahlert, *Tonleben,* esp. 207–12.

51. [Christian] G.[ottfried] W.[ilhelm] Fink, "Music in Germany," in [Hach], *The Musical Magazine* 3 (May 22, 1841): 145–53 and (June 5, 1841): 161–68.

CHAPTER SIX

1. [E. T. A. Hoffmann], "Recension," *Allgemeine musikalische Zeitung* 12 (July 4 and 11, 1810): 630–42, 652–59; trans. F. John Adams, Jr., in *Beethoven: Symphony No. 5 in C minor,* ed. Elliot Forbes (New York: W. W. Norton, 1971), 150–63. Among the valuable works relating to Hoffmann's music criticism, see E. T. A. Hoffmann, *Schriften zur Musik, Nachlese,* ed. Friedrich Schnapp (Munich: Winkler-Verlag, 1963); Peter Schnaus, *E. T. A. Hoffmann*

als Beethoven-Rezensent der Allgemeinen musikalischen Zeitung (Munich and Salzburg: Musikverlag Katzbichler, 1977); *Selected Letters of E. T. A. Hoffmann,* ed. and trans. Johanna C. Sahlin (Chicago and London: University of Chicago Press, 1977); R. Murray Schafer, *E. T. A. Hoffmann and Music* (Toronto and Buffalo: University of Toronto Press, 1975); and *E. T. A. Hoffmann's Musical Writings: "Kreisleriana," "The Poet and the Composer," "Music Criticism,"* ed. David Charlton, trans. Martyn Clarke (Cambridge and New York: Cambridge University Press, 1989).

2. J. S. Dwight, "Academy of Music—Beethoven's Symphonies," *The Pioneer,* ed. J. R. Lowell and R. B. Carter (January–February 1843): 26–28, 56–60. The first section comprises Dwight's impressions of the Symphony no. 2 in D, op. 36, which he heard in rehearsal as well as its first complete American performance on November 12, 1842. (For the date, see Johnson, *First Performances in America,* 32.)

3. Dwight, "Academy of Music," 56.

4. [Hoffmann], "Recension," 633–34, 652, 658; trans. Adams, 152–53, 158, 163. See the important discussion about Hoffmann's criticism of the Fifth Symphony in a Continental context in Wallace, *Beethoven's Critics,* 20–26, 128–32, 135–36, 139–40.

5. See also Wallace, *Beethoven's Critics,* 128–30. For a literary perspective, see Horst S. Daemmrich, *The Shattered Self: E. T. A. Hoffmann's Tragic Vision* (Detroit: Wayne State University Press, 1973).

6. William S. Porter, *The Musical Cyclopedia: or the Principles of Music Considered As a Science and an Art; Embracing a Complete Musical Dictionary, And the Outline of a Musical Grammar, and of the Theory of Sounds and Laws of Harmony; With Directions for The Practice of Vocal and Instrumental Music, And A Description of Musical Instruments* (Boston: James Loring, 1834), 385. Porter describes the genre of the symphony according to an earlier eighteenth-century model as consisting of "several movements, generally a slow introduction, a spirited movement in 2 parts, a minuet and trio, & finally a quick movement. The composition of symphonies has called forth the talents of the most eminent modern composers Haydn, Mozart, & Beethoven."

7. Dwight, *Select Minor Poems,* B, 436–37.

8. For performance dates, see the *Boston Daily Evening Transcript* (February 4 and 24, and March 26, 1842) and Johnson, *First Performances in America,* 36–38. For announcements of Dwight's lectures, see the *Boston Daily Evening Transcript* (January 29; February 3, 10, 17, 23, 24; and March 9, 10, 16, 17, 23, 24, 30, 31, 1842).

9. [H. Theodor Hach], "Beethoven's Symphonies," *The Musical Magazine* 3 (April 24, 1842): 392–406; see also 420.

10. G.[ottfried] W.[ilhelm] Fink, "Symphonie oder Sinfonie," in *Encyclopädie der gesammten musikalischen Wissenschaften, oder Universal-Lexicon der Tonkunst,* ed. Gustav Schilling (Stuttgart: Franz Heinrich Kühler, 1835–1838), 6:541–51.

11. See John Warrack, "Fink, (Christian) Gottfried Wilhelm," in *The New Grove Dictionary of Music and Musicians,* ed. Stanley Sadie (London: Macmillan, 1980), 6:584; Wolfgang Boetticher, "Fink, Gottfried Wilhelm," in *Die Musik in Geschichte und Gegenwart,* ed. Friedrich Blume (Kassel and Basel: Bärenreiter, 1955), 4:cols. 223–27; Kurt-Erich Eicke, *Der Streit zwischen Adolph Bernhard Marx und Gottfried Wilhelm Fink um die Kompositionslehre* (Regensburg: Gustav Bosse Verlag, 1966).

12. J. R. Lowell and R. B. Carter, eds., "Introduction," *The Pioneer,* 1–3. Authors normally received ten dollars per contribution, a competitive rate according to Martin Duberman, *James Russell Lowell* (Boston: Houghton Mifflin, 1966), 47.

13. Dwight, "Academy of Music," 57.

14. Fink, "Symphonie oder Sinfonie," 545.

15. [Hoffmann], "Recension," 633–34, 640–41, 658; trans. Adams, 153, 156, 162–63; G. W. Fink, "*Ueber die Symphonie,* als Beitrag zur Geschichte und Aesthetik derselben," *Allgemeine musikalische Zeitung* 34 (August 26, 1835): 557–63. Earlier parts of that article appeared in *Allgemeine musikalische Zeitung* 31 (August 5, 1835): 505–11 and 32 (August 12, 1835): 521–24.

16. Fink, "Symphonie oder Sinfonie," 547–48.

17. Hoffmann, *Schriften zur Musik, Nachlese,* 19, 24, cited in Carl Dahlhaus, *The Idea of Absolute Music,* trans. Roger Lustig (Chicago and London: University of Chicago Press, 1989), 11–12.

18. Hoffmann, *Schriften zur Musik, Nachlese,* 19.

19. Fink, "Symphonie oder Sinfonie," 548–49; [Hach], "Beethoven's Symphonies," 394.

20. [Hoffmann], "Recension," 633–34; trans. Adams, 152–53.

21. According to Fink, Beethoven's music made "heroes, spirits, magicians, and fairies intermingle with our human doings, and lightnings from the dark night above strike over the mountain peaks into the fertile valley." (Trans. mine.) See [Hoffmann], "Recension," 633–34; trans. Adams, 152–53; Fink, "Symphonie oder Sinfonie," 550; [Hach], "Beethoven's Symphonies," 395.

22. [Hach], "Beethoven's Symphonies," 393–94, based on Fink, "Symphonie oder Sinfonie," 547: "aus welcher ein Spiel vielfacher Charaktere, um einen Hauptcharakter und eine Haupt-Lebensansicht in gar mannigfachen Situationen sich drehend, zu einem einzigen bestimmten Zwecke sich ergiebt."

23. [Hach], "Beethoven's Symphonies," 396, based on Fink, "Symphonie oder Sinfonie," 550: "Irgend einen Empfindungsinhalt, irgend eine psychologische Entwickelung eines der Masse nicht wildfremden oder ganz unzugänglichen Gefühlsganges, der zu einer Tendenz führt, muss sie haben; ohne dies wären es ja nur nichtssagende Töne."

24. [Hach], "Beethoven's Symphonies," 397.

25. Ibid., 397–403.

26. Ibid., 397–98. See also "Dr. Sch." [Schilling], "Tonart—C-Moll," in *Encyclopädie der gesammten musikalischen Wissenschaften, oder Universal-Lexicon der Tonkunst,* ed. Gustav Schilling (Stuttgart: Franz Heinrich Kühler, 1835–1838), 2:266–67.

27. Rita Steblin, *A History of Key Characteristics in the Eighteenth and Early Nineteenth Centuries* (Ann Arbor, Mich.: UMI Research Press, 1983), 121–22, 174–75, 181–84, 227–31.

28. Dwight, "Academy of Music," 26.

29. Ibid., 57.

30. I am indebted for this idea to J. Stephen Parkany's unpublished paper "Presentiments of the Colossal: E. T. A. Hoffmann and the Critical Tradition of Symphonic Drama" (presented at the Fifty-Fourth Annual Meeting of the American Musicological Society, Baltimore, November 4, 1988).

31. Dwight, "Academy of Music," 57–59.

32. Emily Anderson, coll., trans., and ed., *The Letters of Beethoven* (London: Macmillan, 1961; repr., New York and London: W. W. Norton, 1985), 1:312–13, and 3:1355–359.

33. Schindler, *The Life of Beethoven,* 1:130–37, 265–85; 2:150–51. See also [Arnim], *Goethe's Correspondence with a Child.* A footnote reference in Dwight's volume of poetry translations indicates that he had known this work in 1838 in the original German edition of 1835; see Dwight, *Select Minor Poems,* B, 364–65.

34. Dwight, "Academy of Music," 59–60.

35. Johnson, *First Performances in America,* 30–31.

36. Dwight, "Academy of Music," 57–58.

37. J. S. Dwight, "Haydn," *The United States Magazine, and Democratic Review* 14 (January 1844): 17–25. The earlier essays are "Handel and his 'Messiah,'" ibid. 12 (March 1843): 264–79, and "Mozart," ibid. 13 (November 1843): 465–73.

38. Dwight, "Haydn," 20–22.

39. Ibid., 25.

40. *Boston Musical Visitor, Devoted to Vocal and Instrumental Music, and Published by A Musical Association* 3 (October 24, 1843): 177–78.

41. I. [Isaac] B. Woodbury, *The Elements of Musical Composition and Thorough-Base* [sic]: Together With Rules For Arranging Music For The Full Orchestra and Military Bands (Boston: Charles H. Keith, 1844), 132.

42. Ibid., unpaged [iv].

43. See Peter Kivy's use of the term in *The Corded Shell: Reflections on Musical Expression* (Princeton: Princeton University Press, 1980), esp. 3–9 and 143–49. According to Kivy, "emotive description" is not merely subjective. He argues that "criteria of musical expressiveness can be identified with those of human expression" to provide a rational foundation for emotive criticism that is both "scientific" and "humanistic." See also Ian D. Bent, "Analysis," in *The New Grove Dictionary of Music and Musicians,* ed. Stanley Sadie (London: Macmillan, 1980), 1:340–88.

CHAPTER SEVEN

1. "Records of the Harvard Musical Association. 1840. From Its Formation in 1837," 35, Harvard Musical Association, and Hepner, *Pro Bono Artium Musicarum,* 9–13.

2. H. W. Pickering, Manuscript "Librarian's Report" (August 25, 1841), 2, Harvard Musical Association.

3. Bernard Roelker, Manuscript "Librarian's Report" (August 26, 1845), 1, Harvard Musical Association.

4. Dwight, "Academy of Music," 28.

5. Ibid., 56.

6. [J. S. D.], "*Musical Review.* Music in Boston During The Last Winter," *The Harbinger* 1 (August 2, 1845): 124. This and all subsequent citations refer to the complete set of *The Harbinger* located in the Rare Book and Special Collections Division of the Library of Congress, Washington, D.C.

7. [J. S. D.], "*Musical Review.* Music in Boston During The Last Winter—No. III: Concerts of the Boston Academy of Music," *The Harbinger* 1 (August 16, 1845): 154–57.

8. [J. S. D.], "*Musical Review.* Music in Boston During The Last Winter. No. IV," *The Harbinger* 1 (August 30, 1845): 188–89. I shall discuss this essay in Chapter 8.

9. Paul DeKeyser, "Kalkbrenner, Frédéric," in *The New Grove Dictionary of Music and Musicians,* ed. Stanley Sadie (London: Macmillan, 1980), 9:777–79. Kalkbrenner's transcriptions of Beethoven's symphonies are not listed there.

10. A contact between them is discussed in Nathan Broder, "An Unknown Letter by Beethoven," *Juilliard Review* 4 (Winter 1956–57): 16–20.

11. Fréd.[éric] Kalkbrenner, "Note des Éditeurs," *Collection Complète des Symphonies de Beethoven Arrangées pour Piano seul* (Paris: Schonenberger, [1840]), 10 vols. in 1:3.

12. Kalkbrenner, "Symphonie de Beethoven en Ut mineur," in *Collection Complète,* 5:6.

13. Ibid., 6–9. As examples of early editions of orchestral scores, see Ludwig van Beethoven, *Cinquième Sinfonie en ut mineur: C moll de Louis van Beethoven. Oeuvre 67. Partition* (Leipzig: Breitkopf & Härtel, [1826]); see also Beethoven, *Siebente Grosse Sinfonie in A dur von Ludwig van Beethoven. 92tes Werk. Vollständige Partitur* (Vienna: S. A. Steiner und Comp., [1816]), and *Sixième Sinfonie Pastorale en fa majeur: F Dur de Louis van Beethoven. Oeuvre 68. Partition* (Leipzig: Breitkopf & Härtel, [1826]).

14. Programs of the Chamber Concerts for 1844 and 1845, Harvard Musical Association.

15. Hach to R. E. Apthorp, January 2, 1845.

16. D. [Dwight], "Concerts of the Past Winter," 131.

17. [J. S. D.], *"Musical Review.* Music in Boston During The Last Winter," *The Harbinger* 1 (August 2, 1845): 123–24.

18. Michael Broyles, "Music and Class Structure in Antebellum Boston," *Journal of the American Musicological Society* 44 (1991): 482–88. See also Broyles, *"Music of the Highest Class,"* 236, 260, 263–64.

19. J. S. D., "Music, as a Branch," 9–10.

CHAPTER EIGHT

1. Lowens, "Writings about Music," 73–74.

2. Crowe, *George Ripley,* 196, 182.

3. *Oeuvres Complètes de Charles Fourier* (Grenoble: éditions anthropos, 1966–68), 12 vols., with introduction by Simone Debout Oleszkiewicz.

4. Jonathan Beecher and Richard Bienvenu, trans. and ed., with introduction, *The Utopian Vision of Charles Fourier: Selected Texts on Work, Love, and Passionate Attraction* (Boston: Beacon Press, 1971), 22–30, 46–50. See also Dolores Hayden, *Seven American Utopias: The Architecture of Communitarian Socialism, 1790–1975* (Cambridge, Mass. and London: MIT Press, 1976), 149–57, and Frank E. Manuel and Fritzie P. Manuel, *Utopian Thought in the*

Western World (Cambridge, Mass.: Harvard University Press, Belknap Press, 1979), 641–75.

5. *Albert Brisbane, A Mental Biography with a Character Study by his wife, Redelia Brisbane* (Boston: Arena Publishing Company, 1893), 63–85. This is a posthumously published autobiography that Brisbane had dictated to his wife, who edited it and wrote an introduction.

6. Ibid., 171–73, 181, 196–98.

7. Albert Brisbane, *Social Destiny of Man: or, Association and Reorganization of Industry* (Philadelphia: C. F. Stollmeyer, 1840).

8. Ibid., 280.

9. Guarneri, *The Utopian Alternative,* 104.

10. Brisbane, *Social Destiny of Man,* 319–450.

11. [George Ripley], *"Record of the Months.* Select List of Recent Publications," *The Dial* 1 (October 1840): 265–66.

12. Samuel Osgood, autograph letter signed to John S. Dwight, November 21, 1840, Ms. E.4.1 no. 29, Dwight Papers, Rare Book Room, Boston Public Library.

13. Samuel Osgood, autograph letter signed to John S. Dwight, April 9, 1841, Ms. E.4.1 no. 31, Dwight Papers, Rare Book Room, Boston Public Library.

14. Guarneri, *The Utopian Alternative,* 35–52.

15. Ibid., 2, 53–54, 83–84, 232; Crowe, *George Ripley,* 172–75.

16. Albert Brisbane, "On Association and Attractive Industry," *The United States Magazine, and Democratic Review* 10 (1842): 30, 167, 321, 560, and Brisbane, *A Concise Exposition of the Doctrine of Association, or Plan for a Re-organization of Society* (New York: J. S. Redfield, 1843).

17. Guarneri, *The Utopian Alternative,* 233. This method was developed by Pierre Galin, Aimé and Nanine Paris, and Émile Chevé.

18. [Jean-Jacques Rousseau], "Projet Concernant de Nouveaux Signes pour la Musique, Lu par l'Auteur à l'Académie [Royale] des Sciences, le 22 Août 1742," and "Dissertation sur la Musique moderne," in *Traités Sur la Musique* (Geneva, 1781), 5–25, 29–208. See also Bernarr Rainbow, "Galin-Paris-Chevé Method," in *The New Grove Dictionary of Music and Musicians,* ed. Stanley Sadie (London: Macmillan, 1980), 7:99–100, and Daniel Heartz, "Rousseau, Jean-Jacques," in *The New Grove Dictionary of Music and Musicians,* 16:270–73.

19. Guarneri, *The Utopian Alternative,* 208–9, 235–37.

20. John S. Dwight, *A Lecture on Association, in its Connection with Education, Delivered before the New England Fourier Society, in Boston, February 29th, 1844* (Boston: Benjamin H. Greene, For the Society, 1844).

21. Charles A. Dana, *A Lecture on Association, in its Connection with Religion, Delivered before the New England Fourier Society, in Boston, March 7th, 1844* (Boston: Benjamin H. Greene, For the Society, 1844), 41.

22. Dwight, *A Lecture on Association,* 11–22.

23. In addition to Lindsay Swift's account, other valuable personal remembrances or descriptions of life at Brook Farm are Marianne Dwight Orvis, *Letters from Brook Farm, 1844–1847,* ed. Amy L. Reed, with a note on Anna Q. T. Parsons by Helen Dwight Orvis (Poughkeepsie, N.Y.: Vassar College, 1928); Edith Roelker Curtis, *A Season in Utopia: The Story of Brook Farm* (New York: Nelson, 1961); Georgianna Bruce Kirby, *Years of Experience* (New York: Putnam, 1887); and John Thomas Codman, *Brook Farm: Historic and Personal Memoirs* (Boston: Arena Publishing Co., 1894; repr., New York: AMS Press, 1971).

24. Dwight, *A Lecture on Association,* 3–10, esp. 5.

25. [J. S. D.], "Individuality in Association," *The Harbinger* 1 (October 4, 1845): 264–66.

26. [J. S. D.], "*Musical Review,*" *The Harbinger* 1 (June 14, 1845): 12–13.

27. Ibid., 13.

28. [J. S. D.], "*Musical Review.* Music in Boston During The Last Winter," *The Harbinger* 1 (August 2, 1845): 124.

29. [J. S. D.], "*Musical Review.* Music in Boston During The Last Winter.—No. III: Concerts of the Boston Academy of Music," *The Harbinger* 1 (August 16, 1845): 154–57, esp. 154–55.

30. [J. S. D.], "*Musical Review.* Music in Boston During The Last Winter. No. IV," *The Harbinger* 1 (August 30, 1845): 188–89.

31. Ibid., 189.

32. [J. S. D.], "*Musical Review.* Music in Boston," *The Harbinger* 1 (November 1, 1845): 329.

33. Ibid., 329–32.

34. Adolph [Adolf] Bernhard Marx, *Die Lehre von der musikalischen Komposition, praktisch-theoretisch, zum Selbstunterricht, oder als Leitfaden bei Privatunterweisung und öffentlichen Vorträgen* (Leipzig: Breitkopf & Härtel, 1838), 2:497–501, esp. 498.

35. A.[nton] Reicha, *Vollständiges Lehrbuch der musikalischen Composition,* trans. from French of *Cours de composition musicale* by Carl Czerny (Paris: Gambaro, 1816–1818; Vienna: Ant. Diabelli & Comp., [1832]) 1:317–19, 335, but esp. 317–18. See also William S. Newman, *The Sonata Since Beethoven,* 3d ed. (New York and London: W. W. Norton, 1983), 29–33; Bent, "Analysis," 1:350–51; and Alice L. Mitchell, "Czerny, Carl," in *The New Grove Dictionary of Music and Musicians,* ed. Stanley Sadie (London: Macmillan, 1980), 5:138–41.

36. [J. S. D.], *"Musical Review.* Music in Boston," *The Harbinger* 1 (November 1, 1845): 330.

37. Ibid.

CHAPTER NINE

1. Henry W. Bellows, autograph letter signed to John S. Dwight, October 5, 1841, Ms. E.4.1 no. 36, Dwight Papers, Rare Book Room, Boston Public Library.

2. *Boston Daily Evening Transcript* (January 29; February 3, 10, 17, 23, 24; and March 9, 10, 16, 17, 23, 24, 30, 31, 1842).

3. John S. Dwight, autograph letter signed to Henry W. Bellows, November 17, 1842, Bellows Papers, Massachusetts Historical Society.

4. H. W. Bellows, autograph letter signed to John S. Dwight, December 15, 1842, Ms. E.4.1 no. 39, Dwight Papers, Rare Book Room, Boston Public Library.

5. H. W. Bellows, autograph letter signed to John S. Dwight, December 18, 1842, Ms. E.4.1 no. 41, Dwight Papers, Rare Book Room, Boston Public Library.

6. [J. S. D.], "Fourier's Writings," *The Harbinger* 1 (November 1, 1845): 333–35.

7. Ibid., 334.

8. A.[lbert] Brisbane, autograph letter signed to John S. Dwight, December 2, [18]45, Ms. E.4.1 no. 52, Dwight Papers, Rare Book Room, Boston Public Library.

9. A.[lbert] B.[risbane], autograph letter signed to John S. Dwight, December 15, 1845, Ms. E.4.1 no. 53, Dwight Papers, Rare Book Room, Boston Public Library.

10. A.[lbert] B.[risbane], autograph letter signed to John S. Dwight, December 30, [18]45, Ms. E.4.1 no. 54, Dwight Papers, Rare Book Room, Boston Public Library.

11. See, for example, the early expression of this thought in Brisbane, *Social Destiny of Man,* 209–10.

12. J.[érôme] J.[oseph] de Momigny, *La Seule Vraie Théorie de la Musique Utile à ceux qui excellent dans cet Art comme à ceux qui en sont aux premiers Élémens, ou Moyen le plus court pour devenir Mélodiste, Harmoniste, Contrepointiste et Compositeur* (Paris: Au Magasin de Musique de l'Auteur, [1821]).

13. J.[érôme]-J.[oseph] de Momigny, *Cours Complet d'Harmonie et de*

Composition, d'après une théorie neuve et générale de la musique (Paris: Chez l'auteur, 1806), 2:646–59. "Qu'est-ce qui fait qu'une consonance est parfaite? C'est son degré d'Unité. Il n'y a point de consonance qui ait plus d'Unité que l'octave, ni de dissonnance [*sic*] qui ait plus de pluralité que la seconde mineure; donc l'octave est la consonnance [*sic*] la plus parfaite, et la seconde mineure la dissonnance la plus grande" (646). ["What makes a consonance perfect? It is its degree of unity. There is no consonance that has more unity than the octave nor dissonance that has more multiplicity than the minor second; thus the octave is the most perfect consonance, and the minor second the biggest dissonance."—Trans. mine.]

14. [J. S. D.], "*Musical Review*. Music in Boston During The Last Winter. No. IV," *The Harbinger* 1 (August 30, 1845): 189.

15. *The New-York Daily Tribune* (March 9, 12, 13, 14, 16, 17, 19, 20, 21, 1846).

16. Ibid. (March 9, 1846) and repeated (March 13, 1846).

17. Ibid. (March 16, 1846).

18. Ibid., City Items (March 17, 1846).

19. *Gazette and Times* (March 12 and 26, 1846).

20. *The New-York Daily Tribune* (March 12 and 14, 1846).

21. Ibid. (March 17, 19, 20, 1846). Margaret Fuller was then a reviewer of books and concerts for the paper and on very friendly terms with Horace Greeley. She is not likely to have written these notices, however; they do not carry her identifying asterisk.

22. Sophia Ripley, autograph letter signed to John S. Dwight, March 14 [1846], Ms. E.4.1 no. 59, Dwight Papers, Rare Book Room, Boston Public Library.

23. J. S. D., autograph letter signed to George Ripley, March 16, 1846, Ms. E.4.1 no. 60, Dwight Papers, Rare Book Room, Boston Public Library.

24. G.[eorge] R.[ipley], autograph letter signed to John S. Dwight, March 19, 1846, Ms. E.4.1 no. 61, Dwight Papers, Rare Book Room, Boston Public Library.

25. Broyles, *"Music of the Highest Class,"* 288. See also, however, his statement on 291: "In spite of Dwight's increasing unease with the virtuoso school, he remained susceptible to its charms throughout much of the 1840s."

26. D. [Dwight], "The Concerts of the Past Winter," *The Dial* 1 (July 1840): 129–31.

27. [J. S. D.], "*Musical Review*. Ole Bull's Concert," *The Harbinger* 1 (June 28, 1845): 44–45.

28. [J. S. D.], "*Musical Review*. Music in Boston During The Last Winter," *The Harbinger* 1 (August 2, 1845): 124.

29. [J. S. D.], "*Musical Review*. Music in Boston During The Last Winter," *The Harbinger* 1 (August 9, 1845): 140–41.

30. [J. S. D.], "*Musical Review*. Music in Boston During The Last Winter.—No. III: Concerts of the Boston Academy of Music," *The Harbinger* 1 (August 16, 1845): 154.

31. [J. S. D.], "*Musical Review*. Music in Boston," *The Harbinger* 1 (November 1, 1845): 329.

32. [J. S. D.], "*Musical Review*. The Virtuoso Age in Music. The New School of Pianists and Violinists," *The Harbinger* 1 (November 15, 1845): 362–64.

33. [J. S. D.], "*Musical Review*. The Virtuoso Age in Music. The New School of Pianists and Violinists," *The Harbinger* 1 (November 22, 1845): 378–81.

34. [J. S. D.], "*Musical Review*. Leopold De Meyer," *The Harbinger* 1 (November 29, 1845): 396–97.

35. [J. S. D.], "*Musical Review*. Mr. Edward Walker," *The Harbinger* 2 (April 25, 1846): 315–17.

36. Guarneri, *The Utopian Alternative,* 239.

37. [J. S. D.], "*Musical Review*. Great Concert in New York—The Philharmonic Society—Beethoven's Choral Symphony," *The Harbinger* 2 (May 16, 1846): 361–63.

38. *The Albion or British, Colonial and Foreign Weekly Gazette* 5 (May 16, 1846): 240. See also Vera Brodsky Lawrence, *Strong on Music: The New York Music Scene in the Days of George Templeton Strong, 1836–1875,* vol. 1, *Resonances, 1836–1850* (New York and Oxford: Oxford University Press, 1988), 366–69.

39. "Original Day Book," Castle Garden Manuscript Folder, New York City, 1843–1851, New-York Historical Society.

40. *The Albion or British, Colonial and Foreign Weekly Gazette* 5 (May 23, 1846): 252.

41. *Gazette and Times* (May 21, 1846).

42. There were several public "trials" before the London première, however. See David Benjamin Levy, "Early Performances of Beethoven's Ninth Symphony: A Documentary Study of Five Cities" (Ph.D. diss., Eastman School of Music, University of Rochester, 1980), 155, 160–62, 166, and 173. Levy traces the performance history of the Ninth Symphony in Vienna, London, Paris, Leipzig, and Berlin.

43. Ibid., 202–37, 241.

44. William Henry Channing, "Notice To the Associationists of the United States," *The Harbinger* 3 (June 13, 1846): 14–15.

45. Johnson, *First Performances in America,* 43. Johnson quotes short excerpts from Dwight's review of the U.S. première (42–43). For brief discussion of that first performance, see also Howard Shanet, *Philharmonic: A History of New York's Orchestra* (Garden City, N.Y.: Doubleday, 1975), 103–4.

46. [J. S. D.], "*Musical Review.* The Festival Concert in New York.—Beethoven's Choral Symphony," *The Harbinger* 3 (June 13, 1846): 9–11.

47. Ibid., 11.

48. Maynard Solomon, "The Ninth Symphony: A Search for Order," *Beethoven Essays* (Cambridge, Mass., and London: Harvard University Press, 1988), 3–32, esp. 30.

49. [J. S. D.], "*Musical Review.* The Festival Concert in New York.—Beethoven's Choral Symphony," *The Harbinger* 3 (June 13, 1846): 11.

CHAPTER TEN

1. [J. S. D.], "*Musical Review.* The Prospects For The Season," *The Harbinger* 3 (October 17, 1846): 301.

2. See [J. S. D.], "*Musical Review.* Boston Philharmonic Society," *The Harbinger* 4 (February 27, 1847): 185–86, and [J. S. D.], "*Art Review.* Music in Boston," *The Harbinger* 8 (January 6, 1849): 79.

3. [William W. Story], "*Musical Review.* Sixth Concert of the Boston Academy," *The Harbinger* 2 (March 7, 1846): 204.

4. [J. S. D.], "*Musical Review.* Boston Academy of Music. Boston Philharmonic Society," *The Harbinger* 4 (January 9, 1847): 77.

5. [J. S. D.], "*Review. Papers on Literature and Art.* By S. Margaret Fuller. In Two Parts . . . ," *The Harbinger* 3 (September 26, 1846): 250–52.

6. [J. S. D.], "*Musical Review.* 'Father Heinrich' in Boston," *The Harbinger* 3 (July 4, 1846): 58–59. Dwight did not list a specific work by Heinrich. However, it is identified on the program of that concert held on June 13, 1846. The program is included in William Treat Upton, *Anthony Philip Heinrich: A Nineteenth-Century Composer in America* (New York: Columbia University Press, 1939), this material follows p. 196.

7. [J. S. D.], "*Musical Review.* The Prospects For the Season," *The Harbinger* 3 (October 17, 1846): 301; [J. S. D.], "*Musical Review.* Sivori's Last Concert in Boston. The Boston Academy of Music," *The Harbinger* 3 (November 21, 1846): 381.

8. Bonds, *Wordless Rhetoric,* 163, 172.

9. Edward A. Lippman, "The Tonal Ideal of Romanticism," in *Festschrift*

Walter Wiora, ed. Ludwig Finscher and Christoph-Hellmut Mahling (Kassel: Bärenreiter, 1967), 419.

10. See Eggebrecht, *Zur Geschichte der Beethoven-Rezeption,* as cited in Leo Treitler, "History, Criticism, and Beethoven's Ninth Symphony," *Nineteenth-Century Music* 3 (1980): 201.

Works Cited

Primary Sources

The Albion or British, Colonial and Foreign Weekly Gazette 5 (May 16, 1846): 240 and (May 23, 1846): 252.

Apthorp, William Foster. "John Sullivan Dwight." *Boston Evening Transcript* (September 5, 1893). Reprinted in Apthorp, *Musicians and Music-Lovers and Other Essays.* 5th ed. New York: Charles Scribner's Sons, 1908. Reprint. Freeport, N.Y.: Books for Libraries Press, 1972, 277–86.

[Arnim, Bettina Brentano von]. *Goethes Briefwechsel mit einem Kinde.* Berlin: F. Dümmler, 1835. Translated, in part, by [Arnim] as *Goethe's Correspondence with a Child.* London: Longman, Orme, Brown, Green, and Longman, 1839.

Beethoven, Ludwig van. *Cinquième Sinfonie en ut mineur: C moll de Louis van Beethoven. Oeuvre 67. Partition.* Leipzig: Breitkopf & Härtel, [1826].

———. *Siebente Grosse Sinfonie in A dur von Ludwig van Beethoven. 92tes Werk. Vollständige Partitur.* Vienna: S. A. Steiner & Comp., [1816].

———. *Sixième Sinfonie Pastorale en fa majeur: F Dur de Louis van Beethoven. Oeuvre 68. Partition.* Leipzig: Breitkopf & Härtel, [1826].

Bellows, Henry W. Autograph letter signed to John Sullivan Dwight, October 25, 1836. Ms. E.4.1 no. 10. Dwight Papers, Rare Book Room, Boston Public Library.

———. Autograph letter signed to John S. Dwight, October 5, 1841. Ms. E.4.1 no. 36. Dwight Papers, Rare Book Room, Boston Public Library.

———. Autograph letter signed to John S. Dwight, December 15, 1842. Ms. E.4.1 no. 39. Dwight Papers, Rare Book Room, Boston Public Library.

———. Autograph letter signed to John S. Dwight, December 18, 1842. Ms. E.4.1 no. 41. Dwight Papers, Rare Book Room, Boston Public Library.

Boston Daily Evening Transcript. Performance and lecture dates and announcements (January, February, and March 1842).

Boston Musical Visitor, Devoted to Vocal and Instrumental Music, and Published by A Musical Association 3 (October 24, 1843): 177–78.

Brisbane, Albert. *A Concise Exposition of the Doctrine of Association, or Plan for a Re-organization of Society.* New York: J. S. Redfield, 1843.

Brisbane, Albert. *Albert Brisbane, A Mental Biography with a Character Study by his wife, Redelia Brisbane.* Boston: Arena Publishing Company, 1893.

Brisbane, A.[lbert]. Autograph letter signed to John S. Dwight, December 2, [18]45. Ms. E.4.1 no. 52. Dwight Papers, Rare Book Room, Boston Public Library.

B.[risbane], A.[lbert]. Autograph letter signed to John S. Dwight, December 15, 1845. Ms. E.4.1 no. 53. Dwight Papers, Rare Book Room, Boston Public Library.

B.[risbane], A.[lbert]. Autograph letter signed to John S. Dwight, December 30, [18]45. Ms. E.4.1 no. 54. Dwight Papers, Rare Book Room, Boston Public Library.

Brisbane, Albert. "On Association and Attractive Industry." *The United States Magazine, and Democratic Review* 10 (1842): 30–44, 167–81, 321–36, 560–80.

Brisbane, Albert. *Social Destiny of Man: or, Association and Reorganization of Industry.* Philadelphia: C. F. Stollmeyer, 1840.

Brooks, Charles Timothy. Autograph letter signed to John Sullivan Dwight, March 12, 1834. Autograph File. Houghton Library, Harvard University.

———. Autograph letter signed to John Sullivan Dwight, May 26, 1834. Autograph File. Houghton Library, Harvard University.

———. Autograph letter signed to John S. Dwight, May 11, 1837. Autograph File. Houghton Library, Harvard University.

Carlyle, Thomas. Autograph letter signed to John Sullivan Dwight, March 14, 1839. Amy Lowell Autograph Collection. Houghton Library, Harvard University.

[Carlyle, Thomas]. *The Life of Friedrich Schiller: Comprehending an Examination of His Works.* London: Taylor and Hessey, 1825.

Channing, William Ellery. *Charge.* Boston: [Weeks, Jordan, and Company], 1840.

Channing, William Henry. "Notice to the Associationists of the United States." *The Harbinger* 3 (June 13, 1846): 14–15.

Charlton, David, ed., and Martyn Clarke, trans. *E. T. A. Hoffmann's Musical*

Writings: "Kreisleriana," "The Poet and the Composer," "Music Criticism." Cambridge and New York: Cambridge University Press, 1989.

[Chorley, Henry F.] F. C. "Foreign Correspondence." *The Athenaeum: Journal of English and Foreign Literature, Science, and the Fine Arts* 527 (December 2, 1837): 881.

C., H. F. [Chorley, Henry F.] "Review. *The London and Westminster Review.* April–July 1839. Article III. *The Pianoforte.*" In [Hach and Hayward], *The Musical Magazine* 1 (July 20, 1839): 232–35; (August 3, 1839): 248–52; (August 17, 1839): 261–65; (September 14, 1839): 293–98; (October 12, 1839): 323–28.

Codman, John Thomas. *Brook Farm: Historic and Personal Memoirs.* Boston: Arena Publishing Company, 1894. Reprint. New York: AMS Press, 1971.

Dana, Charles A. *A Lecture on Association, in its Connection with Religion, Delivered before the New England Fourier Society, in Boston, March 7th, 1844.* Boston: Benjamin H. Greene, For the Society, 1844.

Dwight, J. S. "Academy of Music—Beethoven's Symphonies." *The Pioneer.* Edited by J. R. Lowell and R. B. Carter (January–February 1843): 26–28, 56–60.

Dwight, John S. "Address, Delivered Before the Harvard Musical Association, August 25th, 1841." In [Hach], *The Musical Magazine* 3 (August 28, 1841): 257–72.

D., J. S. [Dwight, John S.]. "Art. II.—*The Music of Nature; or, An Attempt to prove that what is passionate and pleasing in the Art of Singing, Speaking, and Performing upon Musical Instruments, is derived from the Sounds of the Animated World. With curious and interesting Illustrations.* By William Gardiner. Boston: J. H. Wilkins & R. B. Carter. 1837. [*sic*] 8vo. pp. 505." *The Christian Examiner and General Review* 25 (September 1838–January 1839): 23–36.

D., J. S. "Art. VI.—*William Tell; a Drama, in five Acts.* From the German of Schiller. Providence: B. Cranston & Co., 1838. 12 mo. pp. 120." *The Christian Examiner* (January 1839): 385–91.

[D., J. S.]. "*Art Review.* Music in Boston." *The Harbinger* 8 (January 6, 1849): 79. This and all subsequent citations to the *Harbinger* refer to the complete set located at the Rare Book and Special Collections Division of the Library of Congress, Washington, D.C.

Dwight, John S. Autograph letter signed to James F. Clarke, March 10, 1837. Ms. E.4.1 no. 12. Dwight Papers, Rare Book Room, Boston Public Library.

Dwight, John S. Autograph letter signed to Henry W. Bellows, November 17, 1842. Bellows Papers. Massachusetts Historical Society.

D., J. S. Autograph letter signed to George Ripley, March 16, 1846. Ms. E.4.1 no. 60. Dwight Papers, Rare Book Room, Boston Public Library.

D. [Dwight]. "The Concerts of the Past Winter." *The Dial* 1 (July 1840): 124–34.

Dwight, John S. Dwight Papers, Ms. E.4.1. Rare Book Room, Boston Public Library.

Dwight, John S., ed. *Dwight's Journal of Music, A Paper of Art and Literature.* Boston, 1852–1881. Reprint. New York and London: Johnson Reprint, 1968.

[D., J. S.]. "Fourier's Writings." *The Harbinger* 1 (November 1, 1845): 333–35.

[Dwight, J. S.]. "H. M. A." Brief manuscript containing a historical sketch of the Harvard Musical Association, 1852. Harvard Musical Association Library, Boston.

Dwight, J. S. "Handel and his 'Messiah.'" *The United States Magazine, and Democratic Review* 12 (March 1843): 264–79.

Dwight, J. S. "Haydn." *The United States Magazine, and Democratic Review* 14 (January 1844): 17–25.

D. [Dwight]. "Ideals of Every-Day Life, I and II." *The Dial* 1 (January and April 1841): 307–11, 446–61.

[D., J. S.]. "Individuality in Association." *The Harbinger* 1 (October 4, 1845): 264–66.

Dwight, John S. *A Lecture on Association, in its Connection with Education, Delivered before the New England Fourier Society, in Boston, February 29th, 1844.* Boston: Benjamin H. Greene, For the Society, 1844.

Dwight, J. S. "Mozart." *The United States Magazine, and Democratic Review* 13 (November 1843): 465–73.

D., J. S. "Music, as a Branch of Popular Education." *Boston Musical Gazette: A Semi-Monthly Journal Devoted to the Science of Music* 1 (May 16, 1838): 9–10.

[D., J. S.]. "*Musical Review.*" *The Harbinger* 1 (June 14, 1845): 12–13.

[D., J. S.]. "*Musical Review.* Boston Academy of Music. Boston Philharmonic Society." *The Harbinger* 4 (January 9, 1847): 76–77.

[D., J. S.]. "*Musical Review.* Boston Philharmonic Society." *The Harbinger* 4 (February 27, 1847): 185–86.

[D., J. S.]. "*Musical Review.* 'Father Heinrich' in Boston." *The Harbinger* 3 (July 4, 1846): 58–59.

[D., J. S.]. "*Musical Review.* The Festival Concert in New York.—Beethoven's Choral Symphony." *The Harbinger* 3 (June 13, 1846): 9–11.

[D., J. S.]. "*Musical Review*. Great Concert in New York—The Philharmonic Society—Beethoven's Choral Symphony." *The Harbinger* 2 (May 16, 1846): 361–63.

[D., J. S.]. "*Musical Review*. Leopold De Meyer." *The Harbinger* 1 (November 29, 1845): 396–97.

[D., J. S.]. "*Musical Review*. Mr. Edward Walker." *The Harbinger* 2 (April 25, 1846): 315–18.

[D., J. S.]. "*Musical Review*. Music in Boston." *The Harbinger* 1 (November 1, 1845): 329–32.

[D., J. S.]. "*Musical Review*. Music in Boston During The Last Winter." *The Harbinger* 1 (August 2, 1845): 123–24.

[D., J. S.]. "*Musical Review*. Music in Boston During The Last Winter." *The Harbinger* 1 (August 9, 1845): 139–41.

[D., J. S.]. "*Musical Review*. Music in Boston During The Last Winter.—No. III: Concerts of the Boston Academy of Music." *The Harbinger* 1 (August 16, 1845): 154–57.

[D., J. S.]. "*Musical Review*. Music in Boston During The Last Winter. No. IV." *The Harbinger* 1 (August 30, 1845): 188–89.

[D., J. S.]. "*Musical Review*. Ole Bull's Concert." *The Harbinger* 1 (June 28, 1845): 44–45.

[D., J. S.]. "*Musical Review*. The Prospects For The Season." *The Harbinger* 3 (October 17, 1846): 301.

[D., J. S.]. "*Musical Review*. Sivori's Last Concert in Boston. The Boston Academy of Music." *The Harbinger* 3 (November 21, 1846): 379–81.

[D., J. S.]. "*Musical Review*. The Virtuoso Age in Music. The New School of Pianists and Violinists." *The Harbinger* 1 (November 15, 1845): 362–64 and (November 22, 1845): 378–81.

[Dwight, John S.]. "On Music." Autograph manuscript. Ms. fC.1.7 v.3. Dwight Papers, Rare Book Room, Boston Public Library.

D., J. S. "On the Proper Character of Poetry and Music for Public Worship." *The Christian Examiner and General Review* 21 (November 1836): 254–63.

Dwight, John S. "The Pierian Sodality and Earlier Musical Clubs of Harvard College. By John S. Dwight. Reminiscences of an Ex-Pierian. (Samuel Jennison). From the Harvard Book, 1875." In a printed account with manuscript cover and marginal annotations in Dwight's hand, Harvard Musical Association Library, Boston. [*The Harvard Book* was compiled by F. O. Vaile and H. A. Clark. Cambridge, Mass.: Welch, Bigelow, 1875].

D. [Dwight]. "The Religion of Beauty." *The Dial* 1 (July 1840): 17–22.

[Dwight, J. S.]. *Report Made at a Meeting of the Honorary and Immediate Members of the Pierian Sodality, in Harvard University, Cambridge, August 30th, 1837, with a Record of the Meeting.* Cambridge, Mass.: Folsom, Wells, and Thurston, 1837. Reprinted in *Boston Musical Gazette* (June 27 and July 11, 1838): 33–34, 42.

D., J. S. "Review of Gardiner's *Music of Nature* By Rev. J. S. Dwight. [From the *Christian Examiner*]." *Boston Musical Gazette: A Semi-Monthly Journal Devoted to the Science of Music* 1 (September 19, 1838): 81–82 and (October 3, 1838): 89–90.

[D., J. S.]. "*Review. Papers on Literature and Art.* By S. Margaret Fuller. In Two Parts . . ." *The Harbinger* 3 (September 26, 1846): 249–52.

[Dwight, J. S.]. "Sacred Music." *The American Monthly Magazine* (November 1836): 447–57.

Dwight, John S., trans. with notes. "Select Minor Poems, Translated from the German of Goethe and Schiller. Boston 1839." Editor's manuscript, Ms. G.38.25. Dwight Papers, Rare Book Room, Boston Public Library.

Dwight, John S., trans. with notes. *Select Minor Poems, Translated from the German of Goethe and Schiller.* Boston: Hilliard, Gray, and Company, 1839.

Felton, Cornelius C. Autograph letter signed, April 25, 1832. Ms. E.4.1 no. 3. Dwight Papers, Rare Book Room, Boston Public Library.

Fétis, François-Joseph. "Beethoven (Louis van)." In *Biographie Universelle des Musiciens et Bibliographie Générale de la Musique.* Brussels: Leroux, 1835, 2:100–112.

Fink, [Christian] G.[ottfried] W.[ilhelm]. "Music in Germany." In [Hach], *The Musical Magazine* 3 (May 22, 1841): 145–53 and (June 5, 1841): 161–68.

Fink, G.[ottfried] W.[ilhelm]. "Symphonie oder Sinfonie." In *Encyclopädie der gesammten musikalischen Wissenschaften, oder Universal-Lexicon der Tonkunst.* Edited by Gustav Schilling. Stuttgart: Franz Heinrich Kühler, 1835–1838, 6:541–51.

Fink, G. W. "*Ueber die Symphonie,* als Beitrag zur Geschichte und Aesthetik derselben." *Allgemeine musikalische Zeitung* 31 (August 5, 1835): 505–11; 32 (August 12, 1835): 521–24; 34 (August 26, 1835): 557–63.

Follen, Charles. Autograph letter signed, July 17, 1832. Ms. E.4.1 no. 4. Dwight Papers, Rare Book Room, Boston Public Library.

Fourier, Charles. *Oeuvres Complètes de Charles Fourier,* 12 vols., with introduction by Simone Debout Oleszkiewicz. Grenoble: éditions anthropos, 1966–68.

Fourteenth Annual Report of The Trustees of the Perkins Institution and Massachusetts Asylum For the Blind, to the Corporation. Cambridge, [Mass.]: n.p., 1846.

Fuller, S. M. Autograph letter signed to J. S. Dwight, May 31, 1837. Ms. E.4.1 no. 15. Dwight Papers, Rare Book Room, Boston Public Library.

F. [Fuller, Margaret]. "Lives of the Great Composers, Haydn, Mozart, Handel, Bach, Beethoven." *The Dial* 2 (October 1841): 148–203.

Gardiner, William. *The Music of Nature; or, An Attempt to Prove that What is Passionate and Pleasing in the Art of Singing, Speaking, and Performing Upon Musical Instruments, Is Derived From the Sounds of the Animated World.* London: Longman, Orme, Brown, & Longman, 1832. Reprint. Boston: J. H. Wilkins & R. B. Carter, 1838.

————, comp. *Sacred Melodies, from Haydn, Mozart and Beethoven, Adapted to the best English Poets, and Appropriated to the use of the British Church.* London: Clementi, [1812, 1815].

Gazette and Times (March 12 and 26, 1846; May 21, 1846).

[Hach]. "Advancement of Music." *The Musical Magazine* 3 (January 9, 1841): 19–23.

[Hach]. "The Art of Music in Our Periodical Literature." *The Musical Magazine* 3 (October 23, 1841): 330–34 and (November 6, 1841): 345–50.

Hach, H. Theodor. Autograph letter signed to R. E. Apthorp, January 2, 1845. "Correspondence on Chamber Concerts, 1844–1846." Harvard Musical Association Library, Boston.

[Hach, H. Theodor]. "Beethoven's Symphonies." *The Musical Magazine* 3 (April 24, 1842): 392–406.

[Hach]. "Biography. Beethoven." *The Musical Magazine* 2 (September 12, 1840): 289–96; (October 10, 1840): 321–28; and (October 24, 1840): 356–60.

————. "Concerts." *The Musical Magazine* 2 (January 4, 1840): 15–16.

————. "Concerts." *The Musical Magazine* 2 (March 28, 1840): 110–12.

————. "Concerts." *The Musical Magazine* 2 (February 20, 1841): 63–64.

————. "Fidelio." *The Musical Magazine* 3 (November 20, 1841): 357–61.

————. "Handel and Haydn. The Messiah and The Creation. *Dial.*" In *The Musical Magazine* 2 (August 1, 1840): 256.

————. "Lectures on Music." *The Musical Magazine* 2 (July 18, 1840): 237–40.

————. "The Messiah and The Creation. (From *The Dial*)." In *The Musical Magazine* 2 (August 15, 1840): 263–65.

————. "Music Performed in the Boston Academy of Music's Concerts, During the Past Winter." *The Musical Magazine* 3 (May 8, 1841): 134–35.

————. "Ninth Annual Report of the Boston Academy of Music—1841." *The Musical Magazine* 3 (August 28, 1841): 273–75.

————. "Proceedings of the Musical Convention of 1840." *The Musical Magazine* 3 (April 10, 1841): 122–28.

Hach. "Prospectus." *The Musical Magazine* 3 (January 9, 1841): 1–2.

[Hach, H. Theodor, and T. B. Hayward]. "The Late Musical Season." *The Musical Magazine* 1 (July 20, 1839): 235–39.

————. "Miscellaneous Gleanings, From The Musical Library." *The Musical Magazine* 1 (May 25, 1839): 172–76.

————. "New Musical Publications. *The Life of Haydn* . . ." *The Musical Magazine* 1 (June 8, 1839): 189–90.

————. "Prospectus." *The Musical Magazine* 1 (January 5, 1839): 1–3.

————. "Review. *The Life of Haydn* . . ." *The Musical Magazine* 1 (August 31, 1839): 286–88.

————, eds. *The Musical Magazine; or Repository of Musical Science, Literature, and Intelligence.* Boston: Otis, Broaders and Company, 1839; Boston: George P. Reed, 1840, 1842. All references are to the three-volume set located at the Music Division, Library of Congress, Washington, D.C.

Hoffmann, E. T. A. "The Cadenza." In [Hach], *The Musical Magazine* 1 (August 31, 1839): 280–84; (September 14, 1839): 298–301; (September 28, 1839): 313–18; (October 12, 1839): 328–30; (October 26, 1839): 342–45.

[Hoffmann, E. T. A.]. "Recension." *Allgemeine musikalische Zeitung* 12 (July 4 and 11, 1810): 630–42, 652–59.

Hoffmann, E. T. A. *Schriften zur Musik, Nachlese.* Edited by Friedrich Schnapp. Munich: Winkler-Verlag, 1963.

————. "The Poet and the Composer." In [Hach], *The Musical Magazine* 2 (July 4, 1840): 209–14; (July 18, 1840): 225–31; (August 1, 1840): 241–47.

————. "Thoughts on the High Value of Music." In [Hach], *The Musical Magazine* 3 (March 6, 1841): 65–70.

Hogarth, George. *Musical History, Biography, and Criticism.* London: J. W. Parker, 1835.

Kahlert, [Karl] Aug.[ust]. "On the Romantic in Music." In [Hach], *The Musical Magazine* 2 (May 9, 1840): 149–53.

Kahlert, [Karl] August. *Tonleben. Novellen und vermischte Aufsätze.* Breslau: Georg Philipp Aderholz, 1838.

Kalkbrenner, Fréd.[éric]. *Collection Complète des Symphonies de Beethoven Arrangées pour Piano seul.* Paris: Schonenberger, [1840], 10 vols. in 1.

Kirby, Georgianna Bruce. *Years of Experience*. New York: G. P. Putnam's Sons, 1887.

Lowell, J. R., and R. B. Carter, eds. "Introduction." *The Pioneer* (January 1843): 1–3.

M., AB. [ABM. Marx, Adolf Bernhard]. "Beethoven, Ludwig von." In *Encyclopädie der gesammten musikalischen Wissenschaften, oder Universal-Lexicon der Tonkunst*. Edited by Gustav Schilling. Stuttgart: Franz Heinrich Kühler, 1835–1838, 1:513–20.

Marx, Adolph [Adolf] Bernhard. *Die Lehre von der musikalischen Komposition, praktisch-theoretisch, zum Selbstunterricht, oder als Leitfaden bei Privatunterweisung und öffentlichen Vorträgen*. Leipzig: Breitkopf & Härtel, 1838.

Mason, Lowell, comp. *The Boston Handel and Haydn Society Collection of Church Music*. Boston: Richardson and Lord, 1822. Reprint, with introduction by H. Wiley Hitchcock. New York: Da Capo Press, 1973.

Momigny, J.[érôme]-J.[oseph] de. *Cours Complet d'Harmonie et de Composition, d'après une théorie neuve et générale de la musique*. Paris: Chez l'auteur, 1806.

———. *La Seule Vraie Théorie de la Musique Utile à ceux qui excellent dans cet Art comme à ceux qui en sont aux premiers Élémens, ou Moyen le plus court pour devenir Mélodiste, Harmoniste, Contrepointiste et Compositeur*. Paris: Au Magasin de Musique de l'Auteur, [1821].

The New-York Daily Tribune. Lecture advertisements, reviews, and city items (March 1846).

"Original Day Book." Castle Garden Manuscript Folder, New York City, 1843–1851. New-York Historical Society.

Orvis, Marianne Dwight. *Letters from Brook Farm, 1844–1847*. Edited by Amy L. Reed, with a note on Anna Q. T. Parsons by Helen Dwight Orvis. Poughkeepsie, N.Y.: Vassar College, 1928.

Osgood, Samuel. Autograph letter signed to John Sullivan Dwight, February 24, 1834. Ms. E.4.1 no. 6. Dwight Papers, Rare Book Room, Boston Public Library.

———. Autograph letter signed to John S. Dwight, November 21, 1840. Ms. E.4.1 no. 29. Dwight Papers, Rare Book Room, Boston Public Library.

———. Autograph letter signed to John S. Dwight, April 9, 1841. Ms. E.4.1 no. 31. Dwight Papers, Rare Book Room, Boston Public Library.

Panofka, H.[enry]. "Beethoven's Sonata in A Minor. Extract from the Journal of an Artist." In [Hach and Hayward], *The Musical Magazine* 1 (February 2, 1839): 35–39 and (February 16, 1839): 49–52.

Pickering, H. W. Manuscript "Librarian's Report," August 25, 1841. Harvard Musical Association Library, Boston.

Porter, William S. *The Musical Cyclopedia: or the Principles of Music Consid-ered As a Science and an Art; Embracing a Complete Musical Dictionary, And the Outline of a Musical Grammar, and of the Theory of Sounds and Laws of Harmony; With Directions for The Practice of Vocal and Instrumental Music, And A Description of Musical Instruments.* Boston: James Loring, 1834.

Programs of the Chamber Concerts for 1844 and 1845. Harvard Musical Association Library, Boston.

Quincy, Josiah. Autograph letter signed, April 26, 1832. Ms. E.4.1 no. 2. Dwight Papers, Rare Book Room, Boston Public Library.

"Records of the Arionic Sodality—Cambridge 1813." Bound manuscript book. Harvard Musical Association Library, Boston.

"Records of the Board of Directors of the General Association of Members of the Pierian Sodality." Manuscript book. Harvard Musical Associa-tion Library, Boston.

"Records of the Harvard Musical Association. 1840. From Its Formation in 1837." Manuscript book. Harvard Musical Association Library, Boston.

Reicha, A.[nton]. *Vollständiges Lehrbuch der musikalischen Composition.* Translated from French of *Cours de composition musicale* by Carl Cz-erny. Paris: Gambaro, 1816–1818; Vienna: Ant. Diabelli & Comp., [1832].

Ripley, George. Autograph letter signed to John S. Dwight, July 7, 1840. Ms. E.4.1 no. 24. Dwight Papers, Rare Book Room, Boston Public Library.

R.[ipley], G.[eorge]. Autograph letter signed to John S. Dwight, March 19, 1846. Ms. E.4.1 no. 61. Dwight Papers, Rare Book Room, Boston Public Library.

Ripley, George. *The Claims of the Age on the Work of the Evangelist. A Sermon Preached at the Ordination of Mr. John Sullivan Dwight, As Pastor of the Second Congregational Church in Northampton, May 20, 1840.* Boston: Weeks, Jordan, and Company, 1840.

[Ripley, George]. "*Record of the Months.* Select List of Recent Publications." *The Dial* 1 (October 1840): 265–66.

Ripley, Sophia. Autograph letter signed to John S. Dwight, May 6, [1841]. Ms. E.4.1 no. 34. Dwight Papers, Rare Book Room, Boston Public Library.

———. Autograph letter signed to John S. Dwight, March 14, [1846]. Ms. E.4.1 no. 59. Dwight Papers, Rare Book Room, Boston Public Library.

Roelker, Bernard. Manuscript "Librarian's Report," August 26, 1845. Har-vard Musical Association Library, Boston.

Rousseau, J.[ean] J.[acques]. "Imitation." In *Dictionnaire de Musique*. Paris: la veuve Duchesne, 1768, 253–54.

[Rousseau, Jean-Jacques]. "Projet Concernant de Nouveaux Signes pour la Musique, Lu par l'Auteur à l'Académie [Royale] des Sciences, le 22 Août 1742" and "Dissertation sur la Musique moderne." In *Traités Sur la Musique*. Geneva, 1781.

Schiller, [Friedrich]. ["An die Freude."] "Hymn to Joy." Translated by D. [Dwight]. *The New-England Magazine* 8 (May 1835): 380–81.

Schiller, Friedrich. *On the Aesthetic Education of Man, in a Series of Letters.* Edited and translated by Elizabeth M. Wilkinson and Leonard A. Willoughby. Oxford: Clarendon Press, 1967. Orig. pub. 1795.

"Sch., Dr." [Schilling]. "Tonart—C-Moll." In *Encyclopädie der gesammten musikalischen Wissenschaften, oder Universal-Lexicon der Tonkunst.* Edited by Gustav Schilling. Stuttgart: Franz Heinrich Kühler, 1835–1838, 2:266–67.

[Schindler, Anton Felix]. *The Life of Beethoven, Including His Correspondence with His Friends, Numerous Characteristic Traits, and Remarks on His Musical Works.* Edited by Ignace [Ignaz] Moscheles. 2 vols. London: Henry Colburn, 1841.

Stendhal [Marie-Henri Beyle]. *The Life of Haydn, in a Series of Letters written at Vienna; Followed by The Life of Mozart, with Observations on Metastasio, and on the Present State of Music in France and Italy.* Translated by [Robert Brewin] from the French of L. A. C. Bombet, with Notes by the Author of *The Sacred Melodies* [William Gardiner]. London: John Murray, 1817.

[Story, William W.] *"Musical Review.* Sixth Concert of the Boston Academy." *The Harbinger* 2 (March 7, 1846): 204–5 and (March 14, 1846): 218–20.

Thayer, Alexander Wheelock. *Ludwig van Beethovens Leben.* Translated and edited by Hermann Deiters, 1st ed. in 3 vols. Berlin: F. Schneider, 1866; Weber, 1872, 1879.

T., J. F. [Tuckerman, John Francis]. "Art. III.—*Biographie Universelle des Musiciens,* par. F. J. Fétis.—Paris, 1835. Art. *Beethoven.*" *The Boston Quarterly Review* 11 (July 1840): 332–57.

Wegeler, Franz Gerhard, and Ferdinand Ries. *Biographische Notizen über Ludwig van Beethoven.* Coblenz: K. Bädeker, 1838.

Woodbury, I. [Isaac] B. *The Elements of Musical Composition and Thorough-Base* [sic]: *Together With Rules For Arranging Music For The Full Orchestra and Military Bands.* Boston: Charles H. Keith, 1844.

SECONDARY SOURCES

Abrams, M. H. *Natural Supernaturalism: Tradition and Revolution in Romantic Literature.* New York: W. W. Norton, 1971.

Anderson, Emily, coll., trans., and ed. with introduction. *The Letters of Beethoven.* 3 vols. London: Macmillan, 1961. Reprint. New York and London: W. W. Norton, 1985.

Baltzell, E. Digby. *Puritan Boston and Quaker Philadelphia: Two Protestant Ethics and the Spirit of Class Authority and Leadership.* New York: Free Press; London: Collier-Macmillan, 1979.

Barbour, Brian M., ed. *American Transcendentalism: An Anthology of Criticism.* Notre Dame and London: University of Notre Dame Press, 1973.

Beecher, Jonathan, and Richard Bienvenu, trans. and ed., with introduction. *The Utopian Vision of Charles Fourier: Selected Texts on Work, Love, and Passionate Attraction.* Boston: Beacon Press, 1971.

"Beethoven à Paris." *Revue Internationale de Musique Française* 22 (1987): 7–70.

Bent, Ian D. "Analysis." In *The New Grove Dictionary of Music and Musicians.* Edited by Stanley Sadie. London: Macmillan, 1980, 1:340–88.

Bloom, Peter Anthony. "Critical Reaction to Beethoven in France: François-Joseph Fétis." *Revue belge de musicologie* 26–27 (1972–73): 67–83.

Boetticher, Wolfgang. "Fink, Gottfried Wilhelm." In *Die Musik in Geschichte und Gegenwart.* Edited by Friedrich Blume. Kassel and Basel: Bärenreiter, 1955, 4:cols. 223–27.

———. "Kahlert, Karl August Thimotheus." In *Die Musik in Geschichte und Gegenwart.* Edited by Friedrich Blume. Kassel and Basel: Bärenreiter, 1958, 7:cols. 425–27.

Boller, Paul F., Jr. *American Transcendentalism, 1830–1860: An Intellectual Inquiry.* New York: G. P. Putnam's Sons, 1974.

Bonds, Mark Evan. *Wordless Rhetoric: Musical Form and the Metaphor of the Oration.* Cambridge, Mass. and London: Harvard University Press, 1991.

Boyer, Jean. *Le 'Romantisme' de Beethoven: Contribution à l'Étude de la Formation d'une Légende.* Paris: H. Didier, 1938.

Broder, Nathan. "An Unknown Letter by Beethoven." *Juilliard Review* 4 (Winter 1956–57): 16–20.

Broyles, Michael. "Music and Class Structure in Antebellum Boston." *Journal of the American Musicological Society* 44 (1991): 451–93.

———. *"Music of the Highest Class": Elitism and Populism in Antebellum Boston.* New Haven and London: Yale University Press, 1992.

———, ed. *A Yankee Musician in Europe: The 1837 Journals of Lowell Mason.* Ann Arbor, Mich. and London: UMI Research Press, 1990.

Buell, Lawrence. *Literary Transcendentalism: Style and Vision in the American Renaissance.* Ithaca and London: Cornell University Press, 1973.

Burkholder, J. Peter. *Charles Ives: The Ideas Behind the Music.* New Haven and London: Yale University Press, 1985.

Burnham, Scott. "Criticism, Faith, and the *Idee:* A. B. Marx's Early Reception of Beethoven." *Nineteenth-Century Music* 13 (1990): 183–92.

Call, William Anson. "A Study of the Transcendental Aesthetic Theories of John S. Dwight and Charles E. Ives and the Relationship of These Theories to Their Respective Work as Music Critic and Composer." D.M.A. diss., University of Illinois at Urbana-Champaign, 1971.

Chan, Anne Hui-Hua. "Beethoven in the United States to 1865." Ph.D. diss., University of North Carolina, 1976.

Chmaj, Betty E. "Fry versus Dwight: American Music's Debate over Nationality." *American Music* 3 (1985): 63–84.

Coker, Wilson. *Music and Meaning: A Theoretical Introduction to Musical Aesthetics.* New York: Free Press; London: Collier-Macmillan, 1972.

Comini, Alessandra. *The Changing Image of Beethoven: A Study in Mythmaking.* New York: Rizzoli, 1987.

Cook, Nicholas. *Beethoven: Symphony No. 9.* Cambridge: Cambridge University Press, 1993.

Cooke, George Willis. *John Sullivan Dwight: Brook-Farmer, Editor, and Critic of Music; A Biography.* Boston: Small, Maynard, 1898. Reprint. New York: Da Capo Press, 1969.

Crawford, Richard. "Musical Learning in Nineteenth-Century America." *American Music* 1 (1983): 1–11.

Crowe, Charles. *George Ripley: Transcendentalist and Utopian Socialist.* Athens: University of Georgia Press, 1967.

Curtis, Edith Roelker. *A Season in Utopia: The Story of Brook Farm.* New York: Nelson, 1961.

Daemmrich, Horst S. *The Shattered Self: E. T. A. Hoffmann's Tragic Vision.* Detroit: Wayne State University Press, 1973.

Dahlhaus, Carl. *The Idea of Absolute Music.* Translated by Roger Lustig. Chicago and London: University of Chicago Press, 1989.

DeKeyser, Paul. "Kalkbrenner, Frédéric." In *The New Grove Dictionary of Music and Musicians.* Edited by Stanley Sadie. London: Macmillan, 1980, 9:777–79.

Delano, Sterling F. *"The Harbinger" and New England Transcendentalism: A Portrait of Associationism in America.* Rutherford, N.J.: Fairleigh Dickinson University Press; London: Associated University Presses, 1983.

Dobson, Eleanor Robinette. "Dwight, John Sullivan." In *Dictionary of American Biography.* Edited by Allen Johnson and Dumas Malone. New York: Charles Scribner's Sons, 1930, 5:567–68.

Duberman, Martin. *James Russell Lowell.* Boston: Houghton Mifflin, 1966.

Eggebrecht, Hans Heinrich. *Zur Geschichte der Beethoven-Rezeption: Beethoven 1970.* Mainz: Akademie der Wissenschaften und der Literatur, 1972.

Eicke, Kurt-Erich. *Der Streit zwischen Adolph Bernhard Marx und Gottfried Wilhelm Fink um die Kompositionslehre.* Regensburg: Gustav Bosse Verlag, 1966.

Fertig, Walter L. "Dwight, John Sullivan." In *The New Grove Dictionary of American Music.* Edited by H. Wiley Hitchcock and Stanley Sadie. London: Macmillan; New York: Grove's Dictionaries of Music, 1986, 1:667–68.

———. "John Sullivan Dwight, Transcendentalist and Literary Amateur of Music." Ph.D. diss., University of Maryland, 1952.

Forbes, Elliot, rev. and ed. *Thayer's Life of Beethoven.* Princeton: Princeton University Press, 1967.

Guarneri, Carl J. *The Utopian Alternative: Fourierism in Nineteenth-Century America.* Ithaca and London: Cornell University Press, 1991.

Hatch, Christopher. "The Education of A. W. Thayer." *Musical Quarterly* 42 (1956): 355–65.

———. "Music for America: A Critical Controversy of the 1850's." *American Quarterly* 14 (1962): 578–86.

Hayden, Dolores. *Seven American Utopias: The Architecture of Communitarian Socialism, 1790–1975.* Cambridge, Mass. and London: MIT Press, 1976.

Heartz, Daniel. "Rousseau, Jean-Jacques." In *The New Grove Dictionary of Music and Musicians.* Edited by Stanley Sadie. London: Macmillan, 1980, 16:270–73.

Heath, William G. "John Sullivan Dwight." In *The Transcendentalists: A Review of Research and Criticism.* Edited by Joel Myerson. New York: Modern Language Association of America, 1984, 131–34.

Hepner, Arthur W. *Pro Bono Artium Musicarum: The Harvard Musical Association, 1837–1987.* [Boston]: Harvard Musical Association, 1987.

[Hoffmann, E. T. A.]. "Recension." *Allgemeine musikalische Zeitung* 12 (July 4 and 11, 1810). Translated by F. John Adams, Jr. In *Beethoven: Sym-*

phony No. 5 in C Minor. Edited by Elliott Forbes. New York: W. W. Norton, 1971, 150–63.

Howe, M. A. De Wolfe. *Boston: The Place and the People.* New York: Macmillan, 1903.

Huizinga, Johan. *Homo Ludens: A Study of the Play-Element in Culture.* Translation prepared partly from the author's English trans. New York: Roy Publishers, 1950. Reprint. Boston: Beacon Press, 1955.

Ikeler, A. Abbott. *Puritan Temper and Transcendental Faith: Carlyle's Literary Vision.* Columbus: Ohio State University Press, 1972.

Johnson, H. Earle. *First Performances in America to 1900: Works with Orchestra.* Detroit: Information Coordinators, 1979.

Johnson, James H. "Beethoven and the Birth of Romantic Musical Experience in France." *Nineteenth-Century Music* 15 (1991): 23–35.

Kinkeldey, Otto. "Beginnings of Beethoven in America." *Musical Quarterly* 13 (1927): 217–48.

Kivy, Peter. *The Corded Shell: Reflections on Musical Expression.* Princeton: Princeton University Press, 1980.

Kramer, Lawrence. *Music as Cultural Practice, 1800–1900.* Berkeley and Los Angeles: University of California Press, 1990.

Kunze, Stefan, gen. ed., with Theodor Schmid, Andreas Traub, and Gerda Burkhard. *Ludwig van Beethoven: Die Werke im Spiegel seiner Zeit; Gesammelte Konzertberichte und Rezensionen bis 1830.* Laaber: Laaber-Verlag, 1987.

Lawrence, Vera Brodsky. *Strong on Music: The New York Music Scene in the Days of George Templeton Strong, 1836–1875.* Vol. 1, *Resonances, 1836–1850.* New York and Oxford: Oxford University Press, 1988.

Lebow, Marcia Wilson. "A Systematic Examination of the *Journal of Music and Art* Edited by John Sullivan Dwight: 1852–1881, Boston, Massachusetts." Ph.D. diss., University of California, Los Angeles, 1970.

Levy, David Benjamin. "Early Performances of Beethoven's Ninth Symphony: A Documentary Study of Five Cities." Ph.D. diss., Eastman School of Music, University of Rochester, 1979, 1980.

Lippman, Edward A. "The Tonal Ideal of Romanticism." In *Festschrift Walter Wiora.* Edited by Ludwig Finscher and Christoph-Hellmut Mahling. Kassel: Bärenreiter, 1967, 419–26.

Lowens, Irving. "Writings about Music in the Periodicals of American Transcendentalism (1835–50)." *Journal of the American Musicological Society* 10 (1957): 71–85.

Manuel, Frank E., and Fritzie P. Manuel. *Utopian Thought in the Western World.* Cambridge, Mass.: Harvard University Press, Belknap Press, 1979.

Miller, Perry, ed. *The Transcendentalists: An Anthology.* Cambridge, Mass.: Harvard University Press, 1967.

Mitchell, Alice L. "Czerny, Carl." In *The New Grove Dictionary of Music and Musicians.* Edited by Stanley Sadie. London: Macmillan, 1980, 5:138–41.

Moyer, Birgitte. "Marx, Adolf Bernhard." In *The New Grove Dictionary of Music and Musicians.* Edited by Stanley Sadie. London: Macmillan, 1980, 11:739–41.

Myerson, Joel. *The New England Transcendentalists and the "Dial": A History of the Magazine and Its Contributors.* Rutherford, N.J.: Fairleigh Dickinson University Press; London: Associated University Presses, 1980.

Neubauer, John. *The Emancipation of Music from Language: Departure from Mimesis in Eighteenth-Century Aesthetics.* New Haven: Yale University Press, 1986.

Newman, William S. "The Beethoven Mystique in Romantic Art, Literature, and Music." *Musical Quarterly* 69 (1983): 354–87.

———. *The Sonata Since Beethoven.* 3d ed. New York and London: W. W. Norton, 1983.

Nye, Russel Blaine. *Society and Culture in America, 1830–1860.* The New American Nation Series, vol. 3. New York: Harper and Row, 1974.

Ochs, Michael. "A. W. Thayer, the Diarist, and the Late Mr. Brown: A Bibliography of Writings in *Dwight's Journal of Music.*" In *Beethoven Essays: Studies in Honor of Elliot Forbes.* Edited by Lewis Lockwood and Phyllis Benjamin. Cambridge, Mass.: Harvard University Department of Music, 1984, 78–95; distributed by Harvard University Press.

Parkany, J. Stephen. "Presentiments of the Colossal: E. T. A. Hoffmann and the Critical Tradition of Symphonic Drama." Paper presented at the Fifty-Fourth Annual Meeting of the American Musicological Society, Baltimore, Md., November 4, 1988.

Pemberton, Carol A. *Lowell Mason: His Life and Work.* Rev. ed. of Ph.D. diss., University of Minnesota, 1971. Ann Arbor, Mich.: UMI Research Press, 1985.

Pochmann, Henry A. *German Culture in America: Philosophical and Literary Influences, 1600–1900.* Madison: University of Wisconsin Press, 1957.

Rainbow, Bernarr. "Galin-Paris-Chevé Method." In *The New Grove Dictionary of Music and Musicians.* Edited by Stanley Sadie. London: Macmillan, 1980, 7:99–100.

———. "Mainzer, Joseph." In *The New Grove Dictionary of Music and Musicians.* Edited by Stanley Sadie. London: Macmillan, 1980, 11:539–40.

Rider, Daniel Edgar. "The Musical Thought and Activities of the New England Transcendentalists." Ph.D. diss., University of Minnesota, 1964.

Sablosky, Irving. *What They Heard: Music in America, 1852–1881, from the Pages of "Dwight's Journal of Music."* Baton Rouge and London: Louisiana State University Press, 1986.

Sahlin, Johanna C., ed. and trans. *Selected Letters of E. T. A. Hoffmann.* Chicago and London: University of Chicago Press, 1977.

Saloman, Ora Frishberg. "American Writers on Beethoven, 1838–1849: Dwight, Fuller, Cranch, Story." *American Music* 8 (1990): 12–28.

———. "Continental and English Foundations of J. S. Dwight's Early American Criticism of Beethoven's Ninth Symphony." *Journal of the Royal Musical Association* 119 part 2 (1994): 251–67.

———. "Dwight and Perkins on Wagner: A Controversy Within the American Cultivated Tradition, 1852–1854." In *Music and Civilization: Essays in Honor of Paul Henry Lang.* Edited by Edmond Strainchamps and Maria Rika Maniates, in collab. with Christopher Hatch. New York: W. W. Norton, 1984, 78–92.

———. "Fink, Hach, and Dwight's Beethoven in 1843–44." *Musical Quarterly* 76 (1992): 488–501.

———. "Margaret Fuller on Beethoven in America, 1839–1846." *Journal of Musicology* 10 (1992): 89–105.

———. "Margaret Fuller on Musical Life in Boston and New York, 1841–1846." *American Music* 6 (1988): 428–41.

Schafer, R. Murray. *E. T. A. Hoffmann and Music.* Toronto and Buffalo: University of Toronto Press, 1975.

Schmitz, Arnold. *Das romantische Beethovenbild.* 1927. Reprint. Darmstadt: Wissenschaftliche Buchgesellschaft, 1978.

Schnaus, Peter. *E. T. A. Hoffmann als Beethoven-Rezensent der Allgemeinen musikalischen Zeitung.* Munich and Salzburg: Musikverlag Katzbichler, 1977.

Schrade, Leo. *Beethoven in France: The Growth of an Idea.* 1942. Reprint. New York: Da Capo Press, 1978.

Shanet, Howard. *Philharmonic: A History of New York's Orchestra.* Garden City, N.Y.: Doubleday, 1975.

Solie, Ruth A. "Beethoven as Secular Humanist: Ideology and the Ninth Symphony in Nineteenth-Century Criticism." In *Explorations in Music, the Arts, and Ideas: Essays in Honor of Leonard B. Meyer.* Edited by Eugene Narmour and Ruth A. Solie. Stuyvesant, N.Y.: Pendragon Press, 1988, 1–42.

Solomon, Maynard. "Beethoven and Schiller." In *Beethoven Essays.* Cambridge, Mass. and London: Harvard University Press, 1988, 205–15.

———. "The Ninth Symphony: A Search for Order." In *Beethoven Essays.* Cambridge, Mass. and London: Harvard University Press, 1988, 3–32.

Spalding, Walter Raymond. *Music at Harvard: A Historical Review of Men and Events.* New York: Coward-McCann, 1935. Reprint. New York: Da Capo Press, 1977.

Steblin, Rita. *A History of Key Characteristics in the Eighteenth and Early Nineteenth Centuries.* Ann Arbor, Mich.: UMI Research Press, 1983.

Swift, Lindsay. *Brook Farm: Its Members, Scholars, and Visitors.* 1900. Reprint. New York: Corinth Books, 1961.

Symons, Julian. *Thomas Carlyle: The Life and Ideas of a Prophet.* Freeport, N.Y.: Books for Libraries Press, 1952.

Temperley, Nicholas. "Beethoven in London Concert Life, 1800–1850." *Music Review* 21 (1960): 207–14.

———. *Haydn: "The Creation."* Cambridge: Cambridge University Press, 1991.

Thomas, J. Wesley. "John Sullivan Dwight: A Translator of German Romanticism." *American Literature: A Journal of Literary History, Criticism, and Bibliography* 21 (1949–50): 427–41.

Treitler, Leo. "History, Criticism, and Beethoven's Ninth Symphony." *Nineteenth-Century Music* 3 (1980): 193–210.

Upton, William Treat. *Anthony Philip Heinrich: A Nineteenth-Century Composer in America.* New York: Columbia University Press, 1939.

Vogel, Stanley M. *German Literary Influences on the American Transcendentalists.* New Haven: Yale University Press, 1955.

Wallace, Robin. *Beethoven's Critics: Aesthetic Dilemmas and Resolutions during the Composer's Lifetime.* Cambridge: Cambridge University Press, 1986.

Warrack, John. "Fink, (Christian) Gottfried Wilhelm." In *The New Grove Dictionary of Music and Musicians.* Edited by Stanley Sadie. London: Macmillan, 1980, 6:584.

Waters, Edward. "John Sullivan Dwight: First American Critic of Music." *Musical Quarterly* 21 (1935): 69–88.

Weigand, Hermann J. "Schiller: Transfiguration of a Titan." In *A Schiller Symposium: In Observance of the Bicentenary of Schiller's Birth.* Edited by A. Leslie Willson. Department of Germanic Languages, University of Texas at Austin, 1960, 85–132.

Wellek, René. "The Minor Transcendentalists and German Philosophy." *New England Quarterly* 15 (1942): 652–80.

Wilshere, Jonathan. "Gardiner, William." In *The New Grove Dictionary of Music and Musicians.* Edited by Stanley Sadie. London: Macmillan, 1980, 7:164.

Index